Shawn J. Parry-Giles
and Trevor Parry-Giles

Constructing Clinton

Hyperreality & Presidential Image-Making in Postmodern Politics

PETER LANG
New York • Washington, D.C./Baltimore • Bern
Frankfurt am Main • Berlin • Brussels • Vienna • Oxford

Library of Congress Cataloging-in-Publication Data
Parry-Giles, Shawn J.
Constructing Clinton: hyperreality and presidential image-making
in postmodern politics / Shawn J. Parry-Giles & Trevor Parry-Giles.
p. cm. — (Frontiers in political communication; vol. 3)
Includes bibliographical references and index.
1. Clinton, Bill, 1946– —Relations with journalists. 2. Clinton, Bill, 1946– —
Public opinion. 3. Mass media—Political aspects—United States—History—20th century.
4. Press and politics—United States—History—20th century. 5. Political culture—United
States—History—20th century. 6. Public opinion—United States—History—20th
century. 7. United States—Politics and government—1993–2001.
8. Postmodernism—Political aspects—United States. 9. Virtual reality—Political
aspects—United States. 10. Public relations and politics—United States—History—20th
century. I. Parry-Giles, Trevor. II. Title. III. Series.
E886 .P374   973.929'092—dc21   2001034683
ISBN 0-8204-5695-0
ISSN 1525-9730

Die Deutsche Bibliothek-CIP-Einheitsaufnahme
Parry-Giles, Shawn J.:
Constructing Clinton: hyperreality and presidential image-making
in postmodern politics / Shawn J. Parry-Giles & Trevor Parry-Giles.
–New York; Washington, D.C./Baltimore; Bern;
Frankfurt am Main; Berlin; Brussels; Vienna; Oxford: Lang.
(Frontiers in political communication; Vol. 3)
ISBN 0-8204-5695-0

Cover photo by Jim Mahoney
Cover design by Lisa Dillon

© 2002 Peter Lang Publishing, Inc., New York

All rights reserved.
Reprint or reproduction, even partially, in all forms such as microfilm,
xerography, microfiche, microcard, and offset strictly prohibited.

Constructing Clinton

Lynda Lee Kaid and Bruce Gronbeck
General Editors

Vol. 3

PETER LANG
New York • Washington, D.C./Baltimore • Bern
Frankfurt am Main • Berlin • Brussels • Vienna • Oxford

To Sam and Eli

Table of Contents

Acknowledgments ix

◆ **INTRODUCTION**
Hyperreal Politics, Bill Clinton, and
U.S. Political Culture in the 1990s 1

◆ **CHAPTER ONE**
The Man from Hope:
Hyperreal Intimacy and the
Invention of Bill Clinton 24

◆ **CHAPTER TWO**
Meta-Imaging, *The War Room*,
and the Hyperreal Campaign 52

◆ **CHAPTER THREE**
Political Nostalgia, Hyperreal History,
and the 1996 Presidential Campaign 83

◆ **CHAPTER FOUR**
Primary Colors and the Hyperreal
Authentication of Bill Clinton 118

◆ **CHAPTER FIVE**
Bill Clinton's Hyperreal Legacy 157

◆ **AFTERWORD**
Postmodern Presidentiality
and the Future of Image Politics 187

◆ **BIBLIOGRAPHY** 207

◆ **INDEX** 237

Acknowledgments

We began examining the construction of Bill Clinton early in the 1990s, as this compelling political figure entered the nation's consciousness and became a source of fascination for so many. Along the way, we have been aided by the generous insights and criticisms of many colleagues and friends. Some have read portions of this work as editors, some as respondents, others simply as interested Clinton-watchers or scholars of the presidency. To all of them, we owe and give our gratitude. These colleagues include J. Kevin Barge, Stephen H. Browne, Bonnie Dow, Sonja Foss, Dennis Gouran, Marouf Hasian, Richard J. Jensen, Andrew King, Ron Lee, John M. Murphy, Michael M. Osborn, and Alan Rubin. Thanks also to Herb Simons and Mary Stuckey for examining the manuscript in its final phases and offering their valuable commentary.

Constructing Clinton was developed and written while we were employed at several different institutions. We acknowledge the backing of our colleagues at Monmouth College, St. Ambrose University, and Western Illinois University. We are grateful for the support given in the form of a Faculty and Instructional Grant at Monmouth College, and a Faculty Development Grant from St. Ambrose University. In addition, some good friends in Monmouth—Farhat Haq, Mohsin Masood, Cheryl Meeker, and Clark Scott—challenged our assumptions and provoked many lively discussions about Clinton and his image. We are thankful for their friendship and their insights.

Our current institution, the University of Maryland, provides a highly conducive environment for thinking and writing about the relationships between rhetoric and political culture, and we are very grateful for the support of our colleagues and students in the Department of Communication and at the Center for Political Communication and Civic Leadership. We are grateful for the research assistance provided by two dedicated undergraduate students in our department, Joseph Matukonis and Evan Pitler. And we specifically acknowledge the encouragement of our chair, Edward L. Fink, who actively promotes the research efforts of the faculty in a variety of ways.

Peter Lang Publishing deserves a great deal of credit for their sponsorship of the Frontiers in Political Communication series. Our thanks especially go to series editor Bruce Gronbeck for his careful reading and trenchant comments on this project. We could not have asked for a better editor given Bruce's knowledge of politics, rhetoric, the mass media, and Bill Clinton. Both Bruce Gronbeck and Lynda Kaid are performing a valuable service for those of us who study political communication. Their leadership in editing Peter Lang's series and in pushing the boundaries of political communication in new and challenging directions is tremendous. In addition, the professionals at Peter Lang also have been exceedingly helpful in bringing this project to completion. We are especially appreciative of the patience and diligence of Sophie Appel, Sophy Craze, and Chris Myers. They have answered all our questions, provided clear instructions and direction, and were tireless and cheerful at every step.

Previous portions of this manuscript have appeared in other outlets. Specifically, portions of the Introduction and Chapter One appeared in *Communication Monographs* and *Communication Studies*, portions of Chapter Three appeared in the *Quarterly Journal of Speech*, and an earlier version of Chapter Two appeared in the *Journal of Communication*. We acknowledge the permission granted by the National Communication Association, the Central States Communication Association, and the International Communication Association allowing us to use this material.

Finally, we are very grateful for the constant inspiration of our children. Our sons, Sam Parry-Giles and Eli Parry-Giles, are constant sources of joy, insight, and tolerance as they endured our endless discussions of Bill Clinton. They keep us grounded and it is to them that we dedicate this book.

Introduction

Hyperreal Politics, Bill Clinton, and U.S. Political Culture in the 1990s

The 1990s were a time of considerable political angst in the United States—a time when politics, both nationally and internationally, was in a state of constant flux and transformation. Old paradigms disappeared and new ones emerged. Economies shifted, alliances broke down, and media proliferated. And at the center of this continually changing, constantly morphing time was Bill Clinton, the first "baby-boomer" president, the first Democrat reelected to a second term since FDR, the first post–Cold War president, and the first elected president in history to face an impeachment trial in the United States Senate. Politically speaking, the images and constructions of this one individual dominated the 1990s, as did our never-ending quest to define and explain him. Fundamentally, Bill Clinton personified that decade's political turmoil.

Understanding Bill Clinton requires an acknowledgment that the dominant characteristic of politics in postmodern America is its hyperreality—a condition created by the dominance of representation and the explosion of media. Politics, like much of American life according to semiotician Umberto Eco, "wants to establish reassurance through Imitation."[1] The result is hyperreality, or the idea that because of the saturation of images in contemporary life, it is difficult, if not impossible, to distinguish between that which is "real" and that which is represented or mediated. As such, the distinctions between reality and representation collapse so as to make them meaningless.[2] Hyperreality "implodes the binary concepts of reality and representation into a single concept," according to media critic John Fiske, "and the simulacrum similarly merges the 'copy' with the 'original,' the 'image' with its 'referent.'"[3]

Trying to uncover the "real" Bill Clinton, therefore, is a futile task in a symbolic environment dominated by the hyperreal political image.[4]

This book shuns the search for a political reality behind the "Clinton Image" and explores instead how the images of this individual president were constructed and manipulated. Put another way, we examine how Bill Clinton, his surrogates, and the press put forth verbal and visual portrayals of him for public consumption and the power of those portrayals on U.S. political culture.

Rather than asking, then, "Who is Bill Clinton?" we ask instead, "How did the constructed images of Bill Clinton reflect upon and express the character of U.S. politics?" and "What are the consequences of such images for U.S. political culture?" "Bill Clinton" was a product of the various *images* of Bill Clinton that Americans encountered nationally from 1991 to the present. Some of those images were products of Clinton himself, or his campaign organizations, or his administration. They were carefully crafted, highly scripted exercises in image construction and development, and they deserve our scrutiny. Others were images produced by adversaries, or supposedly disinterested observers. Whatever their sources, these (re)constructions of Bill Clinton's image are the stuff of which this president and our conceptions of his presidency were made in the hyperreal 1990s. And they can tell us a great deal about U.S. politics and the state of contemporary U.S. democratic government.

The Presidency and the Image of Bill Clinton

The presidency, created by Article II of the Constitution, is an institution that continually evolves and changes. But neither its constitutional enactment nor its continuing history fully defines what the presidency means for the U.S. political culture, as expressed in various forms and texts.

The U.S. Constitution puts forth specific parameters for the presidency—the individual must be 35 years of age and so on.[5] Those requirements, though, tell only a part of the story of the American presidency. Specific extra-constitutional requirements of the presidency and its occupant have emerged over the span of American political history such that presidents and presidential candidates must possess certain character qualities, have particular life histories, or share specific occupations. In popular parlance, we discuss whether this candidate or that one appears "presidential." The cultural meaning and expectations for the presidency also come from the heroic *mythos* associated with the office, the White House, and all of its accompanying symbolism. In postmodern, mediated politics, furthermore, demarcations of the presidency combine its mythic dimensions with the intimacies, the privacies, of the individuals in the Oval Office. In sum, beyond its constitutional requirements, there is a rhetoric that helps shape and order the cultural meaning of the institution of the presidency, ideologically defining the office and its occupants.

We label this rhetoric *presidentiality*.[6] Our construct of presidentiality refers to discourses that demarcate the cultural and ideological meaning of the institution of the presidency. Presidentiality is an amalgam of different voices and divergent texts that use as a referent the office of president of the United States and the individuals who hold that office. Presidentiality, thus, is responsive to context and history. Ultimately, it is a rhetoric that constitutes this office and the spectacle that is the presidency of the United States.[7] It also defines, in part, the American community by offering a vision of this central and vital office of the American political system.

Given its constitutive character, *presidentiality* invites the continued scrutiny of the ideologies and boundaries that circumscribe the presidency and presidents in American political discourse. Over time, the presidential role in public life and in political affairs is constantly being reassessed even as it represents the locus of political attention and a metonymy of larger cultural anxieties about politics, the nature of American political life, and the leadership that guides our governmental institutions.[8] Moreover, as media images have come to dominate political discourse, understandings of presidentiality have evolved and changed, as the case of Bill Clinton illustrates, to further complicate this most important institution of the U.S. government.

American political culture is continually revising and reassessing the conception of presidentiality. Such revision is typically a historical process, as we seek to consider the qualities of the men who have occupied the presidency. For some, this effort is fundamental to the preservation of American democracy. Robert A. Wilson's observation that "understanding the depth of character of a presidential candidate" is a responsibility of American citizenship reveals the power of qualification and character to contemporary assessments of the presidency.[9] The measure of character is the extent to which the individual, or the past president, possesses the necessary qualities to occupy the office. How we define those criteria continues to fluctuate, now more than ever.

Our understanding of contemporary presidentialities, of politics, and of Bill Clinton, moreover, is profoundly affected by the advent of the media information age. Conceptions and images of presidentiality are no longer tightly controlled, rare communications, but rather are part of a barrage of data that bombard the citizen daily from a myriad of sources.[10] The president, now, is a bona fide celebrity—his every move documented, filmed, and scrutinized.[11] Media proliferation and presidential celebrity create a communication environment where Americans know more and more about the intimate lives of the individuals in the Oval Office. As they learn more about these leaders, media savvy citizens also display a growing tolerance for moral imperfection, with Clinton as the paradigmatic case of such shifting attitudes toward presidential leadership. "The public has been saturated with postmodern media," concludes Bruce Miroff, "that emphasizes discontinuity and irony over consistency and conviction."[12]

Because of intense media attention on the occupant of the White House, defining the presidency and any particular president necessarily involves scrutiny of the mass media. And such scrutiny must include not only traditional, established journalistic outlets for news, but also non-traditional communication channels and mediums that put forth particular and often competing visions of presidentiality. Our analysis, in particular, examines Bill Clinton's public, mediated image as constructed in specific, though nontraditional, discursive texts. It is through the analysis of these rhetorics of presidentiality, we believe, that a more complete appreciation for the dynamic and evolving image of Bill Clinton is possible.

Images are about character, both as projected to the voters and as perceived by them when making their electoral choices. Presidential image construction is at once concerned with presentation and with the interface of presentation, personality, and policy pronouncements. As such, issues and images are intertwined irrevocably in the campaign process such that voters come to an assessment of a presidential image as "determined by the interaction of [the candidate's] personality and orientation to the world with ours."[13]

Not surprisingly, presidential candidates have always been concerned with projecting an electable image to the voters.[14] Television technologizes and visualizes those images, giving them even greater influence and impact on voters.¹⁵ Rather than ignore or dismiss the imaged nature of contemporary politics, our approach seeks to understand and explain presidential image construction on its own terms, recognizing that political image-making is, and always has been, a central part of presidentiality in the United States. While we do not celebrate or valorize image construction, we also are less quick than some to condemn the power and purpose of image in U.S. politics. We recognize that images are the essence of the postmodern political culture in the United States.

To characterize contemporary U.S. politics as "postmodern" is to recognize that our politics is dominated by the image and is primarily hyperreal in its depiction of individual candidates and leaders. Postmodern politics challenges existing image expectations, interrogating that which is assumed normal and natural. It exists within a postmodern culture "grounded in ambiguity, confusion, and irony."¹⁶ Moreover, the spectacle is the currency of postmodern politics, where visuality predominates and voters expect increasingly new and different information and images of their leaders.¹⁷ It is a politics that deconstructs historicized narratives of presidential leadership as it constructs new narratives and new images. In short, postmodern presidential politics simultaneously rejects and embraces existing presidentialities while it seeks to craft a new presidentiality for a hyper-mediated, hyper-visual, hyperreal time.

We cannot ignore the profound changes under way in U.S. politics as a consequence of postmodernity. As American presidents become increasingly hyperreal products of mass media images, the means of understanding and assessing presidential politics must likewise adjust. Or, as Bruce E. Gronbeck warns, "Turning our back on peek-a-boo politics means that someone is going to kick us in the seat of the pants."¹⁸

In terms of the political culture, then, and for the vast majority of U.S. voters and citizens, there was no "real" Bill Clinton, only a postmodern "Bill Clinton." While there was a physical human being who had a materiality as Bill Clinton, that person was only meaningful for the larger culture because of the images that defined him and that he and his surrogates manipulated. In other words, our interest is not with the "real" Bill Clinton, but with the "hyperreal" President William Jefferson Clinton.

The Dualities of Bill Clinton

Bill Clinton's image was organized, generally, around powerful tensions, inherent dualities that challenged and defined this particular president and what he represented for America's understanding of the presidency. Specifically, those tensions were between the past and the future, between the masculine and the feminine, between war and peace, between "black" and "white," and between public and private. Each of these tensions demarcated, in part, the Clinton persona and the images put forth to define the Clinton presidency.

Both the past and the future occupied important places in Clinton's constructed character. In the 1992 campaign, for instance, the Clinton campaign celebrated both ideals simultaneously. Clinton's own biographical past was featured as a justification for his candidacy in the campaign video *The Man from Hope*. At the same convention where *The Man from Hope* debuted, the Clinton campaign revealed its future-oriented anthem—Fleetwood Mac's "Don't Stop Thinking About Tomorrow." During the 1996 campaign, furthermore, Clinton published a book entitled *Between Hope and History*.[19] This manifesto borrowed from America's mythic past while simultaneously talking about bridges to the twenty-first century.[20]

Clinton came to embody both the past and the future. He was, at once, the chief interpreter of our collective memory of the past (as all presidents are), and a leader trying to take the nation into the new millennium. Of course, Clinton's past and his future were both hyperreal in that there was never a clear sense of what was real and what was appearance. As such, Clinton spun a tale of his own upbringing in *The Man from Hope* solely for its political resonance. He related historical narratives about America's past in *Between Hope and History* and in his 1996 convention film in much the same way, with particular attention to their political efficacies. A master of political nostalgia, Clinton thus warped the line between real and constructed, and between past and future, blurring them increasingly in the service of his personal and political image.[21]

The second duality, or tension, evident in the presidential and personal image of Bill Clinton was the persistent struggle between masculine and feminine. In terms of rhetorical style, Bill Clinton was arguably the most "feminine" of our recent presidents.[22] His rhetoric displayed characteristics of a "feminine style"; it was generally infused with personal examples and was inductive in its reasoning structure, was stylized, and worked to promote a sense of identification with the audience. Simultaneously, though, Clinton's rhetoric was also specific in its masculinity, usually relying on topics and commonplaces of masculine derivation.[23]

This tension was particularly evident in Clinton's powerful construction of his presidential image in *The Man from Hope*. As was often the case in Clinton's discourse, the feminine form and style of this text militated against the masculine focus of the subject matter and topics under discussion. In *The Man from Hope*, the *political* importance of women and their portrayals in general were minimized, deprioritized, and confined to the "private" sphere.[24] The film perpetuated a familial patriarchy that was entrenched within traditional modalities of masculinity and within ideologically powerful frames for understanding electoral politics.

The symbolic constructions of femininity and masculinity via the Clinton image were hyperreal as they worked to both support and resist each other. Bill Clinton used a feminine style of discourse to construct his image in *The Man from Hope* while, inconsistently, tapping into existing and powerful conceptions of masculinity to prove his fitness for the highest office in the land. Of course, this was entirely coherent with the president's actions while in office, where he simultaneously acted as a champion of feminist causes and an alleged sexual harasser of women. While he, thus, embodied both femininity and masculinity, there was no fixed and definable source for the gendered politics that shaped the Clinton image.[25]

Third, Clinton's image reflected the tensions he experienced, and those faced by his entire generation, between the competing demands of war and peace. On the one hand, Bill Clinton was a candidate and a president deeply committed to peaceful and diplomatic problem solving as his peace-making efforts in the Middle East and Northern Ireland demonstrated. He also often went to great lengths to justify and explain, indeed almost rationalize, his uses of military might in foreign conflicts.[26] For many, his foreign and defense policies were confused, befuddled, and rudderless, and this charge frequently surfaced in the campaign rhetorics of George W. Bush and Dick Cheney in the 2000 campaign.[27] Furthermore, Clinton's adversaries would highlight his incapacity to be commander in chief because of his own deficiency of military service. In part, this criticism resulted from Clinton's image as a baby-boomer and ex-war protester—images encouraged by the Clinton campaign as they sought to secure the "baby-boomer" vote in 1992.

Yet, Bill Clinton also frequently employed the language of war and the metaphors of battle to define and explain his political actions. He tapped into the cultural and symbolic importance of militarism in the United States and was willing to capitalize on the political power of such symbolism. So, for instance, the "war room" defined Clinton's 1992 campaign synecdochically, even spawning a documentary film of the same name.[28] *The War Room* defined the Clinton 1992 campaign militarily, as it purported to take its audiences inside the war room operations of the campaign headquarters. His presidency was "ambushed" and "attacked" by a "vast right-wing conspiracy" that was at war with his vision of America and its future. He was fairly quick to involve military forces in overseas operations and to use military force to achieve particular, proportional responses to international incidents. And the conflicts with Newt Gingrich and the Republican Congress, as well as the investigations by Kenneth Starr and the entire impeachment process, were frequently defined in war-like, militaristic terms.

Clinton was, quite simply, trapped between the expectations of his role as commander in chief of the American military, the power of militarism in the definition of American politics, and his deep-seated, historically rooted commitments to nonviolence and peace. Clinton used force, militarism, and violence when it was necessary to bolster his presidential image especially given his status as the first non-military president in recent memory. But Clinton also espoused and championed commitments to nonviolence and even pacifism when it worked to temper his war discourse and make more compassionate his militarism.

Fourth, Bill Clinton frequently turned to questions of race and America's enduring struggle with racial division in the definition of his public and presidential image. Indeed, the president's second term was going to be defined by his Race Initiative.[29] In his Second Inaugural Address, Clinton extolled, "The divide of race has been America's constant curse. . . . We cannot, we will not, succumb to the dark impulses that lurk in the far regions of the soul everywhere. We shall overcome them."[30] Such a rhetorical move was not surprising given the persistent tension between black and white in this president's persona.

Clinton had long been concerned with issues of race and civil rights in America. His own speechwriters believed that his best oratory came when Clinton addressed questions of race and racial tensions.[31] Clinton biographer David Maraniss even maintains, "The forces of light often prevailed when he dealt with African Americans and other minorities,"[32] and as rhetorical critic John Murphy concludes, Clinton was able to "interanimate" the black church and liberal traditions in American politics by appropriating and orchestrating the rhetorical traditions of the civil rights movement.[33] Clinton was so associated with race and civil rights in the United States and around that world that novelist Toni Morrison dubbed him America's first "black" president.[34]

As such, Bill Clinton articulated and expressed the angst and hope of race in America, which may explain, in part, his consistent level of support among African Americans and other marginalized groups and his regular return to questions of race and racial harmony. Yet, Clinton was also a white southerner—the presidential candidate who, in 1992, vigorously attacked Sister Souljah and who shunned Jesse Jackson.[35] This was the same Clinton who, as president-elect, quickly dumped Lani Guinier after her progressive and avant-garde views on racial remedies in the United States caused consternation among critics. Clinton was able to accent and highlight his whiteness[36] just as effectively as he could stress his empathy with African Americans. He was, in many ways, trapped in a hyperreal duality between black and white.

Simultaneously, nothing was ever black and white for Bill Clinton. On Affirmative Action, Clinton found a middle ground with his "Mend it, don't end it" proposals. The clarity of black and white was something Clinton refused to acknowledge and tried to blunt in both his policy pronouncements and his many image reconstructions. In a political and media culture that appreciates and validates stark clarity and polarized positions, Clinton's continuing quest for a compromise (frequently on questions of race) often frustrated and militated against powerful grammars of political understanding.

The final tension was the enduring struggle in the Clinton persona and the Clinton presidency between public and private. By definition, politicians at the presidential level sacrifice a large measure of their privacy in order to achieve electoral success.[37] In the case of Bill Clinton, that sacrifice was partially voluntary. For much of Clinton's political career, at the national level at least, he invited Americans into his personal life and into his family. With *The Man from Hope*, for example, Clinton reminisced about his childhood, the alcoholism and spousal abuse that victimized his family, his marital problems and the birth of his daughter, all in a highly emotive and disclosive exposé.[38]

And in *The War Room*, the Clinton campaign opened to scrutiny the very operations and strategies of the 1992 presidential campaign, highlighting again the intimate image construction strategies that Clinton enacted so successfully with his own biographical narrative.

President Clinton sought, though, to control that which was made public—those aspects of his life and activity that he wanted to reveal to a larger audience. So while he and his family were often forthcoming about private matters, they simultaneously blanched when unflattering or damaging personal information about them became public. This type of publicity became "the politics of personal destruction."[39] The personal or the scandalous, Clinton would suggest, was a private matter that should not be considered in assessing public leadership and political success. Put simply, Clinton's entire persona and image reflected the continual struggle between public and private under way in contemporary American political culture,[40] where prying media institutions dominate and where politicians and presidents negotiate and manipulate their own lives for public consumption and electoral ascendancy.[41] This struggle was powerfully evident in several texts addressing the president, notably Anonymous' *Primary Colors*, a 1996 novel (later adapted into a feature film) that constructed a fictional version of Bill Clinton.

This tension between public and private was thoroughly hyperreal as it engulfed Bill Clinton, his family, and his presidency. In very scripted and managed "intimacies," Clinton revealed himself to the larger public, crafting an image that was highly palatable and electable. Because those texts were so scripted, however, their verisimilitude was suspect, perpetuating an impression of Clinton as overly "political" and planned. The need to offer a "real" portrait of the intimate Bill Clinton gave rise to *Primary Colors*, manifesting an "authentic" rhetoric of image and insight. In many ways, Bill Clinton was trapped by his own tendency to display his private life to voters for electoral purposes and the cultural crusade to get beyond the façade to uncover and authenticate the candidate, the president, and the man identified as Bill Clinton.

Analyzing the Hyperreal Bill Clinton

Our goal with this book is an analysis of unique and, at times, competing texts that expressed and constructed Clinton's image, and that reveal Clinton's continuing legacy for U.S. political culture and discourse in the 1990s and beyond. In so doing, we reflect on the nature of American politics in this postmodern time, highlighting the tensions, traps, and tribulations faced by contemporary political candidates.

First, we offer a close reading of one of the most noteworthy examples of Clinton's personal image construction—the highly stylized and extremely successful 1992 campaign film entitled *The Man from Hope*. *The Man from Hope* debuted at the 1992 Democratic National Convention immediately prior to Clinton's acceptance speech. It was, by design, an attempt to (re)introduce and (re)invent Bill Clinton for the larger public who would be voting in the general election.

This particular text, we assert, reflects and represents the feminized and scopophiliac nature of hyperreal political discourse. *The Man from Hope* presented voters with a very personal and intimate glimpse of Bill Clinton, his family, and his maturation to adulthood. As it ignored politics or political issues, the film highlighted the personal, character-based foci of contemporary politics. In its form, the film was intimately feminine, while relying on masculine themes and constructions to define Bill Clinton. Indeed, the rhetorical resonance and endurance of the images from this film made *The Man from Hope* a central political text in our understanding of Bill Clinton. This initial exercise in image construction demarcated Clinton's presidency, and manifested his perpetual confrontation with the tensions between masculine/feminine and public/private at play in American politics.

Second, we discuss a documentary film entitled *The War Room*. This heralded 1993 release was a *cinéma vérité* account of Clinton's 1992 campaign, with a particular focus on his two chief aides—James Carville and George Stephanopoulos. *The War Room* offered an insider's glimpse of a presidential campaign, allegedly providing unfiltered and "real" insights into the nature of campaigning in the 1990s.

We read the film differently, however, arguing that it is an example of meta-imaging, or the communicative process whereby political campaigns and their chroniclers, in the service of authenticity, publicly display and foreground the art and practice of political image construction. Engaging in meta-imaging offers several distinct advantages for a campaign, and we explore how *The War Room* reflects the strategic nature of meta-imaging within contemporary campaign practice, particularly as it functioned to visually manifest the authenticity of the 1992 Clinton campaign. We also read *The War Room* as an example of the dominance of military emplotments for campaign narratives, noting that such constructions interface powerfully with the hyperreality of American politics and the persistent duality between war and peace.

Third, we examine the power of *Primary Colors* (both the novel and the film) to shape and authenticate the Clinton image. *Primary Colors* emerged at just the time when the American community was asked to reevaluate Bill Clinton as a president—in early 1996. The community's conception of Clinton was so thoroughly hyperreal that determining the authenticity of that perception was difficult at best. *Primary Colors* commented on both the social and political tensions present in Bill Clinton's persona even as its supposedly "authentic" image of Clinton was as hyperreal as all the other images of this president. Our concern is with the portrayal of Clinton (Jack Stanton) in the novel and the film. Moreover, we examine the cultural resonance of *Primary Colors* as a text of political image, reflecting on the assumed verisimilitude of this text as a commentary on Bill Clinton. Indeed, the very fact that the book was released as authored by Anonymous elevated the sense of realism and authenticity that the "novel" represented.

Primary Colors is a significant addition to the list of texts offering an image of Bill Clinton that cannot and will not fully capture the entirety of this complex individual. As such, it entered the hyperreal universe of American politics and was trapped by it, even as it attempted to rise above it as a piece of satirical fiction. In so doing, it spoke to the enduring pull of both the private and the public for Bill Clinton and for American politics.

We then turn our attention to Bill Clinton's efforts in 1996 to secure reelection, particularly examining his book, *Between Hope and History*, and the untitled campaign film shown at the 1996 Democratic convention. Our focus here is Clinton's use of political nostalgia for the purposes of electoral ascendancy. Political discourse has become a prominent source of American collective memory with Bill Clinton, in particular, using history and collective memory skillfully as a tool for political advantage. In the case of Clinton, that demarcation of collective memory transformed into political nostalgia, or the presentation of a distorted rendition of the past for political purposes.

Political nostalgia is a form of hyperreal history. Because of its *affective* power, such nostalgic musings blur distinctions between what may have actually happened in a community's past and what the community longs for or believes might have happened. Clinton, like other political leaders before him, cultivated nostalgic visions of the past to achieve political success, using that version of past events to justify contemporary circumstances. Clinton's appropriation of America's nostalgic fondness for the Founders, the Progressive Era, and the 1950s speaks to the power of hyperreal history in political communication practices and the tension between the past and the future for Clinton.

Ultimately, we conclude that Bill Clinton's image was a product of a textual confluence that may never reveal any sense of who Bill Clinton "really" was but that tells us a great deal about the state of contemporary politics. Our analysis ends with a discussion of the (re)imaging of Clinton after the Monica Lewinsky scandal and his impeachment, paying particular attention to an episode of the MTV series *BIOrhythm* and to the PBS documentary *The American President*. The political culture that was processing and attempting to understand this particular president faced a daunting task, and the Lewinsky scandal only complicated the process further. Because Bill Clinton's image was so thoroughly trapped in hyperreality, because we could never really know who the "real" Bill Clinton was, and because there was no "real" Bill Clinton to understand for the vast majority of Americans, the culture continued producing explanations for this president.

BIOrhythm offered an interpretation that was particularly compelling in the wake of the Lewinsky matter both for its visual and stylistic elements and also for its capacity to use and express the intimately hyperreal dimensions of Bill Clinton's image to maximum effect. The contrast that *BIOrhythm* drew between the uncertainty of Clinton's past and the personal struggles and hardships he endured functions symbolically as a representation of a larger cultural angst concerning this president's impeachment. Through a dramatic retelling of the Clinton saga, with intimate pictures and video of Clinton as a child and teenager, the film positioned the president as a representation of the American Dream, overcoming adversity and psychological trauma to endure and succeed. And just as Clinton transcended the problems of his youth to achieve the American Dream, so too, the film implicitly suggested, can the larger American community overcome the traumas of 1998 to succeed and prosper. To deny the hope that Clinton represents, the film argued, is to deny the hope of America.

The PBS documentary, *The American President*, offered a more institutional assessment of Bill Clinton—an explanation of Clinton's actions and personal misconduct that situated them firmly in the heightened partisan political context of the post-Watergate era. While

MTV explained and defined Clinton by reference to the psychological and the culture, PBS's portrayal was loaded with the mythic and the heroic. Read together, these two documentary renditions of Clinton's story revealed the tensions endemic to the ideal of the presidency in a postmodern, hyperreal time. The American culture, as these media texts suggested, defines our presidents in conflicting and contradictory ways, yet those definitions insure the manifest survival and endurance of the presidency in the face of personal fallibility inherent in the occupants of the office.

As such, *BIOrhythm* and *The American President* are bookend texts to *The Man from Hope* as all three held out an image of Bill Clinton as an agent of hope and survival, albeit in powerfully different ways in vastly different contexts. They represent a confluence of images that speak to the problems of defining a postmodern president in a postmodern time of confusion and uncertainty.

The Clinton Legacy and
Political Culture in the United States

Already the assessments and appraisals of Bill Clinton, his presidency, and his overall impact have begun. Such assessments, sometimes negative, commenced before the end of his term in the White House, and are likely to continue for some time. In Clinton's hands, Bruce Miroff contends, "the image of the presidency has grown more hollow" largely because his "postmodern spectacle" presidency left the U.S. public with a sense of "unease."[42] Calling Clinton's terms in office "the ultimate example of the rhetorical presidency," political scientist George Edwards scolds this president for failing to appreciate the differences between governing and campaigning, and for continuing to "assign strategic primacy to communications [sic]."[43] And borrowing from Stephen Skowronek's formulation of the "preemptive" presidency, Steven Schier labels Clinton the first preemptive president, with limited policy achievements and a "constantly changing personal identity."[44]

Our assessments of Bill Clinton go farther and deeper than simply reactions to his policy failings or clichéd commentaries about his personal predilections and pratfalls. Bill Clinton's enduring legacy will not be his economic record or the success of his foreign policy. Robust economic growth figures or high levels of employment will not define it. We will not look back on this president and recall preeminently his war against Serbia over Kosovo or his battles with Kenneth Starr and his impeachment by Congress. These events, successes, and failures may all figure into our assessment of Bill Clinton, but they will not tell the full story of his meaning for U.S. politics.

Bill Clinton's ultimate legacy will be that he forced the American political culture to examine itself and to question the very nature of leadership and politics in the United States. As he left office in 2001, Clinton elicited competing reactions from an American public forever altered by his presence in their lives. Large majorities of polled respondents approved of Clinton's performance in office, giving this president some of the highest approval ratings in history at anywhere from 65 percent to 68 percent. Those same respondents also generally recorded disapproval or distrust of Clinton as an individual.[45] But these numbers say less about Clinton than they do about the image-based politics of the United States at the turn of the twentieth century.

The temptation among many political commentators and critics, though, is to dismiss or denigrate the image dimensions of electoral decision making, arguing that such a focus debases politics and distorts the governmental processes of the United States.[46] Unfortunately, continually bemoaning the state of American image politics only perpetuates a cynicism and fatalism that corrodes the very substance of democratic governance. Even though many media and political critics complain about the state of contemporary politics, such naysayers ignore the historical reality that campaigns have always addressed process and image rather than content and issues.[47]

Voters and citizens are constructed as more targeted, more fragmented, more scopophiliac, more skeptical than ever before. They are repeatedly told that their political system does not work, that their leaders are dishonest and solely motivated by money and special interests, and that little or nothing can be done to solve intractable problems facing the nation. They are also conditioned to believe that politics is artificial, and they long for a real, genuine, authentic politics, as if such a community has ever existed or will ever be possible. But, having seen politicians come and go and having been television viewers for decades, these voters have learned to peer behind the constructed, to distrust the packaged politician. As we hope to demonstrate, however, American politics is all about packaging and image, and to hope for otherwise is to indulge a fantasy and nostalgically pine for a time and a politics that never were. Bill Clinton profoundly changed U.S. politics, teaching voters that politics rooted in image, powered by artifice, can still effect meaningful change and provide leadership. Toward this end, Clinton's legacy may be that he cemented the power of the constructed image as the bedrock of political culture. Whether this lesson will prevail or will create a backlash remains open to question.

Bill Clinton's place at this moment in history, in this postmodern time of media proliferation and communication flux, amplifies the consequences of his presidency for American political culture and for the future of political discourse. Because of Bill Clinton and the images he has created and that have been created about him, the American political culture will forever be altered. But even as the image ascended and American politics became thoroughly hyperreal in the Clinton years, that same period established again the power of popular voice and public deliberation in our democracy. Amidst all of the images and awash in all the hyperreality, the public's power over events and its impact on public matters grew during the Clinton era, particularly concerning the question of Clinton's impeachment. Such is the nature of American democracy and government. Our system has always privileged image and elevated character to the forefront of political communication. But that same system, whether systemically or culturally, still requires political leaders, as they construct their images and manipulate the artifice of politics for political success, to reckon with a public, a larger sense of democracy in action that continues to rescue American government from the clutches of despotism and despair.

Notes

1. Umberto Eco, *Travels in Hyperreality: Essays*, translated by William Weaver (San Diego, CA: Harcourt Brace Jovanovich, 1986), 57.

2. See Jean Baudrillard, *Simulations*, translated by Paul Foss, Paul Patton, and Philip Beitchman (New York: Semiotext(e), 1983); Jean Baudrillard, "Hyperreal America," translated by David Macey, *Economy and Society* 22 (1993): 243–52; Thomas Carmichael, "Postmodernism, Symbolicity, and the Rhetoric of the Hyperreal: Kenneth Burke, Fredric Jameson, and Jean Baudrillard," *Text and Performance Quarterly* 11 (1991): 319–24; Mike Gane, *Baudrillard's Bestiary* (London: Routledge, 1991); Douglas Kellner, *Jean Baudrillard: From Marxism to Postmodernism and Beyond* (Stanford, CA: Stanford University Press, 1989); Dean MacCannell and Juliet Flower MacCannell, "Social Class in Postmodernity: Simulacrum or Return of the Real?," in *Forget Baudrillard?*, edited by Chris Rojek and Bryan S. Turner (London: Routledge, 1993), 124–45; and Sanford F. Schram, "The Post-Modern Presidency and the Grammar of Electronic Electioneering," *Critical Studies in Mass Communication* 8 (1991): 210–16.

3. John Fiske, *Media Matters: Everyday Culture and Political Change* (Minneapolis: University of Minnesota Press, 1996), 2.

4. Schram, "The Post-Modern Presidency," 216.

5. *U.S. Constitution*, Art. II, sec. 1, cl. 5.

6. To the best of our understanding, the term "presidentiality" is not often used. One notable reference to the concept occurs in a series of memos written to President Gerald Ford by aide Foster Channock concerning the 1976 elections and the necessity of communicating Ford's "presidentiality." See "Thoughts on Presidentiality," Foster Channock Files, Gerald R. Ford Library, Grand Rapids, Michigan. Mark Crispin Miller uses "presidentiality" as a designation for the amalgam of the "presidential" adjectives that George W. Bush lacks. See Mark Crispin Miller, *The Bush Dyslexicon: Observations on a National Disorder* (New York: W. W. Norton, 2001), 32.

7. To label a discourse a "constitutive rhetoric" is to acknowledge its ability to provide substance and meaning that is necessary for the very constitution of a social institution. A clear example is provided by James Boyd White, who sees law as a constitutive discourse that is "the constitution of a world by the distribution of authority within it; it establishes the terms on which its actors may talk in conflict or cooperation among themselves." See James Boyd White, *When Words Lose Their Meaning: Constitutions and Reconstitutions of Language, Character, and Community* (Chicago: University of Chicago Press, 1984), 266. For more on constitutive rhetoric and its ideological dimensions, see also Maurice Charland,

"Constitutive Rhetoric: The Case of the *Peuple Québécois*," *Quarterly Journal of Speech* 73 (1987): 133–50.

8. Joyce Hoffman connects the power of the presidency, at least in part, with Theodore H. White's glorification of the presidency from Kennedy's administration through the 1980s. Hoffman argues that "White's words helped to suffuse Kennedy with the qualities of an all-American superman." See Joyce Hoffman, *Theodore H. White and Journalism as Illusion* (Columbia: University of Missouri Press, 1995), 149. Though not concerned with the presidency as a metonymy, E. J. Dionne offers a telling commentary on the state of American attitudes toward politics. See E. J. Dionne, *Why Americans Hate Politics* (New York: Touchstone, 1992). Kenneth T. Walsh associates the presidency's "diminution" with the "end of the Cold War." See Kenneth T. Walsh, *Feeding the Beast: The White House Versus the Press* (New York: Random House, 1996), 245. Stephen Hess contends that it has just "become harder to run a democratic country" because of the "wide gap between popular expectations of what a president should do and the realities of what a president can do." See Stephen Hess, *Presidents & the Presidency* (Washington, D.C.: The Brookings Institution, 1996), 132. And finally, Robert Shogan argues "that the presidency is an eminently resilient and *dynamic* institution." See Robert Shogan, *The Double-Edged Sword: How Character Makes and Ruins Presidents, From Washington to Clinton* (Boulder, CO: Westview Press, 1999), 256. (emphasis added)

9. Robert A. Wilson, ed., *Character Above All: Ten Presidents from FDR to George Bush* (New York: Simon & Schuster, 1995), 11. A focus on presidential character and personality is also found in James David Barber, *The Presidential Character: Predicting Performance in the White House*, 4th ed. (Upper Saddle River, NJ: Prentice-Hall PTR, 1992); and Shogan, *The Double-Edged Sword*. McGee remarks that assessments of character and leadership are really at the heart of democracy, especially in democratic systems as complex and multifaceted as the United States. In such systems, voters are supremely equipped to evaluate and express judgment about character and leadership, but are less able to confront the vagaries of particular policy positions. See Michael Calvin McGee, "'Not Men, But Measures': The Origins and Import of an Ideological Principle," *Quarterly Journal of Speech* 64 (1978): 141–54.

10. An excellent discussion of this phenomenon is found in Edwin Diamond and Robert A. Silverman, *White House to Your House: Media and Politics in Virtual America* (Cambridge, MA: MIT Press, 1995).

11. For a discussion of the evolving, celebritized presidency, see Neal Gabler, *Life, the Movie* (New York: Vintage Books, 1998); and P. David Marshall, *Celebrity and Power: Fame in Contemporary Culture* (Minneapolis: University of Minnesota Press, 1997).

12. Bruce Miroff, "Courting the Public: Bill Clinton's Postmodern Education," in *The Postmodern Presidency: Bill Clinton's Legacy in U.S. Politics*, edited by Steven E. Schier (Pittsburgh, PA: University of Pittsburgh Press, 2000), 110.

13. For discussions of the relationship between issues, images, and political rhetoric, see Dan Hahn, "The Media and the Presidency: Ten Propositions," *Communication Quarterly* 35 (1987): 254–66; Dan Hahn and Ruth M. Gonchar, "Political Myth: The Image and the Issue," *Today's Speech* 20 (1972): 57–65; Allen Louden, "Voter Rationality and Media Excess: Image in the 1992 Presidential Campaign," in *The 1992 Presidential Campaign: A Communication Perspective*, edited by Robert E. Denton, Jr. (Westport, CT: Praeger, 1994), 169–87; Dan Nimmo and Robert L. Savage, "Political Images and Political Perceptions," *Experimental Study of Politics* 1 (1971): 1–36; M. Timothy O'Keefe and Kenneth G. Sheinkopf, "The Voter Decides: Candidate Image or Campaign Issue?" *Journal of Broadcasting* 18 (1974): 403–12; and Leonard Shyles, "Defining 'Images' of Presidential Candidates from Televised Political Spot Advertisements," *Political Behavior* 6 (1984): 171–81.

14. See Kathleen Hall Jamieson, *Packaging the Presidency: A History and Criticism of Presidential Campaign Advertising*, 3rd edition (New York: Oxford University Press, 1996); Lee Sigelman and David Bullock, "Candidates, Issues, Horse Races, and Hoopla," *American Politics Quarterly* 19 (1991): 5–32; and Gene Wyckoff, *The Image Candidates: American Politics in the Age of Television* (New York: Macmillan, 1968).

15. Roderick P. Hart, *Seducing America: How Television Charms the Modern Voter* (New York: Oxford University Press, 1994); John P. Keating and Bibb Latane, "Politicians on TV: The Image Is the Message," *Journal of Social Issues* 32 (1976): 116–32; and Joshua Meyrowitz, *No Sense of Place: The Impact of Electronic Media on Social Behavior* (New York: Oxford University Press, 1985). Many studies demonstrate the contemporary importance of image in actual voting behavior. See James E. Campbell, "Candidate Image Evaluations: Influence and Rationalization in Presidential Primaries," *American Politics Quarterly* 11 (1983): 293–313; Susan Hellweg, "An Examination of Voter Conceptualizations of the Ideal Political Candidate," *Southern Speech Communication Journal* 44 (1979): 373–85; Susan Hellweg, George Dionisopoulos, and Drew Kugler, "Political Candidate Image: A State-of-the-Art Review," in *Progress in Communication Sciences*, Vol. IX, edited by Brenda Dervin and M. J. Voigt (Norwood, NJ: Ablex, 1989), 43–78; Louden, "Voter Rationality and Media Excess"; O'Keefe and Sheinkopf, "The Voter Decides;" Ronald Rudd, "Issues as Image in Political Campaign Commercials," *Western Journal of Speech Communication* 50 (1986): 102–18; and Shyles, "Defining 'Images' of Presidential Candidates."

16. See Steven E. Schier, "Introduction: A Unique Presidency," in *The Postmodern Presidency: Bill Clinton's Legacy in U.S. Politics*, edited by Steven E. Schier (Pittsburgh, PA: University of Pittsburgh Press, 2000), 1.

17. Visuality refers to the social facts and historically derived techniques of structuring visual images. Thus, whereas vision is a physiological process of sight, visuality involves the discursive determinations of visual meaning. See Hal Foster, ed., *Vision and Visuality* (New York: The New Press, 1988), ix. Of course visuality also involves all of the hyperreal dimensions of postmodern spectacularization. As Craig Owens notes, "In the visual arts we have witnessed the gradual dissolution of once fundamental distinctions—original/copy, authentic/inauthentic, function/ornament." See Craig Owens, "The Discourse of Others: Feminists and Postmodernism," in *The Anti-Aesthetic: Essays on Postmodern Culture*, edited by Hal Foster (New York: The New Press, 1983), 77.

18. Bruce E. Gronbeck, "Rhetoric, Ethics, and Telespectacles in the Post-everything Age," in *Postmodern Representations: Truth, Power, and Mimesis in the Human Sciences and Public Culture*, edited by Richard Harvey Brown (Urbana: University of Illinois Press, 1995), 235.

19. President Bill Clinton, *Between Hope and History: Meeting America's Challenges for the 21st Century* (New York: Times Books, 1996).

20. For a complete discussion of the development of the "bridge" theme in the 1996 Clinton campaign, see Michael Waldman, *POTUS Speaks: Finding the Words That Defined the Clinton Presidency* (New York: Simon & Schuster, 2000), 126–48.

21. We offer one example of Clinton's use of political nostalgia for the purposes of political and personal image construction in an analysis of his speech commemorating the 35th anniversary of the March on Washington. The speech was presented on August 28, 1998, at the apex of the Monica Lewinsky scandal. See Shawn J. Parry-Giles and Trevor Parry-Giles, "Collective Memory, Political Nostalgia, and the Rhetorical Presidency: Bill Clinton's Commemoration of the March on Washington, August 28, 1998," *Quarterly Journal of Speech* 86 (2000): 417–37.

22. For more on the "feminine style" of rhetoric, see Jane Blankenship and Deborah C. Robson, "A 'Feminine Style' in Women's Political Discourse: An Exploratory Essay," *Communication Quarterly* 43 (1995): 353–66; Karlyn Kohrs Campbell, "The Discursive Performance of Femininity: Hating Hillary," *Rhetoric & Public Affairs* 1 (1998): 1–19; Bonnie J. Dow and Mari Boor Tonn, "'Feminine Style' and Political Judgment in the Rhetoric of Ann Richards," *Quarterly Journal of Speech* 79 (1993): 286–302; Kathleen Hall Jamieson, *Eloquence in an Electronic Age: The Transformation of Political Speechmaking* (New York: Oxford University Press, 1988); and Shawn J. Parry-Giles and Trevor Parry-Giles, "Gendered Politics and Presidential Image Construction: A Reassessment of the 'Feminine Style,'" *Communication Monographs* 63 (1996): 337–53.

23. When we speak of masculine themes and subjects, we are generally referring to a "hegemonic masculinity" at the root of much political discourse. Descriptions and typologies of "hegemonic masculinity" are found in Robert Hanke, "Hegemonic

Masculinity in *thirtysomething*," *Critical Studies in Mass Communication* 7 (1990): 231–48; Parry Giles and Parry-Giles, "Gendered Politics," 342–48; and Nick Trujillo, "Hegemonic Masculinity on the Mound: Media Representations of Nolan Ryan and American Sports Culture," *Critical Studies in Mass Communication* 8 (1991): 290–308.

24. The linguistic resources used to marginalize and deemphasize women—and the outright violence committed against them—are illustrated in Tonn et al.'s analysis of a 1988 shooting in Maine. They explore how the woman shot is "symbolically killed" in the press and the trial following the incident. See Mari Boor Tonn, Valerie A. Endress, and John N. Diamond, "Hunting and Heritage on Trial: A Dramatistic Debate Over Tragedy, Tradition, and Territory," *Quarterly Journal of Speech* 79 (1993): 165–81.

25. This theme is developed more fully in connection with Clinton's 1992 presidential campaign film in Parry-Giles and Parry-Giles, "Gendered Politics."

26. In his speech announcing the end of the bombing in Serbia and Kosovo, for example, President Clinton noted, "This victory brings a new hope that when a people are singled out for destruction because of their heritage and religious faith and we can do something about it, the world will not look the other way." This text is available at http://vcepolitics.com/usa/clinton/speeches/990610kosovo.shtml.

27. Notable examples include Governor Bush's speech to the Veterans of Foreign Wars convention on August 21, 2000, and Cheney's speech to the Southern Center for International Studies on August 30, 2000. These texts are available at http://www.georgewbush.com/news/speeches/index.html.

28. Waldman comments frequently about the use of "war rooms" in the Clinton White House to handle crises or to manage domestic priorities and campaigns. See Waldman, *POTUS Speaks*.

29. For more on Clinton's Race Initiative and the Clinton administration's approach to Affirmative Action, see Martín Carcasson and Mitchell F. Rice, "The Promise and Failure of President Clinton's Race Initiative of 1997–1998: A Rhetorical Perspective," *Rhetoric & Public Affairs* 2 (1999): 243–74; George Stephanopoulos, *All Too Human: A Political Education* (Boston: Little, Brown, 1999), 342–75; and Waldman, *POTUS Speaks*, 167–78.

30. There is, of course, a racial dimension to Clinton's description of the impulses driving America's struggle with race as "dark." Such metaphors are compelling and complicated within the contemporary political culture's discernment of racial meaning and interpretation. See "Inaugural Address of President William J. Clinton," January 20, 1997, available at http://www.pub.whitehouse.gov/uri-res/I2R?urn:pdi://oma.eop.gov.us/1997/1/20/6.text.1.

31. These conclusions were offered by Michael Waldman, a Clinton speechwriter from 1993 to 1999 who served as director of the White House Office of Speechwriters, and J. Terry Edmonds, former Clinton speechwriter, at a Smithsonian Institution seminar entitled "All the President's Words," December 5, 1998. As Waldman said at the seminar, "the issue of race is true to him [Clinton]."

32. See David Maraniss, *The Clinton Enigma: A Four-and-a-Half Minute Speech Reveals This President's Entire Life* (New York: Simon & Schuster, 1998), 18.

33. John M. Murphy, "Inventing Authority: Bill Clinton, Martin Luther King, Jr., and the Orchestration of Rhetorical Traditions," *Quarterly Journal of Speech* 83 (1997): 71–89.

34. Toni Morrison, "The Talk of the Town," *The New Yorker*, October 5, 1998, p. 31.

35. Ironically, Clinton and his family turned to Jackson for advice and counsel when the Lewinsky scandal reached its zenith in the late summer of 1998. This relationship took on even more irony when it was revealed in 2001 that Reverend Jackson also was engaged in a long-term extramarital affair that resulted in the birth of a child.

36. See Thomas K. Nakayama and Robert L. Krizek, "Whiteness: A Strategic Rhetoric," *Quarterly Journal of Speech* 81 (1995): 291–309.

37. Various explanations for this phenomenon are offered in the following: Hart, *Seducing America*; Meyrowitz, *No Sense of Place*; Trevor Parry-Giles and Shawn J. Parry-Giles, "Political Scopophilia, Presidential Campaigning, and the Intimacy of American Politics," *Communication Studies* 47 (1996): 191–205; and Schram, "The Post-Modern Presidency."

38. See Parry-Giles & Parry-Giles, "Political Scopophilia"; and Thomas Rosteck, "The Intertextuality of 'The Man from Hope': Bill Clinton as Person, as Persona, as Star?," in *Bill Clinton on Stump, State, and Stage: The Rhetorical Road to the White House*, edited by Stephen A. Smith (Fayetteville: University of Arkansas Press, 1994), 223–48.

39. This phrase has become common in the parlance of Washington. It occurred most notably in President Clinton's speech to the nation following his grand jury testimony on August 17, 1998. See "Address to the Nation on Testimony Before the Independent Counsel's Grand Jury, August 17, 1998," *Public Papers of the Presidents of the United States, William Jefferson Clinton, 1998, Vol. II*, available at http://www.gpo.gov/nara/pubpaps/photoidx.html.

40. See Maurizio Passerin d'Entrèves and Ursula Vogel, eds., *Public & Private: Legal, Political and Philosophical Perspectives* (London: Routledge, 2000); Jürgen Habermas, *The Structural Transformation of the Public Sphere*, translated by Thomas Burger (Cambridge, MA: MIT Press, 1992); and Jeff Weintraub and

Krishan Kumar, eds., *Public and Private in Thought and Practice: Perspectives on a Grand Dichotomy* (Chicago: University of Chicago Press, 1997).

41. See Hart, *Seducing America*.

42. Bruce Miroff, "From 'Midcentury' to *Fin-de-Siècle*: The Exhaustion of the Presidential Image," *Rhetoric & Public Affairs* 1 (1998): 195. Roderick P. Hart also has speculated about the end of the presidency, though in slightly different terms than Miroff. See Roderick P. Hart, "The End of the American Presidency," lecture presented as the Josephine Jones Lecture, University of Colorado, Boulder, CO, March 8, 1999, available at http://www.colorado.edu/Communication/department/endpres.html.

43. George C. Edwards III, "Campaigning Is Not Governing: Bill Clinton's Rhetorical Presidency," in *The Clinton Legacy*, edited by Colin Campbell and Bert A. Rockman (New York: Chatham House, 2000), 33, 47.

44. Steven E. Schier, "American Politics After Clinton," in *The Postmodern Presidency: Bill Clinton's Legacy in U.S. Politics*, edited by Steven E. Schier (Pittsburgh, PA: University of Pittsburgh Press, 2000), 255. For more on the "preemptive" presidency, see Stephen Skowronek, *The Politics Presidents Make: Leadership from John Adams to Bill Clinton* (Cambridge, MA: Belknap Press, 1997).

45. See *National Journal*'s "Polling on National Figures and Institutions," available at http://nationaljournal.com/members/polltrack/2001/national/.

46. See W. Lance Bennett, *The Governing Crisis: Media, Money, and Marketing in American Elections*, 2nd ed. (New York: St. Martin's Press, 1996); E. J. Dionne, Jr., *Why Americans Hate Politics* (New York: Simon & Schuster, 1991); Kathleen Hall Jamieson, *Dirty Politics: Deception, Distraction, and Democracy* (New York: Oxford University Press, 1992); Douglas Kellner, *Television and the Crisis of Democracy* (Boulder, CO: Westview Press, 1990); Timothy Luke, "Televisual Democracy and the Politics of Charisma," *Telos* 70 (1986–1987): 59–80; and David Zarefsky, "Spectator Politics and the Revival of Public Argument," *Communication Monographs* 59 (1992): 411–14.

47. See Lee Sigelman, "There You Go Again: The Media and the Debasement of American Politics," *Communication Monographs* 59 (1992): 407–10.

Chapter One

The Man from Hope: Hyperreal Intimacy and the Invention of Bill Clinton

A particularly telling moment in the 1992 presidential campaign occurred just prior to the New York primary when Bill Clinton appeared on the syndicated talk show *Donahue*. Pressed by the host to address allegations of his extramarital activities, Clinton responded angrily: "We're going to sit here a long time in silence, Phil. I'm not going to answer any more of these questions." As the studio audience cheered, Clinton continued, "You are responsible for the cynicism in this country. You don't want to talk about the real issues."[1] Paradoxically, this presidential candidate, making a rare appearance on a program devoted to a discussion of the personal, sensational, and scandalous, challenged the importance of such concerns for political decision making.

This moment speaks to a simmering tension in contemporary political image construction that illuminates much about the state of the presidency in the United States. Put simply, candidates are forced to construct a heroic image of presidential leadership in an era of televisual intimacy and intrusion.[2] Thus, as Clinton attempted to avoid the personal in order to appear presidential by discussing "real" issues, he simultaneously did so in a media context reliant upon an intimate portrayal of self. For the contemporary political candidate, then, pursuing the presidency presents an ideological conundrum. Moreover, this tension exposes the complex and hyperreal nature of contemporary political image construction in the United States.

Mediated postmodern politics creates the forum in which the hyperreal and intimate features of political discourse operate simultaneously. Television, observes political commentator Roderick P. Hart, "has become the delivery system for intimacy."[3] Similarly, the "intimate medium of television requires that those who speak comfortably through it project a sense of private self, [and] unselfconsciously self-disclose,"[4] concludes Kathleen Hall Jamieson. Such intimacy, though, is a function of hyperreality; it exists in the service of image construction.

Hyperreality masks the simulated intimacies constructed and packaged for public consumption by political candidates adapting to the mass media. In addition, media production practices exploit what Freud called the scopophiliac impulse or the human need to gaze that naturalizes the hyperreal political image and creates an artificial, mediated intimacy. A viewer's gazing impulse is satisfied by these production strategies that manufacture an illusory intimacy and invites and maintains spectator attention by creating highly personal visual cues.[5] Presidential aspirants, though, are trapped in this hyperreality, because as they exhibit an *image* of their intimate selves via television, they sacrifice the interpersonal distance necessary to perform the heroic dimensions of the presidency. That distance is further surrendered to the television cameras that visually invade the personal space of candidates as they seek to maximize their intimacy with the voter.[6]

The hyperreal intimacy that candidates are compelled to offer also fosters the gendered character of political image construction. The contemporary televisual construction of image creates a forum for what Jamieson calls an effeminate style of political communication—a style that is "personal, excessive, disorganized, and unduly ornamental." This effeminate style opposes a more manly style that is "factual, analytic, organized, and impersonal."[7] Because television encourages self-disclosure on the part of political candidates, political communicators of either sex often assume a more womanly, or feminine, style of communication.

Ultimately, while images put forth by candidates may seem intimate, and feminine, they derive their rhetorical power from highly managed, masculine-based institutional affiliations and themes. A political culture may encourage increased femininity on the part of both male and female politicians and concurrently require those same politicians to demonstrate their inherent masculinity through appeals to existing and constraining sexist stereotypes. The hyperreality of contemporary politics forces candidates to negotiate the tension between femininity and masculinity as they seek to communicate gender attributes for political gain in an intimate manner. Of course, both the scopophiliac and gendered attributes of political image-making derive their power and influence from the hyperreality of this postmodern political time.

Nowhere is the overt hyperreal construction of "image" more powerfully on display than in the presidential campaign film—the introductory, biographical media event that usually debuts immediately prior to a candidate's acceptance speech at the national party conventions. Beginning with Ronald Reagan's 1984 film, presidential campaign films have served as "centerpiece[s] of the presidential election campaign."[8] These image rhetorics play a central role in the rituals of presidential campaigning,[9] and they are used for campaign commercials, shown to countless audiences, mailed to contributors, and otherwise distributed widely to voters nationwide. Campaign films are, in this way, meaningful texts of presidentiality, defining the nature of presidential qualification and character and putting forth a vision of the office and the institution to justify a particular candidacy.

Presidential campaign films are significant because they historicize and mythologize the American presidency and situate the featured candidate within that mythology. They are, as such, important texts of presidentiality in contemporary political culture, for, as Joanne Morreale asserts, they "provide comprehensive, structured storehouses of mythical images of the president, the country, and its citizens." In order to image themselves as presidential prospects, candidates rely on historical and "complex symbols . . . [that] embody cultural myths."[10] Yet within the contemporary political environment, such films must also adapt to the other predominant dimension of the televisual age by satisfying the demands of a feminine intimacy that voters expect because of the scopophiliac grammars and conventions of televised politics. Thus, presidential contenders speak to Americans about what the presidency should be, offering a prototypical presidentiality in the process.[11] And they must also do so in a highly personalized and intimate manner to fully adapt to the complexity of political practice and voter expectations in this postmodern age.

In this chapter, we examine the 1992 Clinton campaign film entitled *The Man from Hope*. Our analysis of the film's verbal and visual elements exposes a text that is both intimate and mythic,[12] both feminine and masculine, manifesting the tensions and paradoxes of hyperreal politics. But before turning to the text itself, we consider more fully the reordered and restructured nature of political image construction in the postmodern era.

Political Scopophilia and Gendered Politics in Postmodernity

As presidential candidates strive for presidential viability, electoral success, and public acceptance, their choices and strategies represent a confluence of factors, from the individual and psychological to the social and ideological. The tendency to focus exclusively on the collective, ideological bases for political choices ignores, in the words of Janice Rushing and Thomas Frentz, "the role of the interior world of the psyche in the visualization of a cultural ideal."[13] A greater appreciation of the multiple dimensions of moral choice and political judgment emerges from a consideration of the varied aspects of political images and rhetorics.[14]

One such aspect of contemporary political culture is political scopophilia. Freud theorized that human beings, from early childhood, possess a need to gaze at others, which produces a feeling of pleasure.[15] This impulse is scopophilia. Freud observed that the scopophiliac instinct to gaze represented a phenomenon of infantile sexuality that develops into a normal part of adult sexual behavior. For Freud, looking and displaying are both instinctual and potentially aberrant. He concluded, therefore, that these impulses are present in everyone, but are controlled by social norms, taboos, and rules that prevent their manifestation as perversions. In Freud's theory, while all humans are instinctually driven to look at others, only some perverse individuals (voyeurs) employ this instinct as the sole source of sexual gratification.

The application of Freud's theories of scopophilia in media studies is restricted primarily to cinematic and televisual specularity theory, and focuses predominantly on voyeurism as a sexual perversion. Premised on the technological apparatus of cinema,[16] such theories hold that film (and, for some, television) encourages voyeurism in viewers because the viewing experience allows/commands audiences to gaze at characters who are seemingly unaware of being watched, giving the spectator control and power over the projected images. This secret gazing, many contend, objectifies women in particular, and permits a sexual gratification of sorts on the part of the spectator.[17]

Television and cinema both encourage and invite the scopophiliac *impulse* (as opposed to the voyeuristic perversion) in audiences, not only because of technology, but also because of curiosity and possibility. It is this impulsive need to gaze that most adequately accounts for the intimacy demands of contemporary hyperreal politics. An audience's scopophilia is aroused because television and cinema allow for the possibility of gazing, without guilt, into the private affairs of others. As Freud suggests, there is an epistemophiliac impulse, of which scopophilia is a prime component.[18] Pleasure is derived from knowing (as opposed to the controlling/dominating pleasure emergent from voyeurism), which looking and gazing make possible. Television and cinema technologize that pleasure and extend the scopophilia of the viewers beyond their immediate context.

The visuality of postmodern presidentialities, thus, involves not just the frequently mentioned spectacles of political imaging. There is a visually epistemological sense of politics as well.[19] Because politics is so heavily mediated by technologies dependent upon visual cues and images for their impact, voters come to know and experience politics in profoundly visual ways. They expect to see their candidates in increasingly intimate contexts and the visual evidence presented via the mass media validates their political knowledge and understanding. As television and news proliferate endlessly, voters encounter greater opportunities to gaze at political candidates, both literally and figuratively. Television, as a medium, recognizes and capitalizes on the scopophilia present in its audience. To be successful in the world of "electronic electioneering,"[20] the politician must willingly accommodate this impulse in an audience of voters accustomed to a televisual diet of intimacy and personal display.

Personal revelation and intimacy on the part of presidential candidates, though, is strategically risky. It was Freud who observed that leaders are powerful when they are substitutes for the ego-ideal and distant from their subjects.[21] This distance is part of a powerful presidentiality that is central to the political and moral leadership of the office and the institution.[22]

Candidates for the presidency must negotiate their image construction carefully within this more complicated and perilous scopophiliac environment. They still must strive for a presidential image, and they must utilize and associate the myths and images of the presidency with their candidacy. However, because of the presence of television and the intimate gazing that this medium invites, candidates must exhibit their private and intimate selves to voters in order to appear credible and forthcoming. In addition, political intimacy often occurs within the context of "feminine" symbolism because television requires that political speakers assume a more womanly, or feminine, style of communication.[23]

The Gendered Nature of Scopophiliac Politics

A feminine style of political communication would seem to promote female candidates.[24] "Because the mass media . . . are fixated on differences between the private and public self of public figures," Jamieson argues, "a comfort with expressing instead of camouflaging self . . . is useful for a politician." This usefulness, according to Jamieson, "benefits females."[25]

Others go beyond identifying the utility of the feminine style and claim that a feminine style of discourse may actually represent the beginnings of a feminized politics—a potential shift in public discourse to a more feminist orientation. Feminist critics Bonnie Dow and Mari Boor Tonn conclude, "the characteristics of feminine style are part of a synthesis of form and substance that works to promote an alternative political philosophy reflecting traditionally feminine values."[26] Both the discourse that uses a feminine style and the criticism of that discourse strive toward "the continued formation of 'a discursive space which defines itself in terms of a common identity' but which operates to provide potential for oppositional ideology that counters hegemonic ideas of universality."[27] In short, these critics see the presence of a feminine style in political discourse as potentially revolutionary, with such a style creating the conditions necessary for an "alternative . . . political judgment."[28]

We, too, celebrate the growth of the feminine style in political discourse and recognize its potential for significant political change. But we are reluctant to read too much into this contemporary discursive development. Specifically, while most campaign rhetorics exhibit a feminine style, they simultaneously rely upon prevailing masculine values and themes.[29] Instead of resulting in a feminized political sphere, contemporary campaign rhetorics reflect the continual marginalization of women in the political process and the general exclusion of women from political office and political power.[30] Ideologically, masculinity thus continues to ground and define presidentiality in the United States.

Masculinity is a hegemonic construct defined by Robert W. Connell as "the culturally idealized form of masculine character."[31] Hegemonic masculinity represents "the social ascendancy of a particular version or model of masculinity that, operating on the terrain of 'common sense' and conventional morality, defines 'what it means to be a man.'"[32] Tim Carrigan and his colleagues define hegemonic masculinity as "centrally connected with the institutionalization of men's dominance over women" and is fundamentally a matter of "how particular groups of men inhabit positions of power and wealth, and how they legitimate and reproduce the social relationships that generate their dominance."[33] The power of hegemonic conceptions of masculinity is that they allow for change and evolution while still maintaining the dominance of men over women.[34] Differing formulations of masculinity enter and exit the symbolic environment,[35] and the hegemony allows for such alteration. Conceptions of masculinity are not fixed or natural, and the critical scrutiny of existing hegemonies of masculinity potentially erodes the oppression and domination that such discourses characteristically express.

The symbolic power of social constructions of masculinity for the larger political culture occurs when candidates define their images according to powerful values, ideals, and myths that typically represent masculinity. This process occurs in two ways. First, presidential candidates are associated with institutions and cultural practices that define masculinity for American society. This symbolic association results in the construction of a masculine model of leadership. Second, women are portrayed in this presidential discourse as firmly within their familial, patriarchally determined roles, reinforcing the maleness of presidential candidates and relegating the role of the women in their lives to supportive rather than participatory activities.

The Man from Hope reflects both the gendered dimensions of American politics and also its scopophiliac characteristics. It is, thus, a rhetoric of tremendous relevance to the understanding of presidentiality in the 1990s. *The Man from Hope* offered a presidentiality that clearly and successfully constructed a candidate to fit his times and the office he sought. The film put forth an intimate discourse that invited a scopophiliac gaze via the manipulation of familiar media production practices. Such practices offered visual grammars to guide and encourage viewer gaze and to create voter knowledge about the candidate in ways reliant upon visuality. Furthermore, the candidate's image was grounded in an ideology of masculinity that reified his presidential persona by way of a feminine style of discourse.

Candidate Bill Clinton and the Discourse of Hyperreal Hope

W. Lance Bennett reports that during the 1992 election campaign, the Clinton campaign confronted their candidate's political problems by reconstituting "a human persona that was vulnerable, humble, and accessible to ordinary people."[36] Their plan was reflected in the campaign film produced by Harry Thomason and Linda Bloodworth-Thomason, noted friends of the Clintons and producers of several successful television series. The film received praise from critics and pundits[37]; both Bill and Hillary Clinton were also reportedly moved to tears by its narrative.[38]

The Man from Hope featured many personal reflections and revelations from a variety of individuals close to Bill Clinton as well as from the candidate himself. Where previous presidential campaign films offered mostly direct address from relatively few people (usually the candidate and one or two other people), the Clinton film presented the ruminations of the entire Clinton family, from his mother to his daughter. Their stories were almost entirely about Bill Clinton's upbringing, his personal family life, and his character. The film did not discuss any of the offices held by the candidate or any accomplishments achieved by Clinton as Arkansas' governor. In addition to the film's self-disclosive narratives, the visual production techniques of *The Man from Hope* fostered its intimate appeal, inviting the gaze of spectators and appealing to their scopophiliac impulse in the process. As such, the entire structure and content of the film was consistent with the campaign's goal of (re)inventing Bill Clinton for the voting public.

Visualizing Clinton in *The Man from Hope*

Three production strategies that amplify the intimacy of mediated texts are the use of direct address by a candidate, the reliance on close-up images, and the structure of spectator positioning prompted by camera placement. The "talking head" style of campaign advertising, characterized by direct address from the candidate, is often viewed as a means by which the audience can assess a candidate's personality and character.[39] Furthermore, the camera's focus on the face promotes a political intimacy that encourages what Hart calls "face watching," as faces are turned "into arguments."[40] This focus on the face through direct address invites a response that is heightened by the use of close-up images. According to Paul Messaris, responses to television close-ups are "based in part on the real-world association between interpersonal closeness and involvement,"[41] which are dependent upon the rules of "real-life vision."[42] Thus, as the gaze of a candidate is fixed on or near the camera, the spectators will employ appropriate interpersonal responses and return the gaze, attending to these intimate messages. The screen thus becomes "an 'extended retina' for the viewer,"[43] constructing an illusory intimacy between the candidate and the spectator.

These three production practices elevated the intimacy of *The Man from Hope*. The film interviewed Clinton in a dimly lit room at the Arkansas Governor's Mansion, where his eye gaze is directed just to the left of camera. The filmmakers positioned Clinton in an interview style; the camera zoomed in and out, vacillating from a talking head shot to a full-body image. The use of direct address and close-ups presumed to offer insight into his character and personality, addressing image issues that Clinton confronted in the aftermath of Gennifer Flowers, alleged draft evasion, and Whitewater allegations. These close-up shots of Clinton were often accompanied by self-disclosive comments about his family. The spectator positioning combined with the close-up and eye gaze to create a sense of intimacy, especially when interfaced with self-disclosive messages.

As Clinton narrated his intimate autobiography, he offered what appeared to be a revealing look into his life and past both visually and verbally. When talking about his childhood, for example, Clinton referenced his early separations from his mother. As Clinton's face filled the screen, he related how his mother cried "because she felt so bad that I was leaving" so she could go to nursing school.[44] The extreme nature of the close-up was attention-grabbing; Clinton's invitational gaze elevated the aura of self-revelation and intimacy. In a similarly self-disclosive moment, Clinton recalled vivid memories of an incident when he, at only fourteen years old, confronted his alcoholic stepfather about the domestic violence present in the home. The candidate concluded this memory by reflecting:

> I never stopped loving my stepfather, or thinking he was a really good person. I wish I'd known more about human psychology as a child than I did, because I came to realize that he was a good person and that the problem was not that he didn't love my mother or me or my brother. The problem was that he didn't think enough of himself.

Once again, the close-up of Clinton was extreme, which invited a reciprocal gaze, and called forth an assessment of "personality," especially given the character-based exigencies that plagued Clinton's primary campaign. The audience, conditioned by television, instinctively needed to see and to know this candidate, and the film fulfilled that need by the direct address of the candidate concerning personal matters.

As the film's narrative progressed to Clinton's adult family life, it featured his memories of Chelsea—the candidate's daughter—which once again intersected personal revelation and intimate camera angles. Bill Clinton, for example, revealed his amazement and gratitude at the birth of his daughter. He recounted: "I remember how scwunched up she was when she came out. I still, uh, remember how profoundly grateful I was that, you know, Hillary was okay and that I had lived to see it. I mean, I was very aware at that moment that that's something my father hadn't done." In another particularly intimate revelation, the candidate spoke of watching the Clintons' *60 Minutes* interview with Chelsea. In that interview, to respond to the Gennifer Flowers scandal, both Bill and Hillary Clinton discussed the difficulties in their marriage. Of that moment, Clinton noted how "pretty painful" it was "to have your child watch that." When the Clintons asked Chelsea what she thought of the interview, Chelsea reportedly replied: "I'm glad you're my parents." As the camera zoomed in slowly on Clinton's face, it extended the invitation to gaze into the face of the teary-eyed candidate. He concluded the segment by noting that he knew at that moment that whatever happened with the election, everything "would be all right." The film then switches to "campaign talk" as Clinton discusses the meaning of his quest for the White House, thus tying his private virtues as a father to his public life as a presidential candidate.

While the camera close-ups helped reify Clinton's narrative, the candidate's first person narrative was naturalized further by the use of photographic and filmed images of the Clintons that functioned to elevate the realism of the text's image-making aims. Throughout the film, the Clinton family interviews were enveloped by black and white photographic images of small town life, young Bill Clinton, or significant events in U.S. history. Of course, the use of black and white images heightened the mythology of the past as depicted in the video. So, during the film's opening and conclusion, a black and white photograph of a train station appeared with the sign "HOPE" displayed. Bill Clinton narrated this segment: "I was born in a little town called

Hope, Arkansas, three months after my father died." The candidate then appeared on screen talking about growing up in Hope and going to his "grandfather's grocery store." A black and white photograph of two men standing by a grocery counter and a black and white photograph of a marching band in a parade followed Clinton's image. Clinton thus was encased by the historical images of small town life, which helped naturalize and mythologize the candidate's campaign image.

As the film closed with Clinton's narration, a summarizing series of images were visualized that further accentuated the text's realism. A contemporary vision of an airplane flying at dusk faded into colorized image of a small town Main Street. A black and white film of children jumping into a swimming area then preceded a colorized image of young girls walking out of a house as if to go to school. The next imaged sequence included a colorized film of a marching band and a black and white video of children swimming. The following images connoted home videos of the Clinton family because of the 1989 date that appears on screen. An image of Bill Clinton throwing rocks in a pond with his daughter is followed by a video of the two dancing. These images faded into a Clinton presidential campaign rally followed by a segment of the candidate dancing with his wife, Hillary Clinton. We then witnessed a young Chelsea dancing alone and Bill and Hillary Clinton being showered with confetti during a contemporaneous campaign rally. As the film closed, the famed image of the Clinton-Kennedy handshake emerged in slow motion and faded into the same train station image from Hope, Arkansas. Throughout the visual montage that intersected archival footage, Clinton home videos and photographs, and Clinton campaign footage, we *heard* Bill Clinton say:

> Sometimes late at night on the campaign plane, I look out the window and think how far I am from that little town in Arkansas. And yet in many ways I know that all I am or ever will be came from there. A place and a time when nobody locked their doors at night, everybody showed up for a parade on Main Street, and kids like me could dream of being part of something bigger than themselves. . . . I hope that we as a people will always acknowledge that each child in our country is as important as our own. I still believe these things are possible. I still believe in the promise of America. And I still believe in a place called Hope.

By surrounding Clinton's narration with these archival and historical images, the candidate's persona came to embody the small town myths, the purity and innocence of childhood, the good father and husband personas, and the visions of hope that are symbolized by JFK and by Clinton's birthplace. In a separate scripted and intertextual political moment, Texas governor Ann Richards fused Clinton's persona with the "American Dream" when she introduced the convention campaign film to the Democratic faithful, asserting, "the story of Bill Clinton is a truly American story."

The sequencing of the visual images helped naturalize this simulated and intimate exercise in image-construction. "Two shots joined together in the context of a broader narrative," Paul Messaris maintains, "are 'read' by the viewer as being part of a coherent stream of space, time, and action, even if the shots were in fact taken at widely separate times and places." Even though the editing of the visuals is apparent, Messaris argues that viewers still "succumb to the illusion of false continuity."[45] Thus, as Bill Clinton sought to (re)image himself for the general election in the aftermath of the difficult primary campaign, he centered his image on issues of character extracted from his childhood and his personal life. The visual images that enveloped his intimate narration, the sequencing of those visuals, as well as the camera positioning helped reify his message and encourage a scopophiliac response from the voter.

The intimacy of *The Man from Hope* thus emerged from the character and persona of the candidate, and this film represented a significant departure from previous presidential campaign films.[46] The entire Clinton campaign, Bennett suggests, provided a "daily intimacy" that began with the convention film, and offered voters a "fantasy of renewal and hope."[47] That fantasy was made real by the exhibitionist nature of the campaign film that appealed to the scopophilia at work in the viewing, voting public. Seemingly, the Clinton family secrets were revealed and the viewer was asked to "feel his pain" as Clinton demonstrated his strength of character in conquering that pain. The film allowed the viewer the epistemophiliac pleasure of *knowing* the candidate and invited the viewer through both its narrative and its visual components into his personal life and private matters. Clinton represented, fundamentally, the American Dream of conquering adversity and achieving success. *The Man from Hope* let the viewer see that dream's enactment in Clinton's life and gain pleasure from the knowledge that Bill Clinton personified that dream for all of America, a vision that was essentialized by the visual production techniques and the gendered ideologies upon which the film was based.

Gendered Politics in *The Man from Hope*

The Man from Hope was also a highly feminine campaign discourse, in that it was personal, anecdotal, and inductive in its attempt to achieve identification with the viewer.[48] The film was also ornate in its use of music and entertainment production techniques, which added to the refinement of the campaign film genre as a discursive text that relies on the feminine style in its presentation. The intimate dimensions of the film were further expressed via women (e.g., Clinton's wife, mother, daughter, and mother-in-law) and their prominent place in Bill Clinton's life. In fact, aside from Roger Clinton, who served a subservient role to his older brother, women were the only individuals featured in the film as first-person testifiers for the Democratic presidential nominee. Their task was clearly to substantiate and authenticate Bill Clinton's moral character.

The relationships that exist between issues of morality, the intimate/private sphere, and the feminine are historically grounded. "Female symbols, like the goddess of liberty and Columbia, were favored emblems of civic virtue," finds Mary Ryan. Women's roles within the public/private spheres were thus relegated to the "private nurturance of infant citizens" related to issues of "moral education" designed to protect the male child from "the corrupting influence of the city."[49] Responding to Clinton's "womanizer" image, the discourse from the women in Clinton's life—the women who presumably know him best—endowed him with a rhetoric of civic virtue that was firmly situated within the feminine/private sphere.

Despite its feminine style, *The Man from Hope* also represented a masculine text of presidentiality. As with most campaign rhetorics, this film utilized familiar masculine institutions to establish Clinton's credentials for the presidency. Moreover, the film relegated women to supportive or authenticating roles.[50] This became especially noteworthy in the case of Hillary Rodham Clinton, given her well-known activism and policy influence. The film's reliance on masculinist images and themes revealed how *The Man from Hope* performed the presidency.[51] Thus, even though the film constructed an intimate image of Clinton with its feminine style, its dependence on hegemonic masculinity ideologically comforted those who would fear a weakening of the heroic and mythic presidency. The integration of the feminine (e.g., intimate) style and masculinity evidenced the manner in which *The Man from*

Hope strategically and ideologically negotiated the contemporary paradox of presidentiality. Although unconscious and socially constructed, the film preserved and naturalized the link between masculinity and the presidency through its use of public, mythic, and nostalgic heroes fused with the history of the United States.

Hegemonic constructions of masculinity are partially "defined through occupational achievement" and success within the industrial, capitalist system.[52] The enduring personality traits associated with maleness/work include aggressiveness, competitiveness, and confidence. This is particularly true of the hegemonic masculinity that infuses contemporary presidentialities. Specifically, politics as an occupation serves as the primary institution used by the candidates to demonstrate their preparation for the presidency.

Clinton's campaigners, interestingly, ignored his overtly political work as governor of Arkansas and instead relied on his Boys' Nation experience and martyred, mythologized heroes to construct a political occupation for their candidate. This emphasis, of course, strategically avoided Clinton's record as governor and shifted the focus to the *mythos* of Camelot and the civil rights movement. As such, Clinton's political résumé, his occupational credentials, were constructed as affiliative and ideal rather than direct and experiential. We can almost sense the torch of leadership passing from President Kennedy to a young Bill Clinton as they shake hands during the Boys' Nation photo opportunity on the White House lawn. The film heightened the mythology of this experience through the political icons that Clinton say influenced his civic consciousness: John F. Kennedy, Martin Luther King, Jr., and Robert Kennedy. This gendered-based institution (Boys' Nation) and the male political heroes linked to Clinton implied the exclusionary nature of the presidency as an all-male preserve.

The military acts as the second institution used by candidates to define their qualifications for public office. Connell notes that gendered power is preserved in advanced capitalist societies through control of the military and the police.[53] The use of military images and themes also implies that a candidate possesses the heroism and courage necessary for successful military service. By extension, such traits come to be associated with the presidency and are essential, the texts imply, for effective presidential leadership.

Bill Clinton, of course, lacked a military record and his repeated attempts to avoid service in the Vietnam War were well known by the time *The Man from Hope* debuted in July of 1992. Clinton's battles, as presented in the film, were different—they symbolized a war against poverty and for social justice. The film subtly established a sense of his battle readiness, as Clinton spoke of driving "supplies down into the burned out part of [Washington, DC]" following Martin Luther King Jr.'s assassination. Black and white video clips of African American children seeking cover on the city streets as if to escape the ravages of battle accompanied this statement. We then witnessed archival images of armed police officers riding in trucks against the backdrop of the U.S. Capitol. When detailing the aftermath of King's April 1968 assassination when "Washington burned," numerous black and white video images of burning buildings filled the screen. The implication, of course, was that this was the warlike context in which Clinton risked his life to save others (e.g., African American children) to deliver supplies into the firestorm of battle. Examples like these served to communicate the character of the presidential candidate who might one day lead the country into future wars. Military qualities worked to credential this presidential candidate and were fully complicit with a hegemonic masculinity that privileges military courage and fortitude as important character traits.

The family functions as another institution that serves to shape and define presidential image. Although the family has traditionally been viewed as an institution that features women in powerful roles, the construction of the candidate's family in *The Man from Hope* further revealed the film's reliance on patriarchy. This conception of the family stereotypically portrayed males as the breadwinner, family protector, and father figure.[54] Moreover, the family functioned often as a setting for demonstrations of courage and determination in the face of adversity, which reinforced masculine images of protectionism and control.

Specifically, family experiences in *The Man from Hope* were used to demonstrate the candidate's determination and courage in the face of significant personal tragedy. The film featured, for example, Clinton and his mother (in separate interviews spliced together) discussing Clinton's standoff with his alcoholic stepfather when he was in the ninth grade. Even as he faced the wrath of his intoxicated stepfather, we were told of Clinton's determination to act decisively to prevent further abusive behaviors. Clinton stated: "When I was in the ninth grade I think, he . . . kind of got violent with my mother one night and I just bulled through the door and told him he wasn't going to do that anymore." Virginia

Kelley finished the story by recounting her son's words through her own memory of the event:

> [Bill said] 'Stand up. I have something to say to you,' . . . He got into his face and said, 'Daddy, if you're not able to stand up, I'll help you. You must stand to hear what I have to say.' . . . Bill told him then, 'Don't you ever, ever lay your hand on my mother again.'

Notably, this story established Clinton's controlling, masculine bravery in protecting his fully capable and mature adult mother while only fourteen years old. Clinton's brother Roger even asserted, "my brother took over the leadership role when he was just a kid." The film implied, thus, that just as he worked diligently to unify his family, rescuing his vulnerable and needy mother and brother from danger, Clinton would work just as hard to re-unify the country and protect its most defenseless citizens. His leadership would manifest his own ideals: "we've got to be one country again . . . coming together instead of coming apart." This construction of Clinton's courage interfaced with the familial patriarchy at the foundation of masculine power. Such masculine constructions were reified further through the roles constructed for the women who appeared in the film.

Portraying Women in *The Man from Hope*

"A hegemony is a negotiation among elite and nonelite groups," contends rhetorical critic Celeste Condit, "and therefore always contains interests of nonelite groups."[55] To that end, texts contain complex layers and intermixtures of dominant and radical ideologies working oppositionally. *The Man from Hope*, employing a feminine style of presentation, drew upon enduring traits of socially constructed concepts of masculinity to argue for the presidential character of Bill Clinton. Additionally, the construction of women in the film further illustrated how this feminine style actually worked hegemonically to mask its masculine themes.

Political scholar Virginia Sapiro is right to caution against viewing the public conception of political women through a gendered lens that typecasts them as mothers, housewives, and sex objects.[56] Nevertheless, we are still drawn to the observation that in *The Man from Hope*, women *were* constructed as supportive wives and commentators who offer testimony of the candidate's strength of character and authenticity.[57]

Such portrayals of women in the text reflected a fundamental aspect of hegemonic masculinity that promotes hierarchical and patriarchal relationships between men and women.

Hillary Rodham Clinton offered the possibility that such roles might be challenged and altered. Yet the producers of the Clinton campaign film crafted her portrayal to fit within the confines of the more traditionally feminine role of wife and mother. Her areas of expertise were linked exclusively to the family and in particular to her husband's abilities as a father. For instance, she talked of "Bill's becoming a father and having Chelsea" as "one of the great experiences of his life," evidenced by the fact that "he would sit for hours and look at his daughter . . . trying to take in this miracle." Unlike her husband, who is allowed to speak about family *and* politics, Hillary Clinton has a voice only on issues relating to the family. Rather than speaking of her own law school career, for example, she spoke about the first time she saw "Bill" and her feeling that he was "great looking and . . . fun." After pausing briefly as if to search carefully for her words, Hillary Clinton concluded awkwardly that "[Bill] is just somebody who challenged you and made you happy all the time."

The authenticating role of motherhood was played out further in the film through the testimony offered by the other women in Bill Clinton's life. Virginia Kelley, for instance, testified to her son's sincerity as a reformer in acknowledging that even at age seven, he wanted to help Arkansas "get off the bottom" of a list that rated states according to educational quality. More interestingly, Clinton's mother-in-law, Dorothy Rodham, bore witness to the couple's "synergy" by pointing to the success of their marriage: "I think they deeply love and are committed to one another." Bill Clinton's grandmother was even invoked in the film as the one who reared him and thus socialized him to value reading. The effectiveness of the moral education offered by Virginia Kelley and the grandmother was addressed by perhaps the most innocent participant in the video; Chelsea Clinton concluded that her parents successfully "taught me . . . the Golden Rule." These women who know the candidate best were featured as credible witnesses to the civic virtue of Bill Clinton's intimate character. They addressed Clinton's outstanding campaign challenges and exigencies in an intimate manner, serving as the sole experts of his private, albeit contested, identity.

Absent other father images personally associated with the candidate, Bill Clinton stood as the patriarchal icon of civic virtue fully socialized by the women in his life to venture into the political/public realm of battle against the evil forces of corruption (e.g., the political forces that sought to demean his image). His wife, daughter, mother, and mother-in-law, who see him adoringly, created and corroborated that image. Even Ann Richards, when introducing Clinton's film, affirmed the genuineness of his character—his personal, intimate self:

> Bill Clinton is not a creation of the media or of this party, he's not a cardboard cut-out candidate. He is a real human being—a son, a father, a husband, and a friend. And those of us who know and respect Bill Clinton, want you to know that this Democratic Party has a presidential nominee that you would be proud to call your friend.

Murray Edelman argues that political candidates and officials "who refuse to act chauvinistically are likely to be defined as weak, ineffective, and vulnerable to attack."[58] Clinton's chauvinism was much more subtle in its use of a feminine style and the fusing of his persona and his civic virtue with the women in his life. The symbolic representation of women, particularly Hillary Rodham Clinton, in *The Man from Hope* evidenced the symbolic representation of women in the American political system. Within the rubric of hegemonic masculinity, women in our political system are supportive, nurturing, and honest about personal character issues. Moreover, the feminine style used in the film masked the stereotyped roles of women. The assessment of such discourses may ignore the reactionary power of the film vis-à-vis the role of women in politics and in society. The film thus was dependent on traditional masculine constructions to evidence Clinton's presidential character.

Scopophilia, Feminization, and the Hyperreal Political Culture

As the distance between candidate and the voter shrinks because of the candidate's self-disclosure and the camera's ability to intrude into the candidate's private realm, the image of intimacy encourages the public to believe they are coming to know the "real" candidate—the person behind the campaign artifice. However, these images are thoroughly hyperreal to the extent that it is virtually impossible to know or discern "real" intimacy from planned intimacies. So while *The Man from Hope* seemed intimate and revelatory of the Clintons, we know that the intimacies found in the text were highly orchestrated.[59]

Easily the most disquieting feature of the political construction of intimacy is the use of a feminine style of discourse to mask the patriarchy of contemporary politics. Hegemony exists when those with power are able to secure the consent of the powerless. Accordingly, hegemonic rhetorics will co-opt oppositional discourses to achieve the necessary consent for the exercise of communal power. The result is a condition in which, according to Condit, "to resist the hegemony that is constructed in negotiation with those [elite] groups is always also to resist what is partially of one's own interests."[60] The use of the feminine style in contemporary candidate image construction works as part of the negotiation under way over the nature and exercise of political power in the United States. This presentational manner may persuade those who would oppose existing power relationships that politics are becoming feminized. As such, a feminine style might occlude meaningful opposition to patriarchy. Its use may only reflect a presentational shift that does not violate patriarchal constructions and that does repress the feminine. Thus, both the masculine and the feminine co-exist in a symbiotic whole, achieving a hegemonic outcome of some consequence.

Voters gaze at candidates and television invites more and more viewers to the spectacle of presidential politics. And voters come to expect and gain pleasure from knowing and seeing more of their presidential candidates. But these same voters are trapped in a contradiction, as is the entire presidential election process. On the one hand, voters are sold (by the media, candidates, parties, and consultants) a nostalgic, mythic leadership that is powerful and symbolically meaningful in the electoral choices that they make. Such leadership is remote, paternal, and largely inaccessible. On the other hand, voters are accustomed to a televisual culture that exploits and manipulates both the scopophilia and its accompanying epistemophilia for profit and ratings. Quite expectantly, that culture encroaches upon political behavior and motive, providing both scopophiliac pleasure and shame to a citizenry possessing large levels of intimate knowledge about political leaders. Confusion results, as voters seek distant, heroic leadership while responding to strategies that manipulate the intimacy of contemporary politics.

Such confusion is an outgrowth, though, of a dynamic, evolving political culture, questioning its ideological assumptions, and challenging its political practices. *The Man from Hope* constructed a presidentiality that offered an intimate and highly feminine portrait of the candidate firmly grounded in a masculinist ideology. Its rhetoric simultaneously naturalized the masculine essence of the presidency and Clinton's fitfulness for the office and responded to the demands of an increasingly feminized media culture that requires increased political intimacies. The paradoxes and tensions that characterize contemporary American political culture, and that were expressed in *The Man from Hope*, emerge in other texts that construct the Clinton image. We proceed, in the next chapter, to examine the political hyperreality and intimacy found in the Clinton campaign's attempt to control the image-making process further during the 1992 campaign as it orchestrated and managed a documentary film crew's access to its campaign "war room."

Notes

1. An account of this episode is found in Jack Germond and Jules Witcover, *Mad as Hell: Revolt at the Ballot Box, 1992* (New York: Warner Books, 1993); and Peter Goldman, Thomas M. DeFrank, Mark Miller, Andrew Murr, and Tom Mathews, *Quest for the Presidency 1992* (College Station: Texas A&M University Press, 1994).

2. See Thomas A. Bailey, *Presidential Greatness* (New York: Appleton-Century-Crofts, 1966); Murray Edelman, *Constructing the Political Spectacle* (Chicago: University of Chicago Press, 1988); Walter R. Fisher, "Romantic Democracy, Ronald Reagan, and Presidential Heroes," *Western Journal of Speech Communication* 46 (1982): 299–310; and Sarah Russell Hankins, "Archetypal Alloy: Reagan's Rhetorical Image," *Central States Speech Journal* 34 (1983): 33–43. See also Robert E. Denton, Jr., *The Symbolic Dimensions of the American Presidency: Description and Analysis* (Prospect Heights, IL: Waveland Press, 1982); Dan Hahn, "The Media and the Presidency: Ten Propositions," *Communication Quarterly* 35 (1987): 254–66; Barbara Hinckley, *The Symbolic Presidency: How Presidents Portray Themselves* (New York: Routledge, 1990); Timothy Luke, "Televisual Democracy and the Politics of Charisma," *Telos* 70 (1986–1987): 59–80; Robert Schmuhl, *Statecraft and Stagecraft: American Political Life in the Age of Personality* (Notre Dame, IN: University of Notre Dame Press, 1992).

3. Roderick P. Hart, *Seducing America: How Television Charms the Modern Voter* (New York: Oxford University Press, 1994), 11. See also Joshua Meyrowitz, "New Sense of Politics: How Television Changes the Political Drama," *Research in Political Sociology* 7 (1995): 117–38.

4. Kathleen Hall Jamieson, *Eloquence in an Electronic Age: The Transformation of Political Speechmaking* (New York: Oxford University Press, 1988), 81.

5. This is not unrelated to the phenomenon of "parasocial interaction" where television viewers come to feel a personal relationship with characters or individuals they encounter on their television screens. A comprehensive discussion of the various dimensions of parasocial interaction is found in Alan M. Rubin and Elizabeth M. Perse, "Audience Activity and Soap Opera Involvement: A Uses and Effects Investigation," *Human Communication Research* 14 (1987): 246–68. See also Michael J. Papa, Arvind Singhal, Sweety Law, Saumya Pant, Suruchi Sood, Everett M. Rogers, and Corinne L. Shefner-Rogers, "Entertainment-Education and Social Change: An Analysis of Parasocial Interaction, Social Learning, Collective Efficacy, and Paradoxical Communication," *Journal of Communication* 50 (2000): 31–56; Janice Peck, "TV Talk Shows as Therapeutic Discourse: The Ideological Labor of the Televised Talking Cure," *Communication Theory* 5 (1995): 58–81; and Alan M.

Rubin, Elizabeth M. Perse, and Robert A. Powell, "Loneliness, Parasocial Interaction, and Local Television News Viewing," *Human Communication Research* 12 (1985): 155–81.

6. See Sanford F. Schram, "The Post-Modern Presidency and the Grammar of Electronic Electioneering," *Critical Studies in Mass Communication* 8 (1991): 210–16.

7. Jamieson, *Eloquence in an Electronic Age*, 67–89.

8. Joanne Morreale, *A New Beginning: A Textual Frame Analysis of the Political Campaign Film* (Albany: State University of New York Press, 1991), 3.

9. Joanne Morreale, *The Presidential Campaign Film: A Critical History* (Westport, CT: Praeger, 1993), 178.

10. Morreale, *The Presidential Campaign Film*, 6. See also David M. Timmerman, "1992 Presidential Candidate Films: The Contrasting Narratives of George Bush and Bill Clinton," *Presidential Studies Quarterly* 26 (1996): 364–73.

11. See Fisher, "Romantic Democracy;" and Herb W. Simons and Don J. Stewart, "Network Coverage of Video Politics: 'A New Beginning' in the Limits of Criticism," in *Television and Political Advertising: Signs, Codes, and Images*, Vol. 2, edited by Frank Biocca (Hillsdale, NJ: Lawrence Erlbaum Associates, 1991), 203–28.

12. The mythic and characterological dimensions of *The Man from Hope* are discussed in Bruce E. Gronbeck, "Characterological Argument in Bush's and Clinton's Convention Films," in *Argument and the Postmodern Challenge: Proceedings of the Eighth SCA/AFA Conference on Argumentation*, edited by Raymie E. McKerrow (Annandale, VA: Speech Communication Association, 1993), 392–7.

13. Janice H. Rushing and Thomas S. Frentz, "Integrating Ideology and Archetype in Rhetorical Criticism," *Quarterly Journal of Speech* 77 (1991): 403.

14. Analyzing contemporary rhetoric using psychoanalytic theory and Freud's work is increasingly popular. See Barbara A. Biesecker, "Rhetorical Studies and the 'New' Psychoanalysis: What's the Real Problem? or Framing the Problem of the Real," [review essay], *Quarterly Journal of Speech* 84 (1998): 222–40; Dana L. Cloud, *Control and Consolation in American Culture and Politics: Rhetoric of Therapy* (Thousand Oaks, CA: Sage, 1998); Thomas S. Frentz and Janice H. Rushing, "Integrating Ideology and Archetype in Rhetorical Criticism, Part II: A Case Study of *Jaws*," *Quarterly Journal of Speech* 79 (1993): 61–81; Michael J. Hyde, "Jacques Lacan's Psychoanalytic Theory of Speech and Language," *Quarterly Journal of Speech* 66 (1980): 96–118; John J. Makay, "Psychotherapy as a Rhetoric for Secular Grace," *Central States Speech Journal* 31 (1980): 184–96; Tullio Maranhão,

Therapeutic Discourse and Socratic Dialogue (Madison: University of Wisconsin Press, 1986); James P. McDaniel, "Fantasm: The Triumph of Form (An Essay on the Democratic Sublime)," *Quarterly Journal of Speech* 86 (2000): 48–66; Stephen D. O'Leary and Mark H. Wright, "Psychoanalysis and Burkeian Rhetorical Criticism," *Southern Communication Journal* 61 (1995): 104–21; David Payne, *Coping with Failure: The Therapeutic Uses of Rhetoric* (Columbia: University of South Carolina Press, 1989); David Payne, "*The Wizard of Oz*: Therapeutic Rhetoric in a Contemporary Media Ritual," *Quarterly Journal of Speech* 75 (1989): 25–39; Lloyd S. Pettegrew, "Psychoanalytic Theory: A Neglected Rhetorical Dimension," *Philosophy & Rhetoric* 13 (1977): 46–59; Robert E. Terrill, "Put on a Happy Face: *Batman* as Schizophrenic Savior," *Quarterly Journal of Speech* 79 (1993): 319–35; and Robert E. Terrill, "Spectacular Repression: Sanitizing the Batman," *Critical Studies in Media Communication* 17 (2000): 493–509. In addition, the decidedly rhetorical nature of psychoanalysis and the therapeutic process is the source of some anxiety to those who cling to psychoanalysis as a scientific process. Donald P. Spence predicts that unless the power of rhetoric is diminished, "the fate of psychoanalysis as a creative enterprise would seem in jeopardy." See Donald P. Spence, *The Rhetorical Voice of Psychoanalysis* (Cambridge, MA: Harvard University Press, 1994), 4. Nevertheless, the link between psychoanalysis and rhetoric is a powerful one, and it may well be the case that psychoanalysis is impossible without the tools and practices of rhetoric. See Mikkel Borch-Jacobsen, *The Emotional Tie: Psychoanalysis, Mimesis, and Affect* (Stanford, CA: Stanford University Press, 1992).

15. Sigmund Freud, "Three Essays on the Theory of Sexuality, in *The Standard Edition of the Complete Psychological Works of Sigmund Freud*, Vol. 7, edited and translated by James Strachey (London: The Hogarth Press, 1905/1957), 123–246; and Sigmund Freud, "Instincts and Their Vicissitudes" in *The Standard Edition of the Complete Psychological Works of Sigmund Freud*, Vol. 14, edited and translated by James Strachey (London: The Hogarth Press, 1915/1957), 109–40.

16. Theresa Hak Kyu Cha, ed., *Apparatus* (New York: Tanam Press, 1980).

17. See John Ellis, *Visible Fictions* (London: Routledge & Kegan Paul, 1982); John Fiske, *Television Culture* (London: Methuen, 1987); Sandy Flitterman, "Woman, Desire and the Look: Feminism and the Enunciative Apparatus in Cinema," in *Theories of Authorship: A Reader*, edited by John Caughie (London: Routledge & Kegan Paul, 1981), 242–50; Sandy Flitterman-Lewis, "Psychoanalysis, Film, and Television," in *Channels of Discourse: Television and Contemporary Criticism*, edited by Robert C. Allen (Chapel Hill: University of North Carolina Press, 1987), 172–210; Annette Kuhn, *Women's Pictures: Feminism and Cinema* (London: Routledge & Kegan Paul, 1982); Christian Metz, *The Imaginary Signifier: Psychoanalysis and the Cinema*, translated by Celia Britton, et al. (Bloomington: Indiana University Press, 1982); and Laura Mulvey, "Visual Pleasure and the Narrative Cinema," *Screen* 16:3 (1975): 6–18.

18. See Sigmund Freud, "Notes Upon a Case of Obsessional Neurosis," in *The Standard Edition of the Complete Psychological Works of Sigmund Freud*, Vol. 10, edited and translated by James Strachey (London: The Hogarth Press, 1905/1955), 155–318; and Paula Rabinowitz, "Voyeurism and Class Consciousness: James Agee and Walter Evans, *Let Us Now Praise Famous Men*," *Cultural Critique* 21 (1992): 143–170.

19. For further discussions of visual epistemology, see Martin Jay, *Downcast Eyes: The Denigration of Vision in Twentieth-Century French Thought* (Berkeley: University of California Press, 1993); and David Michael Levin, ed., *Modernity and the Hegemony of Vision* (Berkeley: University of California Press, 1993).

20. Schram, "The Post-Modern Presidency," 210.

21. In his analysis of group psychology, Freud examines the power of leaders in primitive societies and links that power to the influence of hypnotists. As he reveals, "it is precisely the sight of the chieftain that is dangerous and unbearable for primitive people, just as later that of the Godhead is for mortals." Leaders are successful when they are "of a masterful nature, absolutely narcissistic, self-confident and independent." See Sigmund Freud, "Group Psychology and the Analysis of the Ego," in *The Standard Edition of the Complete Psychological Works of Sigmund Freud*, Vol. 18, edited and translated by James Strachey (London: The Hogarth Press, 1921/1955), 124–5. See also Borch-Jacobsen, *The Emotional Tie*; and Ian Craib, *Psychoanalysis and Social Theory* (Amherst: University of Massachusetts Press, 1990).

22. Hinckley, *The Symbolic Presidency*.

23. Jamieson, *Eloquence in an Electronic Age*, 84. For more on the nature of the postmodern political spectacle, see Ryan Barilleaux, *The Post-Modern Presidency: The Office After Ronald Reagan* (New York: Praeger, 1988); Michael Gurevitch and Anandam P. Kavooris, "Television Spectacles as Politics," *Communication Monographs* 59 (1992): 415–20; Douglas Kellner, *Television and the Crisis of Democracy* (Boulder, CO: Westview, 1990); Schmuhl, *Statecraft and Stagecraft*; Schram, "The Grammar of Electronic Electioneering"; David L. Swanson, "The Political-Media Complex," *Communication Monographs* 59 (1992): 397–400; and David Zarefsky, "Spectator Politics and the Revival of Public Argument," *Communication Monographs* 59 (1992): 411–14.

24. Jamieson, *Eloquence in an Electronic Age*; Kathleen Hall Jamieson, *Beyond the Double Bind: Women and Leadership* (New York: Oxford University Press, 1995).

25. Jamieson, *Beyond the Double Bind*, 95.

26. Bonnie J. Dow and Mari Boor Tonn, "'Feminine Style' and Political Judgment in the Rhetoric of Ann Richards," *Quarterly Journal of Speech* 79 (1993): 287.

27. Dow and Tonn, "'Feminine Style,'" 287.

28. Dow and Tonn, "'Feminine Style,'" 289.

29. Our focus, in this analysis, is on the gendered nature of contemporary political communication, though such concerns are usually "treated as marginal to or outside of the subject matter of political theory." See Mary Lyndon Shanley and Carole Pateman, eds., *Feminist Interpretations and Political Theory* (University Park: The Pennsylvania State University Press, 1991), 3. We maintain that gender roles and categories of behavior are the result of socialization and naming rather than reflective of any essential or natural linkage to biological sex. See Judith Lorber, *Paradoxes of Gender* (New Haven, CT: Yale University Press, 1994). The veneration of the "feminine" style reifies this style of discourse and may suggest the acceptance of a "polarity" of the sexes. See Dow and Tonn, "'Feminine Style'"; Anne F. Mattina, "'Rights as Well as Duties': The Rhetoric of Leonora O'Reilly," *Communication Quarterly* 42 (1994): 196–205; and Patricia A. Sullivan, "Women's Discourse and Political Communication: A Case Study of Congressperson Patricia Schroeder," *Western Journal of Communication* 57 (1992): 530–45. In addition, our usages of "masculine" and "patriarchy" are distinct and purposeful. "Masculine" is typically used as a modifier of characteristics, traits, myths, etc., or as part of the phrase "hegemonic masculinity." We use "patriarchy" to refer to embedded and socially derived systems of power and control through which males are accorded superiority over females. As with our usages of "feminine," these terms are not meant to suggest natural or biological bases for gendered constructions.

30. Some commentators claim that while a feminine style of communication may characterize much contemporary political discourse, such discourse continues to marginalize women (and others) from the political process. See Edelman, *Constructing the Political Spectacle*; and Schram, "The Post-Modern Presidency." Others point to the very nature of democratic liberalism that highlights values of individuality, autonomy, and freedom as exclusionary and powerful forces for political theory and voting behavior. See Ronald D. Hedlund, Patricia K. Freeman, Keith E. Hamm, and Robert M. Stein, "The Electability of Women Candidates: The Effects of Sex Role Stereotypes," *Journal of Politics* 41 (1979): 513–24; and Nancy J. Hirschmann, "Freedom, Recognition, and Obligation: A Feminist Approach to Political Theory," *American Political Science Review* 83 (1989): 1227–44.

31. Robert W. Connell, "An Iron Man: The Body and Some Contradictions of Hegemonic Masculinity," in *Sports, Men, and the Gender Order: Critical Feminist Perspectives*, edited by Michael A. Messner and Donald F. Sabo (Champaign, IL: Human Kinetics Books, 1990), 83.

32. Robert Hanke, "Hegemonic Masculinity in *thirtysomething*," *Critical Studies in Mass Communication* 7 (1990): 232.

33. Tim Carrigan, Bob Connell, and John Lee, "Toward a New Sociology of Masculinity," *Theory and Society* 14 (1985): 592–4.

34. See Jeff Hearn and David H. J. Morgan, "Men, Masculinities, and Social Theory," in *Men, Masculinities and Social Theory*, edited by Jeff Hearn and David H. J. Morgan (London: Unwin Hyman, 1990), 1–20.

35. See Elizabeth W. Mechling and Jay Mechling, "The Jung and the Restless: The Mythopoetic Men's Movement," *Southern Communication Journal* 59 (1994): 97–111.

36. W. Lance Bennett, "The Cueless Public: Bill Clinton Meets the New American Voter in Campaign '92," in *The Clinton Presidency: Campaigning, Governing, and the Psychology of Leadership*, edited by Stanley A. Renshon (Boulder, CO: Westview Press, 1995), 108. See also Goldman et al., *Quest for the Presidency*.

37. Thomas A. Rosteck, "The Intertextuality of 'The Man from Hope': Bill Clinton as Person, as Persona, as Star?," in *Bill Clinton on Stump, State, and Stage: The Rhetorical Road to the White House*, edited by Stephen A. Smith (Fayetteville: University of Arkansas Press, 1994), 223–48.

38. Goldman et al., *Quest for the Presidency*, 287.

39. See Jefferson Hunter, *Image and Word: The Interaction of Twentieth-Century Photographs and Texts* (Cambridge, MA: Harvard University Press, 1987), 115; and Larry J. Sabato, *The Rise of Political Consultants: New Ways of Winning Elections* (New York: Basic Books, 1981), 123.

40. Hart, *Seducing America*, 40, 38.

41. Paul Messaris, *Visual Persuasion: The Role of Images in Advertising* (Thousand Oaks, CA: Sage, 1997), xv.

42. Paul Messaris, *Visual Literacy: Image, Mind, & Reality* (Boulder, CO: Westview Press, 1994), 13.

43. Joshua Meyrowitz, "Television and Interpersonal Behavior: Codes of Perception and Response," in *Inter/Media: Interpersonal Communication in a Media World*, edited by Gary Gumpert and Robert Cathcart (New York: Oxford University Press, 1982), 226.

44. Harry Thomason and Linda Bloodworth-Thomason (producers), *The Man from Hope* (West Lafayette, IN: Public Affairs Video Archives, 1992). All citations of the text are from this source.

45. Messaris, *Visual Literacy*, 36.

46. For a comparison of intimate appeals and scopophilia in recent presidential campaign films, see Trevor Parry-Giles and Shawn J. Parry-Giles, "Political Scopophilia, Presidential Campaigning, and the Intimacy of American Politics," *Communication Studies* 47 (1996): 191–205.

47. Bennett, "The Cueless Public," 101.

48. Our formulation of the "feminine" style into an analytically useful framework of discourse draws from several different sources that have explicated this rhetorical style. That framework defines the "feminine" style as personal, organized in inductive or nonlinear patterns, stylized and ornamental, reliant on anecdotes and examples, and likely to encourage identification between a speaker and audience. See Karlyn Kohrs Campbell, *Man Cannot Speak for Her: A Critical Study of Early Feminist Rhetoric*, Vol. I (New York: Praeger, 1989); Jamieson, *Eloquence in an Electronic Age*.

49. Mary P. Ryan, "Gender and Public Access: Women's Politics in Nineteenth-Century America" in *Habermas and the Public Sphere*, edited by Craig Calhoun (Cambridge, MA: MIT Press, 1992), 266–7.

50. The concept of authenticity is variously associated with conceptions of morality, self-realization, truth, and individualism. See Chapter Four; Imantis Baruss, *Authentic Knowing: The Convergence of Science and Spiritual Aspiration* (West Lafayette, IN: Purdue University Press, 1996); Alessandro Ferrar, *Reflective Authenticity: Rethinking the Project of Modernity* (London: Routledge, 1998); and Charles Taylor, *The Ethics of Authenticity* (Cambridge, MA: Harvard University Press, 1992).

51. See Judith Butler's discussion of "performing gender" in "Performative Acts and Gender Constitution: An Essay in Phenomenology and Feminist Theory" in *Performing Feminisms: Feminist Critical Theory and Theater*, edited by Sue-Ellen Case (Baltimore, MD: Johns Hopkins University, 1990), 270–82. See also Judith Butler, *Gender Trouble: Feminism and the Subversion of Identity* (New York: Routledge, 1990).

52. Nick Trujillo, "Hegemonic Masculinity on the Mound: Media Representations of Nolan Ryan and American Sports Culture," *Critical Studies in Mass Communication* 8 (1991): 291. See also Hanke, "Hegemonic Masculinity," 236; and Gwenyth H. Edwards, "The Structure and Content of the Male Gender Role Stereotype: An Exploration of Subtypes," *Sex Roles* 27 (1992): 533–51.

53. Robert W. Connell, *Gender and Power: Society, the Person, and Sexual Politics* (Stanford, CA: Stanford University Press, 1987).

54. See Trujillo, "Hegemonic Masculinity," 291.

55. Celeste Michelle Condit, "The Rhetorical Limits of Polysemy," *Critical Studies in Mass Communication* 6 (1989): 119. See also Celeste Michelle Condit, "Hegemony in a Mass-Mediated Society: Concordance about Reproductive Technologies," *Critical Studies in Mass Communication* 11 (1994): 205–30.

56. Virginia Sapiro, "The Political Uses of Symbolic Women: An Essay in Honor of Murray Edelman," *Political Communication* 10 (1993): 141–54.

57. See Virginia Sapiro, *The Political Integration of Women: Roles, Socialization, and Politics* (Urbana: University of Illinois Press, 1983).

58. Edelman, *Constructing the Political Spectacle*, 61.

59. For a discussion of the fusion of intimacy and celebrity, particularly as related to the Gennifer Flowers scandal and *The Man from Hope*, see Bruce E. Gronbeck, "Character, Celebrity, and Sexual Innuendo in the Mass-Mediated Presidency," in *Media Scandals: Morality and Desire in the Popular Culture Marketplace*, edited by James Lull and Stephen Hinerman (New York: Columbia University Press, 1997).

60. Condit, "The Rhetorical Limits," 119.

Chapter Two

Meta-Imaging, *The War Room,* and the Hyperreal Campaign

In *The Man from Hope*, Bill Clinton's campaign for the presidency was constructed as a quest for an idealistic vision of a better nation for all its people. Just as Clinton fought to preserve his family, just as he loved his wife and daughter, just as he endured the "hits" in the 1992 campaign, so too would he bring to the presidency a hope and a dedication for a better tomorrow. By the time of the Democratic convention in 1992, and the formal introduction of Clinton as the Democrats' candidate for president, only the most politically aware and active voters knew who Bill Clinton was and what he stood for. As such, *The Man from Hope* was, for many voters, the first extended introduction they had to Bill Clinton and it was a powerful rhetoric of presidential image construction.

The Man from Hope, though, was only the beginning. Over the course of his eight years as president, Bill Clinton would produce countless image texts to define himself, his family, and his presidency. We turn now to another of these image texts, a unique and compelling rhetoric in the Clinton lexicon of images—the 1993 film, *The War Room*.

The War Room represents a developing and relatively new form of image politics—the meta-image. *Meta-imaging* is the communicative act whereby political campaigns and their chroniclers publicly display and foreground the art and practice of political image construction. Meta-imaging is now a common form of political discourse. It is a political-rhetorical genre wherein campaign outsiders attempt to get "inside" presidential campaigns to unmask the image of the "real" candidate.

The 1992 campaign, for instance, yielded a photographic collection of the Clinton campaign, advertised as "candidate Clinton's private visual diary—the diary he might have kept, had he the time and objectivity."[1] *Newsweek* also produced an "insider" account of the 1992 campaign, later expanded into a book, where the Clintons were singled out in the preface for "daring to be so open, even in their moments of highest stress and deepest gloom."[2] During the 1996 presidential campaign, *60 Minutes* was granted "exclusive" access to the "behind-the-scenes" moments prior to the Kansas announcement of Jack Kemp as Bob Dole's running mate. Following the 1996 election, *Newsweek* and *Time* both featured "insider" accounts of the campaign. *Newsweek* billed their special issue as a "previously confidential account of the behind-the-scenes campaign."[3] *Time* boasted a look "through the keyhole and into the lives of the two presidential candidates," in a photographic spread called "Inside the Campaign."[4] This form of political communication offers so-called "insider" access to campaigns and the process of political image construction. Such accounts appear as insightful investigative journalism or diligent documentary filmmaking. These rhetorics of political imaging, however, are highly managed and controlled by the campaigns to put the best image forward of a candidate and a campaign. Politically, meta-images signal the openness of a campaign and its honesty and candor. They provide campaigns with exposure and enhance the reach of political discourse beyond immediate circumstance or context. In this way, their appearance as "journalistic acumen" or "documentary" style filmmaking is a simple illusion that masks their overtly political nature.

The War Room is a compelling example of meta-imaging and we examine the film as a reflection of both the strategic and ideological power of meta-imaging for U.S. political culture. This film offered its audiences a *visual* "insider" account of Bill Clinton's first presidential campaign, reliant on the "genre memory"[5] or the historical remembrances of such journalistic insider accounts as Theodore White's famous *The Making of the President* series and Timothy Crouse's *The Boys on the Bus*.[6] The coupling of the visual with the so-called insider narrative, though, is significant as the visuals worked to *authenticate* the content of the film even though the "documentary" offered minimal substantive insight into what its producers promoted as the "frenzy of Bill Clinton's unorthodox 1992 presidential campaign."[7] What the film demonstrated most clearly is the symbiotic relationship between politics and the media and the means by which campaigns work to influence the media coverage of the campaign. Rather than viewing the campaign through the gaze of the media, as is the case of many journalistic insider accounts, *The War Room* inverted the gaze, offering a vision of the media through the perspectival lens of campaign operatives. Such an inverted gaze undoubtedly helps explain why the actual film appears with some regularity in clips and still photographs. Indeed, *The War Room* is an enduring part of our political culture, with an ideological force that frequently surfaces in political discourse.

In order to explicate the presence and influence of meta-imaging, we analyze *The War Room* in two ways. First, we evidence how the rhetorical power of this example of meta-imaging derived primarily from the film's reflection and manipulation of the hyperreality endemic to American politics. Strategically, *The War Room* revealed the hyperreality of American politics; it functioned simultaneously as a "real" depiction of the campaign highly dependent on the visual authentication of its content *and* a highly planned and controlled rhetoric of image construction and maintenance. The assumption of verisimilitude in *The War Room* made this documentary account of the campaign of significant strategic importance, even though it was released following the 1992 election.

Second, we argue that *The War Room* is an illustration of the ideological dimensions of hyperreal presidential politics. Discourse that is hyperreal is more intense and immediate in its impact on audiences. As such, the defining metaphors, narratives, and myths that govern mediated political communication are of greater influence in defining the nature of politics itself. In the case of *The War Room*, the hyperreal structuring of politics according to military metaphors worked toward the edification of image-making as a normative, masculine, and white campaign process.

Military motifs are common in political campaigning and the coverage of those campaigns. But when politics is hyperreal, when there is no distinction between the metaphors that represent politics and the actual acts of political campaigning, those metaphors acquire even more salience. In *The War Room*, this particular usage of militarized images and metaphors worked to imbue and naturalize the language and influence of political campaigning into the fabric and ideological systems of American politics. This symbolic process occurred polysemically, as the militarized campaign metaphors expressed both the factionalization of politics and the unification that politics provides for the community. Ideologically, then, the hyperreality of meta-imaging in *The War Room* amplified and restored a powerful, albeit illusory, equilibrium to an American political system characterized by angst and uncertainty in the postmodern political system.

The War Room

Billed as an "adventure story filled with cliff-hanging suspense," *The War Room* was a film shot in *cinéma vérité* style, that profiled two campaign strategists, George Stephanopoulos and James Carville, and their activities between the Democratic National Convention in New York and Election Day, 1992.[8] It began during the New Hampshire primary and, using footage from other media sources,[9] it chronicled the Clinton campaign confronting charges of infidelity and draft evasion. The focus of the film eventually shifted to Carville and Stephanopoulos at the convention, when the filmmakers—Chris Hegedus and Da Pennebaker—were given access and permission to shoot the campaign staff at work. Most of the 96-minute film displayed them at various stages throughout the campaign, most notably in the Little Rock campaign headquarters—the "war room"—and at various important locations (e.g., the sites of the presidential debates). The film featured discursive moments (meetings, strategizing sessions, staff briefings, and speeches) that are highly dependent on visual representations for their authentication. In this sense, *The War Room* invited the inference that it was about actual issues of an actual campaign. The film, though, centered on image, and served as a representation of a representational campaign in an era of representational politics.

Presented as a documentary, *The War Room* implied a high degree of verisimilitude, disinterestedness, and accuracy, characteristics exacerbated by the visual authentication strategies inherent in the film's camera work. Indeed, to say that *The War Room* is an example of meta-imaging put forth by the Clinton campaign would seem incongruous given its generic classification. The film is clearly offered as what Bruce E. Gronbeck would classify as an "ostensibly descriptive" documentary.[10] According to its promoters, *The War Room* simply was an observational glimpse at the life of the Clinton campaign with little interference by the filmmakers. At least in its presentation, the documentary denied any reflexivity, any sense of "metacommentary" about its "process of representation."[11]

Yet it is quite clear that the Clinton campaign (Carville and Stephanopoulos in particular) maintained considerable control over the making and content of the film.[12] *The War Room*, thus, was not the dispassionate reflection of the reality of the 1992 Clinton campaign that its producers suggested. Rather, it was a calculated and controlled example of meta-imaging—an attempt by the Clinton campaign to put forth their image of the presidential election process. Such image-making strategies, though, were masked by the visual techniques at work, which functioned to naturalize and heighten the feeling of insider access. While the film may not have influenced the 1992 election,[13] it nonetheless fed the perpetuality of political campaigning, insuring that its effectiveness transcended the campaign that it allegedly infiltrated. Not only did it work to establish the "image" of Clinton's campaign, it also significantly critiqued the Republican presidential hegemony that would persist beyond 1992 were Clinton to have lost the general election. Read in this way, *The War Room* illuminated the meta-image as a new form of political communication of some significance.

Meta-Imaging as Campaign Strategy

Historically, campaigns and candidates hid or minimized the processes of image construction with good reason. To reveal the process of political packaging and imaging would open up the "backstage" areas of political life, undermining claims to authority and stature that are often necessary for political success. "'Greatness' manifests itself," Joshua Meyrowitz reveals, "in the onstage performance and, by definition, in its isolation from backstage behaviors."[14]

Only via investigative "insider" (journalistic) accounts or via academic analyses of the process are voters given a glimpse into the "packaging" of the presidency.[15] These texts attempt to accentuate the credibility of journalists and academics while unmasking the strategies of the image-makers, bringing to the forefront this genre of journalism designed to make public the so-called private side of politics. All premised on the discovery of something previously hidden, these projects seek to tear away some of the mystery of the presidential campaign process, offering a vision of campaigns from the perspective of outsiders (e.g., journalists, academics).

The War Room, however, expressed and represented an important shift in the discursive enactment of political campaigns. This film manifested the Clinton campaign's explicit acknowledgment of the centrality of image construction to the campaign process and, thus, evidenced the existence of meta-imaging as a campaign strategy. Herbert W. Simons theorizes that when rhetors "go meta," they are engaging in a "strategic, reflexive, and frame-altering process that either responds to another's message or to the shared message context."[16] Meta-imaging, like Simons's conception of "going meta," is strategic, reflexive, and frame-altering as a response to the entirety of the American political context, rather than to the individualized discursive events. As the political campaigns compete with media organizations for control of the candidate's image,[17] meta-imaging provides a means by which campaigns can assume greater definitional power over that image.

The War Room as Strategic Campaign Rhetoric

A meta-image is strategic in its ability to orient the image construction of a presidential candidate in particular, self-promotional ways. By foregrounding the image construction process, a campaign expands the image process to include the candidate as well as the image-makers. If done under the cover of documentary or news, moreover, the meta-image can capitalize on the hyperreal nature of political images wherein issues of image and reality are altered, confused, and distorted for the typical viewer. Regardless of the particular strategy, the choice of a campaign to "go meta" with its image construction process is a calculated, strategic, and ultimately self-serving decision, transcending the campaign and extending the livelihood of the image-making process.

Some evidence for the strategic nature of *The War Room* as a campaign rhetoric comes from the extra-textual reporting that addressed the film's production. Because of its uniqueness, the film attracted considerable attention and generated ample media coverage, revealing the strategic decisions and calculations involved in granting access to the documentarists. For instance, Hegedus and Pennebaker were granted limited access to the campaign headquarters in Little Rock. They only shot 35 hours of footage there, even though their filming of the campaign ran from July to November of 1992.[18] Put differently, in the span of four months, the filmmakers were only allowed to shoot less than two full days worth of activity. Beyond that, Jerry Hagstrom reports that Carville and Stephanopoulos determined what was filmmable and unfilmmable, and that there was some feeling by the film's producers that "they saved up stuff for us." Hagstrom, in fact, concludes that *The*

War Room might be seen as the "ultimate in Carville's and Stephanopoulos's personal spin control skills."[19]

A clear and influential relationship also existed between Carville and Stephanopoulos and the documentarists. Pennebaker remarked in several sources that Carville and Stephanopoulos were the most interesting people to film in the room.[20] He concluded that they "were like inspirational links between Clinton and the sea of young people working on his campaign."[21] Carville and Stephanopoulos, likewise, greatly admired the documentarists. Stephanopoulos praised Pennebaker, calling him a "genius."[22] Expressing the strategic power of *The War Room* best, Stephanopoulos concluded: "I hope this film will show people how a modern campaign is run and the passion behind it, and that they'll come away with a little more respect for the political process."[23]

The text of *The War Room* also demonstrated the film's strategic role for the Clinton campaign through the characters' responses to the camera and via the issues that served as the centerpieces of the film. First, the film's strategic role can be found in the ways in which the campaign managers responded to the camera. Both Carville and Stephanopoulos appeared keenly aware of the camera's presence throughout the film, often insuring that their backs were not to the camera when speaking. Other individuals registered their awareness of the camera as well. In one instance, the film recorded an Election Day meal with Carville and Mandy Grunwald, the campaign's advertising specialist. On at least three occasions, Grunwald looked nervously at the camera and laughed or smiled, revealing how obtrusive the camera was for some of the individuals in the documentary.

In addition to the keen awareness of the camera's location, Carville and Stephanopoulos repeatedly called attention to the image-making process. The cameras, for example, were permitted access to at least a portion of the strategizing for Clinton's victory speech. Even though Stephanopoulos told Clinton on the telephone that he "should speak from the heart," earlier scenes suggested the collaborative nature of the speechwriting process, involving Paul Begala (a campaign consultant who traveled with Clinton), Stephanopoulos, and others, sans Clinton. In the end, Stephanopoulos seemed to supervise the editing process, sending staffers off to revise the speech text. During the final hours of the campaign, Carville also acknowledged his role in Clinton's image construction. After watching Clinton assert, "if you'll be my voice tomorrow, I'll be your voice for four more years," Carville smiled and said, "I thought of that, didn't I? . . . I'll take credit for it." Such attribution was commonplace in the film, to the extent that when Stephanopoulos paid tribute to Carville's campaign genius, he asserted: "one person wrote what I call haiku about five months ago: 'change versus more of the same'; 'the economy—stupid'; and 'don't forget about health care.'" Thus, instead of celebritizing Clinton's rhetorical powers, the film clearly shifted the gaze of the camera and centered the rhetorical dimensions of the campaign in the "war room"—the campaign headquarters. Rather than hide the ghostwritten nature of the campaign, the Clinton team advertised and celebrated the process while simultaneously managing that meta-image.

What such editing suggested is the existence of visual "insider" access for the documentarists with minimal access to *actual* campaign strategizing. Further evidence of such censored access to the verbal conversations is represented in the few informal occasions where Clinton appears. In one scene, Clinton (clad in a t-shirt, running shorts, and a baseball cap) received a telephone call in his hotel room. After motioning Carville, Stephanopoulos, Begala, and Dee Dee Meyers (press liaison for the campaign) to quiet their voices, the film cut away to the Gennifer Flowers press conference as if the documentarists were censored from the actual telephone conversation. On another occasion, Clinton and Stephanopoulos were having a quiet conversation as the latter hurriedly ate. Their voices were hushed, and even though certain words were distinguishable, the subject of the conversations was inaccessible as we entered after it began and cut away before it ended.

Clearly, while the documentarists were granted visual access, or the *appearance* of "insider" access at times, they were routinely barred from documenting many conversations. Such limited access evidences the controlled nature of the film's content. Of course, it is impossible to argue how these subjects might have behaved absent the camera's presence, but there was a clear sense from the film that they were acutely aware of its place in the room and its power to record events, which simultaneously suggests the managed nature of the film's content.

Also instructive were the issues addressed in the film. At times, Carville especially seemed to construct messages for the producers, just as they suspected. Tellingly, Carville's speeches debased George Bush's image rather than built up Clinton's. In one such speech, directed toward an unknown recipient in what looks like a hotel room, Carville argued, "why can't we talk about the lowest economic growth in the last fifty years?" In a separate conversation with a journalist at the convention, Carville urged, "why doesn't he [Bush] run the economy and not run his mouth? . . . If he can't, get outta the way." In another instance, which seemed to be articulated for the camera in the "war room," Carville questioned whether Bush could be the first "incumbent president [to give] an acceptance speech and not mention his economic record."

Apart from Carville's "speeches," much of the film's content was quite mundane. We saw the campaign strategists follow the news of the campaign by watching television or reading newspapers. We watched Stephanopolous blow bubbles with his gum as he awaited a telephone call. We listened in as campaign workers debated the merits of handmade signs over official campaign signs. We also watched a campaign worker play with her hair as she asked Stephanopoulos insipid questions about his emotional state. In fact, much of the inside information offered in *The War Room* bordered on the banal rather than the "adventure story" that the film purported to offer.

Yet, we do gain insight into the symbiotic nature of politics and the media because of the pervasiveness of the news media in *The War Room*'s narrative. Before the general election began, the news media provided much of our insight into the campaign. When we revisited the Gennifer Flowers press conference, for example, we not only reviewed excerpts from that conference but were shown the last second frenzied preparations for the conference that are seldom aired on the news. We also witnessed Mary Matalin teasing a television reporter before he interviewed her; both were laughing, revealing a more casual relationship. Once the interview began, however, the interviewer assumed a very professional persona devoid of such interpersonal antics.

In other instances, however, the news media framed the campaign narrative. Throughout the primaries, the film's narrative was often chronicled by such newspaper headlines as "Clinton Takes Florida," "Native son takes South," and "CLINTON WINS BIG VICTORY IN 2 MIDWESTERN PRIMARIES." The film let us watch the campaign staff as they obtained much of their information about Bush and Perot from television news; they occasionally kept track of their own candidate through the same medium. When inside the war room, multiple televisions were on, broadcasting multiple stations simultaneously. When outside the war room, the media was likewise omnipresent, surrounding the candidate and the other celebrities of the campaign (i.e., the image-makers).

Once the general campaign began and the action centered in the war room, however, the film inverted the normal gaze of insider accounts. When the media frame an insider account, we are generally invited to view the campaign through the eyes of the journalist; we witness the campaign, thus, from the outside in. *The War Room*, however, offered a view from the campaign's perspective; we see the campaign from the inside out. A more extended example evidenced this inverted gaze and illustrated the modes of spin. The film's producers showcased an event that followed the Republican National Convention, where a Clinton campaign staffer discovered that some Bush campaign materials were produced in Brazil. The event revealed how the Clinton team tried to create a media scandal by relaying the story to the media. Using his media connections, Carville initially contacted a Washington journalist that he referred to as "the woman in *Broadcast News*." When CBS and other media outlets refused to air the story, believing the Bush campaign's explanation that the materials were purchased with private monies, the matter was dropped. Angered over the lack of attention to the issue, Carville took the opportunity to chastise the media's "double standard" before the camera:

> I believe that on any number of things that we are held to a different standard. I think it is absolutely ludicrous that no one ever asked George Bush about Iran-Contra. Two cabinet secretaries saying that Bush was lying. No one ever said a damn thing . . . [and James Baker], he's beyond being questioned. He gives everybody tickets to the opera. We can't question him.

Despite the fact that the Brazil "scandal" was a non-issue that was totally inconsequential to the campaign, this event occupied roughly ten minutes, or 10 percent, of the entire documentary. Throughout this scene, however, our gaze became Carville's gaze. The media's response was filtered through the person who first attempted to set the agenda for the nightly news only to chastise the media agenda-setters for failing to comply with his direction. The inversion of the gaze was clear; we're offered insight into how the campaign attempted to influence the news rather than into how the news framed the campaign, furthering the strategic dimension of this film for the campaign and the self-reflexive aim of the film's content. To that end, the film educated us in the means by which campaign operatives attempt to impact their own image, the image of their opposition, and the overall tenor of the campaign.

There is, however, a second strategic dimension to this incident. This scene and the other critiques of Bush and the Republican Party represented the transcendence of image-making and meta-imaging beyond the campaign. Regardless of who won in the end, Carville clearly was given a forum for attacking the Republican Party and its leader. Second, because the incident was featured in *The War Room*, it became a real event, a part of the campaign history. In a hyperreal manner, what was not a part of the campaign as it happened becomes a real part of the campaign's narrative. As such, the events of the real campaign become less important, less significant than the *telling* of those events—even to their very ontological essence as events at all.[24] The image of the campaign and its reality were collapsed in this one segment wherein Carville rescued from obscurity an event that was not a public part of the 1992 presidential campaign but will remain a part of its history via *The War Room*.

Strategy, Authenticity, and Hyperreality

While offering a visual glimpse into the campaign's strategies, the success of *The War Room* derived arguably from its documentary motif and the visual techniques that are commonly associated with documentary filmmaking. Documentaries ordinarily shun aesthetics—they seek a reflection of reality in as pure a manner as possible.[25] In the case of *visual insider access* framed as documentary, the visual images and the camera techniques work to naturalize the content of the film.

The importance of visual imagery to the authentication or realism of political activity is profound.[26] Establishing the importance of visuals, W. J. T. Mitchell argues that the "image" represents "the sign that pretends not to be a sign, masquerading as . . . natural immediacy and presence,"[27] promoting the impression that "moving pictures" represent a "form of actuality, a medium through which reality can be genuinely and authentically captured and presented."[28] Keith V. Erickson locates the force of visual images in "political reality," which "frequently emerges from the strategic use of visuals that cue spectators' emotive impulses, unspoken agreements, and cultural recollections," creating an "impression of authenticity or naturalness."[29]

In *The War Room*, there are multiple ways in which the content of the film is authenticated by its visual techniques and representations. In the opening frames of the film, *The War Room*'s producers relied on the assumption that the camera is "an extension of the eye";[30] the camera positioned us *outside* the Clinton war room in New Hampshire and then immediately situated us *inside* that war room in the next frame. This act of taking us visually from the street side of politics to a closed-door zone of political activity represented an integral technique of visual insider access; these private spheres function as *sites of authenticity* that heightened the narrative's verisimilitude and its perceived depth of insight.

Throughout with film, *The War Room* offered multiple sites of authenticity that enhanced its authority and realism. The Little Rock war room, which was the subject of the film and the title, of course, functioned as the highest form of authentication. Yet the producers guide us from backstage site to backstage site, giving us access to places most have never glimpsed before. The cameras situated our gaze, for example, behind closed hotel doors with Clinton during private moments with his campaign staff and on the campaign plane, overseeing the presidential candidate doing a crossword puzzle. We were backstage at the Democratic national convention and the presidential debates, gazing at Clinton from behind curtains. We were often positioned behind Clinton during speeches, behind the campaign strategists, and even behind the sea of news media cameras at campaign events, which communicated the depth of backstage that the cameras were allowed to infiltrate to offer views seldom shown on television. And, we were "on the bus," gazing out at the people on the streets, seeing the scene from the same perspective as the candidate, the campaign workers, and allegedly the documentarists. Such authentications, thus, not only naturalized the content, but simultaneously exacerbated the ethos of the film's producers, who were the individuals invited in from outside the campaign. The perception exists, Joshua Meyrowitz maintains, that such "backstage behavior" seems "more 'real' or honest than front region behavior."[31]

Once backstage, we were often positioned in conversations, which furthered the feeling of insider access. During the Democratic national convention in 1992, for example, the camera situated us in a conversation between Carville and at least three male journalists who encircled the campaign strategist. Initially, the camera gaze bounced around Carville's face as we are allowed to look toward him at close range. The camera then swung rapidly around (like our own heads do when conversing with a group of people) past one reporter to a second and then down to a close-up shot of the reporter's hands as he took notes. In this scenario as in many others, the camera functioned as our "extended retina."[32] We moved beyond, though, "feeling informed"[33] about the Clinton campaign to feeling included in it because of the near invisibility of the camera.[34] Such feelings of *virtual inclusivity* brought about by the visual nature of the access worked to overwhelm all other senses, eliminating questions about the banality of the film's content.

The use of *cinéma vérité* filming style combined with what appeared as camera glitches and accentuated the *The War Room*'s verisimilitude because of the assumption that such filming techniques "make us see the world as it is."[35] Throughout the film, the camera was often in constant motion. Some of the movement was purposeful as the camera swiveled to catch the conversational exchanges in a way we would do if present. In other instances, the movement reflected the rapidity of activity on the campaign trail as when the camera followed Stephanopoulos down the backstage hallway at the end of a debate as he rushed to his spin post. Such *cinéma vérité* signposts suggested that the documentarists were on the scene catching the fast-paced action of the campaign, which necessitated a filming technique and editing style that lacked the aesthetic purity of a nightly newscast. The dim lighting in certain frames, the blurriness of others, or the existence of bright lights that blinded us as we rise above Clinton during media frenzies helped further authenticate the film's content, which inherently contained the technical glitches that are seemingly necessitated by live-action filming. Rather than editing out such rough spots that offered no insight into the substance of the campaign, the documentarists instead included many such shots, which function as a strategic component of meta-imaging's visual insider access.

Although not an explicit aspect of the visual nature of insider access, the sounds of the campaign narrative worked to authenticate the film's verisimilitude even further. Some of these sound effects appeared contrived while others functioned as synchronous sound.[36] In one instance when the producers relied on a sound track, we heard the music of a marching band; we watched a band playing from inside the Clinton bus, which was driving at a relatively fast speed through a small town. The music was loud and uninhibited by bus sounds or the sound of air breezing by the bus windows. Even though the scene exhibited a total absence of location sound,[37] such sound acted to center our gaze on the image[38] (i.e., the band), which was viewed through our backstage vantage point from inside the bus.

In other instances, the producers featured synchronous sound, which helped establish the meaning of the images because of their congruence with the visuals.[39] Therefore, we heard the convention sounds as Carville walked among the delegates. We heard the birds singing as Clinton and his campaign strategists read the morning newspapers on an outdoor patio. We heard television and radio voices during war room interactions. And we detected the air hitting the camera microphones when its operators chased campaign strategists. Whether the sound drew attention to the visual images or naturalized the film's narrative, it helped bring an image together at a particular time "with a spectator especially desirous of seeing that very image"[40] and of defining that image as actualized insider access.

Other content features could likewise further the authenticity of the film, particularly its more mundane content and the omnipresence of the news media. For many, politics is a banal activity,[41] which includes the ever-present media that offered background noise throughout the film in much the same way that television and radio do in our own homes or our cars. To hear NBC journalist Andrea Mitchell's voice in the background, for example, accentuated the realism of the film and naturalized the whole of its content because the media's presence in the film is so familiar to us.

Through its presentational strategies, thus, the film worked to highlight the distinction between reality and representation and to subvert any conception of hyperreality. However, meta-imaging represents a campaign strategy, and *The War Room* acted as a successful meta-image, precisely because politics in the United States are so thoroughly hyperreal. That which is political reality is only real by virtue of its representation. Meta-imaging tries to subvert the hyperreality of politics by providing a more "real" sense of imaging from a visual insider's perspective. Yet at the same time, meta-imaging relies on the hyperreality of politics as a controlled representation of political reality. As such, while *The War Room* claimed to offer a "true," "real," insider," documentary account of the Clinton campaign, that account was a masterfully controlled and highly managed exercise of political image construction and representation. We are presented, thus, with what Meyrowitz calls a "middle region behavior," where we see "parts of the former backstage area along with parts of the traditional onstage area."[42]

This middle region, though, is as controlled as a carefully crafted public image of a political campaign.

The choice to engage in meta-imaging is a strategic one for a campaign that reflexively acknowledges the role and power of image construction in American politics. The strategic benefits of such a move are evident from *The War Room* and the positive portrayals put forth of the image-makers and, by extension, of the candidate. By utilizing the documentary form for such meta-imaging, the campaign capitalized on the perceived, but illusory, truth value of this genre,[43] tapping into the existing and powerful hyperreality of American political discourse. Yet, because of its presentation as a documentary, the subjective, political nature of this self-promotion and partisan attack were masked.

The War Room and the
Ideological Consequences of Meta-Imaging

While strategic, meta-imaging is also ideological by virtue of its discursive contribution to the systems of meaning and political vocabularies that maintain collective identity and control. In addition, because meta-imaging is hyperrealistic, it magnifies and amplifies its ideological messages. We define ideology as those patterns of thought and language that enact systems of power and influence in public, communal existence. Ideology is composed of the commitments, narratives, myths, metaphors, etc., that work to persuade people to believe in particular concepts or to act in certain ways that may or may not be in their personal best interests.[44] Moreover, ideology is powerful because of the texts that express it and the people who personify it. When those texts reflect hyperreality, they make the useful distinction between reality and representation disappear and, thus, enhance the power of the ideological persuasion under way in such discourse.

Hyperreality potentiates a shift to metaphors and, in the case of *The War Room*, a shift to a militaristic conception of political campaigning. "Metaphors are not simply stylistic devices," argue Dennis Mumby and Carole Spitzack, "they actually structure experience."[45] In the case of *The War Room*, this is powerfully evident. Political observers Edwin Diamond and Robert A. Silverman conclude that *The War Room* "vividly demonstrated the warrior state of mind of modern campaigns."[46] Indeed, *The War Room* offered a specific ideological interpretation of presidential campaigning that was dominated by military metaphors and narrative emplotments. Mark Johnson maintains that metaphors are "based on systems of related or interlocking mappings that connect one experiential domain to another."[47] The metaphorical process is, John B. Thompson argues, profoundly ideological, and works as "an effective way of mobilizing meaning in the social-historical world, and that, in certain contexts, the meaning mobilized thereby may be embroiled with power and may serve to create, sustain and reproduce relations of domination."[48]

Employing a militaristic metaphor to define the 1992 presidential campaign invoked long-standing interpretive vocabularies common in American politics.[49] War metaphors have particularly salient ideological force in an America struggling with its communal identity in the aftermath of the Cold War. Commenting on the presence of "tragic fear" in the Persian Gulf War, Robert L. Ivie maintains that the "rhetorical legacy of the Cold War is a tragic framework of interpretation that constitutes the perils of *hubris* in the image of a heroic nation struggling globally to redeem itself by contesting the relentless forces of chaos and establishing a New World Order." The consequence of this legacy, Ivie continues, is the requirement that the United States "find and fight evil everywhere in the hope of creating and preserving an international utopia of freedom and democratic principles, thereby saving America's own soul and insuring its material security."[50]

The political hyperreality that engulfed and was expressed by *The War Room* enhanced its polysemic ideological message. Because of its supposed reality, the film naturalized as dehistoricized, unpolitical truth the militaristic nature of campaigns, even while such militarism was of central importance to the image of campaigning offered by the film and its subjects. By locating image-making within the common interpretive framework of "campaigns as war," image-making comes to occupy an important, legitimate, and "real" function in the practice of the "war." Factionalism and division are privileged, and the nature of politics was defined by these characteristics.

Simultaneously, the consequence of such militarism is a reassertion of national unity and ascendance. As Robert Burgoyne demonstrates, depictions of war and martial conflict are common tropes of national identity and unity.[51] They tap into existing and powerful reservoirs of meaning that bind and bond individuals to the nation as mythically created in the depictions. In this sense, *The War Room* reinscribed a sense of order, unity, and structure to a postmodern and uncertain political environment. Within that environment, the militaristic framework suggested, political consultants (the image-makers—here Carville and Stephanopoulos) were ascendant and were the personification of order and unification. They guide the candidate (in this case, Clinton) to the achievement of political unity and they offered the symbols and images that define that national identity. In this way, the war metaphors remind us that even though we may have different viewpoints, politics, and party affiliations, the important cultural ideal is that the nation is our "primary form of belonging."[52]

The War Room's Militaristic Vision of the 1992 Campaign

We identify four military themes or motifs that were present in *The War Room*. The first military image that emerged from the film occurred in its opening credits. As the words *The War Room* appeared on the screen, an explosion of fireworks was displayed. Both messages were militaristic in nature. *The War Room*, as a metaphor, connoted a headquarters or central location for the conduct of war, much like the Situation Room in the White House. The "war room" metaphor conjures powerful images: past generals coordinating war efforts, enemy targets identified by brightly lit maps, and past presidents poised by a telephone ready to issue the next orders. The "war room" concept was furthered by the appearance of t-shirts that Carville and other staffers wore emblazoned with "War Room Staff" on one side, and the slogan "Speed Killed Bush" on the other. The fireworks in the opening credits also reinforced these mental images, as they were loud, spectacular, and reminiscent of guns and explosive devices. Both the title of the film and the opening fireworks immediately expressed the bellicosity of this particular interpretation of the 1992 campaign.

The second militaristic message put forth in the film was the powerful construction of the enemy (George Bush and the Republican Party) that pervaded the discourse of *The War Room*. Of course, constructing Bush and the GOP as enemies was part of the strategic power of the film, as we have already discussed. But such constructions also work ideologically by putting forth a particular version of political campaigns premised on confrontation and the finality of victory or defeat, symbolically eliminating the possibility of compromise or accommodation. As Murray Edelman argues, the construction of political enemies helps to "give the political spectacle its power to arouse passions, fears, and hopes, the more so because an enemy to some people is an ally or innocent victim to others."[53]

Constructing the enemy in the campaign was the main topic of Carville's speech to the New Hampshire Clinton campaign staff at the very beginning of *The War Room*. The Republican Party, according to Carville, was responsible for most of the unsavory revelations about Clinton. As he stated, "It's going to come out that Roger Ailes is behind a lot of this stuff before the election, that you've been seeing about Governor Clinton." He went on to attack Georgette Mosbacher, a key Republican campaign contributor, who, Carville argued, "can't wait until this election's over so she can get her Mazeratti and her jewels back." To the applause of the assembled campaign operatives, he concluded with a charge: "don't forget who the real enemy is in here and don't forget what we're really campaigning against." Interestingly, the speech occurred in the midst of the New Hampshire primary and the Gennifer Flowers incident, with Bill Clinton's nomination still very much in doubt.[54]

Third, *The War Room* converted Carville and Stephanopoulos metaphorically and hyperrealistically into military heroes—those who because of their perseverance and skill were able to win the "war" of the general election campaign against heavy odds. The heroism of these campaign operatives occurred, first, by virtue of the film's focus on them as the center of all action. They were even identified as the "stars" of the film, when after the title, the credits read, "Featuring James Carville and George Stephanopoulos." By positioning Carville and Stephanopoulos at the center of all activity, *The War Room* suggested that they were the real heroes of the campaign, and that campaigns are really about what political consultants—the image-makers—do and say.

The heroism of Carville, in particular, was clearest when Stephanopoulos paid tribute to him on Election Eve. Stephanopoulos said, in introducing Carville, that "besides Bill Clinton, one person really gave this campaign focus. . . . He's about to pass from the role of regular human being into the role of a legend." Carville then presented a very sentimental speech. This speech functioned as a bookend to the speech at the beginning of *The War Room* given to the New Hampshire campaign staff. The first speech functioned as a rallying speech, much like the speech a general would give to troops prior to battle. The speech at the conclusion of the film worked as a victory address at the end of a long fight, in which praise was offered to those who have sacrificed. The battle was contextualized within the larger struggle or war. Near the end of the speech, through tears, Carville concluded that "We've changed the way campaigns are run," as if giving the "fight" some meaning and purpose. Ultimately, the heroism of Carville and Stephanopoulos was perhaps most clearly evident when the film showed several of the "war room's" staff taking pictures of the two operatives as they spoke the night before the election.

Such a vision of heroism is decidedly masculine and white. As established, Carville and Stephanopoulos were the center of activity as the camera directed our gaze to their actions and the activities of other peripherally portrayed white men involved in the campaign (e.g., speechwriters, pollsters). Of equal importance to the image-makers' prominence, though, were the ways in which white women were positioned in relation to the image-makers. Women were often the laugh track for Carville or the ones with whom Stephanopoulos shared his feelings in quiet moments. As Carville conducted a radio interview from the war room, two white women staffers sat on the floor and look up at him in an adoring and interested manner as he talked about his relationship with Mary Matalin. And though Matalin was featured as an active image-maker, her prominence was clearly established in relation to Carville's celebrity status. As P. David Marshall argues, the discursive power that accompanies celebrity offers the individual "a voice above others, a voice that is channeled into the media systems as being legitimately significant."[55]

Seldom were women's voices awarded such discusive power. In the Brazil printing issue, for example, a white woman was shown handing information to Carville as he talked on the telephone to journalists. Mandy Grunwald was another exception to the submissive campaign workers, yet she was featured as a voice on a conference call who is positioned in opposition to Carville because her views on a proposed ad conflicted with the opinions of the film's hero. She lacked visuality in this scene and a voice in the conflict at the end of the team meeting over her alleged recalcitrance; to that end, Grunwald as well as the other white women in the film, lacked a complete representation in the body politic. As Moira Gatens contends, women are often depicted as incomplete or dependent on men in political discourse, which works to naturalize "women's differential treatment" in the larger public, political sphere.[56]

Such traditional portrayals of gender and politics appeared as normalized as the invisibility of whiteness in *The War Room*.[57] Apart from a fleeting image of Betty Currie (Clinton's future administrative assistant in the White House), the war room presented a racially homogenized image of presidential politics that reified the centrality of whiteness in the public sphere. Herman Gray maintains that 1980s Reaganism "served as a key point of rearticulation for disparate political, social, historical, and cultural investments in an aggressive discourse of whiteness," which "functioned as the cultural and historical sign, for many whites, of the 'real' or 'authentic America.'"[58] Ronald Reagan's whiteness legacy is the political context out of which Bill Clinton's image-construction practices emerged. As we have argued elsewhere, Bill Clinton "accent[ed] and highlight[ed] his whiteness just as effectively as he . . . stressed his empathy with African-Americans."[59] The lack of diversity in Clinton's war room could suggest minimally two revealing conclusions. First, Clinton's commitment to multiculturalism and equality represented part of his public persona but not part of his private actions (whether consciously or unconsciously) in his behind-the-scenes war room. Second, because the Clinton campaign viewed *The War Room* as an exercise in image-making, its operatives sought to highlight the candidate's commitment to whiteness in the war room just as they did in the entirety of the 1992 campaign so as to more fully position Clinton as a Southern, centrist, New Democrat. At bottom, the image of the Clinton war room and the image-makers' heroism was predicated on a masculine, white, and militarized vision of power and celebrity.

Finally, *The War Room* was replete with examples of militaristic language. In Carville's rallying speech to the New Hampshire headquarters, he spoke of the "tough fight" to come and the propensity of Republicans to "ambush" Democrats. He cautioned the audience to know what they are "fighting" against before the Republicans "beat us back." The militaristic language was also found in Stephanopoulos's spin concerning the final presidential debate, when he argued to the press, "Another good night for Bill Clinton—three debates, three wins. Bush was on the defensive all night." Later, the film featured Clinton himself saying on television to an airport rally right before the election, "We fought for a year, we've got two days to go. . . . Fight on, don't give up." Even at a lighter, more humorous point in the film, the language of war still appeared to control the perspective of the campaign. *The War Room* featured Carville and Stephanopoulos, on Election Day, speculating about the likelihood of Clinton's defeat and composing a fake concession speech. In it, Carville joked, "It is not that we have lost this battle; it's whether we endure in the larger war."

The Implications of Meta-Imaging for U.S. Political Culture

There are several implications that emerge from this analysis of *The War Room*. This film is simply a case study—an exemplar—of larger political, ideological systems at work in postmodern American politics. That system is reordering conceptions of image, leadership, presidentiality, and national identity via the texts that express its ideology. We use *The War Room* as our springboard to address this reordering.

First, meta-imaging represents one more example of the symbiotic relationship between media and politics.[60] The media interlopers want a unique vantage point from which to narrate their story of the campaign, while the image-makers seek further control over the public image of their campaign and their candidate. Media reporters are likely, furthermore, to promote the authenticity of their "insider" accounts so as to further market these stories. As such, media meta-images are put forth as documentaries, news, or other "objective" genres of discourse.

In the age of image-making, capturing the real, the actual, the authentic, seems appealing to a public fascinated by celebrities and the intimacies of their private lives.[61] In an attempt to capture attention, and to entice journalists and their audiences, so-called intimate access is converted into media events that are simply another means of image control under the guise of realism.[62] The representation that is the meta-image comes to be the reality of political campaigning via the forms of documentary and news and their illusions of objectivity. And in the case of *The War Room*, that reality was amplified by the frequent inverted gaze at the campaign.

The meta-image, then, restructures the relationships between media and political campaigns. Meta-imaging interrogates the entire journalistic enterprise, suggesting that access, when granted, may simply be a political tool or ploy of image construction. The journalistic establishment becomes, thus, complicit in the image construction of political candidates. Such complicity may be unwitting, further enhancing the power of these hyperreal depictions of American political campaigns.

A second implication of this understanding of meta-imaging regards the power of image-based politics in a postmodern era. Presidents and presidential candidates have always used and manipulated their images for political purposes, but the hyperreality of the meta-image entices publics into the belief that such imaging can be unmasked and revealed. We are invited by the meta-image into the world of campaigning and image construction with the promise, the guarantee, that what we see is real.

In a meaningful way, meta-imaging provides cover for publics swayed by campaign imagery and political persuasion. Americans experience two symbolic constructions of presidential campaigns or two different versions of a history that rearticulates new presidentialities for the community. First there is the campaign itself and then the series of meta-images offered of the campaign in the weeks and years following. Politics is restructured in the public mind by these meta-images, and the larger presidentiality of the polity shifts. Moreover, the leadership of the presidents we elect is further demystified and personified through the meta-imaging process. The fact that such meta-imaging is put forth as realistic enhances its influence in the public conceptions of leadership and campaign history.

For *The War Room* and Bill Clinton, the 1992 campaign was constructed as an adventure story with militaristic overtones and dedicated soldiers. In a sense, Bill Clinton's leadership was remote and secondary to the influence of Carville and Stephanopoulos. Nevertheless, the film still reflected favorably on Clinton, defining him as the candidate who assembled this dynamic, compelling army and providing him and his partisans with a forum for presenting their views. In this sense, at least, the strategic choice to meta-image was successful for the Clinton campaign.

Third, *The War Room* exemplifies the tendency within political communication to define campaigning according to easily accessed and understood metaphors and narratives. Such metaphors, as in this film, generally invoke images of competition, power, and winning—usually with sports or military vehicles. The construction of image-making in this metaphorical rubric is of significant consequence for postmodern American politics.

If a political campaign is a war, with the stakes and outcomes of battle, the soldiers/generals in that war become important and crucial to its conclusion. The result is a portrayal of politics in America that masks or repudiates its republican character. There is no sense in most examples of meta-imaging of the representative, constitutional foundations of American government. Voters are simply numbers on a printout that are aggregated into Electoral College votes or partisan, crowd participants eager to glimpse or touch their political heroes. If the presidential campaign is a metonymy of American democracy, then meta-images assert a view of campaigning where all that matters is image-making, even more than the image itself. In this sense, the democratic process is materialized into a war or battle where the important decisions with any real consequence are made by those who possess no legitimate, constitutional power at all.

Another consequence of the representations offered in such meta-images is the perpetuation of a naturalized, militaristic perspective of politics that shapes and controls actual governance and policy. Rather than negotiation and compromise,[63] the processes of government becomes an extension of campaign battles. Meetings are defined in the media by what was lost or won, Congress becomes deadlocked in endless disputes with little support for negotiation or accommodation, resulting in a process of governing dominated by a rhetoric of power. Certainly the budget battles of 1995 and 1996 evidenced how a rhetoric of confrontation superseded any rhetoric of negotiation in policy-making. And even when negotiation and compromise do emerge, the media and its pundits feverishly try and calculate the political wins and losses of such negotiation.

The use of war metaphors of competition and power also manifests a sense of unity and nationalism that emerge from such meta-imaging. While militarism may structure politics to highlight difference and division, such metaphors also value and uphold the political creed of the American political system. Meta-imaging is, thus, polysemic. At once, we are invited to see the divisions that define our different political orientations and to celebrate a political system that gives order and unity to our national identity. There is always, in such meta-imaging, a strong sense of unity and commitment to an American political system. Even though deeply divided over budgetary disputes and alleged presidential perjury issues, political officials are quick to remind international audiences that the United States will fight, in a unified manner, any outside aggression. Because such discourse is so thoroughly hyperreal, this unity is given shape and reality by such depictions of American politics.

On a final level, the inherent hyperreality of all postmodern political rhetorics mitigates against the metaphors of war and confrontation that they put forth to demarcate political action. Politics is not about life, death, and battles, but about the images and representations of these weighty issues. Meta-images are, thus, snared in a postmodern, hyperreal trap of their own creation. Democracy in the United States is simply a representation in the postmodern media/information age. In a strange paradox, political rhetorics like *The War Room* cling to an outdated and modernist conception of politics as war and battle while those rhetorics simultaneously use the postmodern tools of symbolism and representation to express political realities. Meta-imaging, then, may be the ultimate expression of the confusion and angst of a politics adrift in a postmodern age of representation.

Notes

1. P. F. Bentley, *Clinton: Portrait of Victory* (New York: Warner Books, 1993).

2. Peter Goldman, Thomas M. DeFrank, Mark Miller, Andrew Murr, and Tom Mathews, *Quest for the Presidency, 1992* (College Station: Texas A&M University Press, 1994), x.

3. "Victory March," *Newsweek*, November 18, 1996, p. 28.

4. "Inside the Campaign," *Time Extra: The Election of 1996*, Fall, 1996, pp. 38–9.

5. Bakhtin asserts that genres (e.g., journalistic insider access narratives) are able to infer a past while simultaneously adapting new strategies that are appropriate for the context in which they are produced. Thus, visual insider narratives rely on the memory of the earliest journalistic insider accounts yet adapt to the increasing visuality of U.S. culture and expand the genre in new ways. In the process, such genres help insure that social expectations are passed down to future generations. See Mikhail Bakhtin, *Speech Genres and Other Late Essays*, translated by Vern W. McGee (Austin: University of Texas Press, 1986). See also Robert Burgoyne, *Film Nation: Hollywood Looks at U.S. History* (Minneapolis: University of Minnesota Press, 1997); and Gary Saul Morson and Caryl Emerson, *Mikhail Bakhtin: The Creation of a Prosaics* (Stanford, CA: Stanford University Press, 1990), 89, 295–7.

6. See Timothy Crouse, *The Boys on the Bus* (New York: Ballantine, 1972); Theodore H. White, *America in Search of Itself: The Making of the President, 1956–1980* (New York: Warner Books, 1982); Theodore H. White, *The Making of the President 1960* (New York: Atheneum, 1961); Theodore H. White, *The Making of the President 1964* (New York: Atheneum, 1965); Theodore H. White, *The Making of the President 1968* (New York: Atheneum, 1969); Theodore H. White, *The Making of the President 1972* (New York: Atheneum, 1973). For a compelling analysis of the power of White's construction of the presidency and particularly of JFK, see Joyce Hoffman, *Theodore H. White and Journalism as Illusion* (Columbia: University of Missouri Press, 1995).

7. Chris Hegedus and Da Pennebaker, *The War Room* (Canada: MCA Home Video, 1993). All subsequent citations of the film's text come from our transcription of its dialogue and content.

8. Upon its release, *The War Room* elicited considerable critical praise. Most of the acclaim celebrated the unparalleled insights and understandings of presidential campaigning that the film offered. *The War Room* achieved the pinnacle of filmmaking recognition when it was nominated for an Academy Award in the Best Documentary Feature category. See Jonathan Alter, "Documentary: The James and George Show," *Newsweek*, November 8, 1993, p. 78; Janet Maslin, "Another

Making of a President, Starring the New Spin Doctors," *The New York Times*, October 13, 1993, p. C15; and Terence Rafferty, "The Battle of Little Rock," *The New Yorker*, November 8, 1993, pp. 124–6.

9. Jonathan Alter, "Documentary: The James and George Show," *Newsweek*, November 8, 1993, p. 78.

10. See Bruce E. Gronbeck, "Celluloid Rhetoric: On Genres of Documentary," in *Form and Genre: Shaping Rhetorical Action*, edited by Karlyn Kohrs Campbell and Kathleen Hall Jamieson (Falls Church, VA: Speech Communication Association, 1990), 145. See also Dan Armstrong, "Wiseman and the Politics of Looking: Manoeuvre in the Documentary Project," *Quarterly Review of Film Studies* 11 (1990): 35–50; Susanna Hornig, "Television's *NOVA* and the Construction of Scientific Truth," *Critical Studies in Mass Communication* 7 (1990): 11–23; Martin J. Medhurst, and Thomas W. Benson, "*The City*: The Rhetoric of Rhythm," *Communication Monographs* 48 (1981): 54–72; Miles Orvell, "Documentary Film and the Power of Interrogation: *American Dream* and *Roger and Me*," *Film Quarterly* 48 (1994–95): 10–19; Trevor Parry-Giles, "Ideological Anxiety and the Censored Text: *Real Lives—At the Edge of the Union*," *Critical Studies in Mass Communication* 11 (1994): 54–72; and Paula Robinowitz, *They Must Be Represented: The Politics of Documentary* (London: Verso, 1994). Documentaries are popular texts for rhetorical and critical analysis. Benson and Anderson, for example, subject the films of Frederick Wiseman to careful and detailed critical analysis. And the political impact of documentary is the focus of Rosteck's analysis of *See It Now* and McCarthyism. Much of this work emphasizes the reflexivity of film and the rhetorical dimensions of documentary in particular. See Thomas W. Benson and Carolyn Anderson, *Reality Fictions: The Films of Frederick Wiseman* (Carbondale: Southern Illinois University Press, 1989); and Thomas Rosteck, *See It Now Confronts McCarthyism: Television Documentary and the Politics of Representation* (Tuscaloosa: University of Alabama Press, 1994).

11. Bill Nichols, *Representing Reality: Issues and Concepts in Documentary* (Bloomington: Indiana University Press, 1991), 56.

12. Amy Bernstein, "The Hidden Life of the War Room." *U.S. News & World Report*, April 12, 1993, p. 21; and Susan Karlin, "Filming Inside Clinton's Camp," *The New York Times*, sec. IX, January 31, 1993, pp. 15, 16.

13. Edwin Diamond and Robert A. Silverman, *White House to Your House: Media and Politics in Virtual America.* (Cambridge, MA: MIT Press, 1995).

14. Joshua Meyrowitz, *No Sense of Place: The Impact of Electronic Media on Social Behavior* (New York: Oxford University Press, 1985), 167.

15. For journalistic insider accounts, see Joe McGinniss, *The Selling of the President 1968* (New York: Pocket Books, 1969); and White, *America in Search of Itself.* For

academic analyses of the political process, see Kathleen Hall Jamieson, *Packaging the Presidency: A History and Criticism of Presidential Campaign Advertising*, 3rd edition (New York: Oxford University Press, 1996); Dan Nimmo, *The Political Persuaders: The Techniques of Modern Election Campaigns* (Englewood Cliffs, NJ: Prentice-Hall, 1970); and Larry J. Sabato, *The Rise of Political Consultants: New Ways of Winning Elections* (New York: Basic Books, 1981). We should note that Da Pennebaker, the producer/director of *The War Room*, has filmed previous campaign efforts. In particular, he produced *Primary*, a 1960 documentary that followed John F. Kennedy around as he solicited votes, and *Campaign Manager*, a profile of Barry Goldwater's 1964 campaign manager, John Grenier. Neither film achieved the notoriety and exposure of *The War Room*. See Jerry Hagstrom, "War Room Secrets," *National Journal*, March 20, 1993, pp. 703–5.

16. Herbert W. Simons, "Going Meta: Definition and Political Applications," *Quarterly Journal of Speech* 80 (1994): 469.

17. Diamond and Silverman, *White House to Your House*.

18. J. Senior, "Hollywood on the Potomac," *The New York Times*, December 12, 1993, sec. IX, pp. 1, 7.

19. Hagstrom, "War Room Secrets," p. 705. See also Janet Maslin, "Another Making of a President," p. C15.

20. See Hagstrom, "War Room Secrets," pp. 703–5; and Karlin, "Filming Inside Clinton's Camp," pp. 15, 16.

21. Karlin, "Filming Inside Clinton's Camp," p. 15.

22. George Stephanopoulos, personal communication, January 27, 1997.

23. Karlin, "Filming Inside Clinton's Camp," p. 16.

24. Burgoyne, *Film Nation*.

25. Bill Nichols, *Ideology and the Image* (Bloomington: Indiana University Press, 1981), 170–2.

26. During antiquity, questions of authenticity were associated with distinctions between the genuine and the fake. In the post-Industrial Age, such authenticity queries centered on the tension between the nineteenth century "culture of imitation" and the twentieth century "culture of authenticity." To be authentic, Imants Baruss contends is to be "that which is true to its own nature." At the end of the twentieth century, Doug Rossinow associates authenticity quests with "identity politics" and the "new left's agenda" associated with "alienation, powerlessness, racism, war, [and] sexism." See Imants Baruss, *Authentic Knowing: The*

Convergence of Science and Spiritual Aspiration (West Lafayette, IN: Purdue University Press, 1996); Alexander Nehamas, *Virtues of Authenticity: Essays on Plato and Socrates* (Princeton: Princeton University Press, 1999), xxxii; Miles Orvell, *The Real Thing: Imitation and Authenticity in American Culture, 1880–1940* (Chapel Hill: University of North Carolina Press, 1989), xvi, xv; Doug Rossinow, *The Politics of Authenticity: Liberalism, Christianity, and the New Left in America* (New York: Columbia University Press, 1998), 4, 343. The concept of political authenticity and image-making is developed more fully in Chapter Four.

27. W. J. T. Mitchell, *Iconology: Image, Text, Ideology* (Chicago: University of Chicago Press, 1986), 43.

28. Philip Schlesinger, *Putting 'Reality' Together: BBC News* (London: Constable, 1978), 128.

29. Keith V. Erickson, "Presidential Rhetoric's Visual Turn: Performance Fragments and the Politics of Illusionism," *Communication Monographs* 67 (2000): 144, 140.

30. Joel Snyder, "Picturing Vision," in *The Language of Images*, edited by W. J. T. Mitchell (Chicago: University of Chicago Press, 1980), 225.

31. Joshua Meyrowitz, "New Sense of Politics: How Television Changes the Political Drama," *Research in Political Sociology* 7 (1995): 122.

32. See Joshua Meyrowitz, "Television and Interpersonal Behavior: Codes of Perception and Response," in *Inter/Media: Interpersonal Communication in a Media World*, edited by Gary Gumpert and Robert Cathcart (New York: Oxford University Press, 1982), 226.

33. See Nichols, *Ideology and Image*, 241.

34. See Roderick P. Hart's discussion of "feeling informed" in Roderick P. Hart, *Seducing America: How Television Charms the Modern Voter* (New York: Oxford University Press, 1994), 53–76.

35. See J. Dudley Andrew, *The Major Film Theories: An Introduction* (London: Oxford University Press, 1976), 104. See also Jacques Aumont, Alain Bergala, Michel Marie, Marc Vernet, *Aesthetics of Film*, trans. Richard Neupert (Austin: University of Texas Press, 1992).

36. Nichols, *Ideology and Image*, 199.

37. Nichols, *Ideology and Image*, 199.

38. Rick Altman, "Television/Sound," in *Studies in Entertainment: Critical Approaches to Mass Culture*, edited by Tania Modleski (Bloomington: Indiana University Press, 1986), 46.

39. Nichols, *Ideology and Image*, 199–200.

40. Altman, "Television/Sound," 51.

41. James Jasinski, "(Re)constituting Community Through Narrative Argument: *Eros* and *Philia* in *The Big Chill*," *Quarterly Journal of Speech* 79 (1993): 480.

42. Meyrowitz, "New Sense of Politics," 124.

43. See Nichols, *Ideology and the Image;* and Roger Silverstone, "The Right to Speak: On a Poetic for Television Documentary," *Media, Culture and Society* 5 (1983): 145–52.

44. Michael Calvin McGee, "The 'Ideograph': A Link Between Rhetoric and Ideology," *Quarterly Journal of Speech* 66 (1980): 1–16; and John B. Thompson, *Ideology and Modern Culture* (Stanford, CA: Stanford University Press, 1990).

45. Dennis K. Mumby and Carole Spitzack, "Ideology and Television News: A Metaphoric Analysis of Political Stories," *Central States Speech Journal* 34 (1983): 166.

46. Diamond and Silverman, *White House to Your House,* 108.

47. Mark Johnson, *Moral Imagination: Implications of Cognitive Science for Ethics* (Chicago: University of Chicago Press, 1993), 9–10. See also George Lakoff and Mark Johnson, *Metaphors We Live By* (Chicago: University of Chicago Press, 1980).

48. Thompson, *Ideology and Modern Culture,* 64.

49. See Samuel L. Popkin, *The Reasoning Voter: Communication and Persuasion in Presidential Campaigns* (Chicago: University of Chicago Press, 1991); and Theodore O. Windt, Jr., "Presidential Rhetoric: Definition of a Field of Study," *Central States Speech Journal* 35 (1984): 24–34.

50. Robert L. Ivie, "Tragic Fear and the Rhetorical Presidency: Combating Evil in the Persian Gulf," in *Beyond the Rhetorical Presidency*, edited by Martin J. Medhurst (College Station: Texas A & M University Press, 1996), 176.

51. Burgoyne, *Film Nation*.

52. Michael Ignatieff, *Blood and Belonging: Journeys into the New Nationalism* (New York: Noonday Press, 1993), 5.

53. Murray Edelman, *Constructing the Political Spectacle* (Chicago: University of Chicago Press, 1988), 66.

54. Carville's speech to the New Hampshire organization is the harshest construction of Bush and the Republicans presented in the film. Later, during an interview at the Democratic Convention, Carville constructs Bush as a consummate politician, which may work to further manufacture an enemy for the general election. He says: "George Bush is an ultimate politician. His political skills are awesome. He may be a joke as the president, but as a politician, I have a great deal of respect for him." Of course, this quotation not only villifies Bush, given the general cultural condemnation of politicians, but it also works to heighten expectations about Bush's political skills.

55. P. David Marshall, *Celebrity and Power: Fame in Contemporary Culture* (Minneapolis: University of Minnesota Press, 1997), x.

56. Moira Gatens, *Imaginary Bodies: Ethics, Power and Corporeality* (London: Routledge, 1996), 21, xi.

57. According to Fiske, "whiteness" represents "a strategic deployment of power" that "contains a limited but varied set of normalizing positions from which that which is not white can be made into the abnormal; by such means whiteness constitutes itself as a universal set of norms by which to make sense of the world." See Fiske, *Media Matters,* 42.

58. Herman Gray, *Watching Race: Television and the Struggle for "Blackness"* (Minneapolis: University of Minnesota Press, 1995), 16. See also Michael Rogin, *Ronald Reagan: The Movie* (Berkeley: University of California Press, 1987).

59. Shawn J. Parry-Giles and Trevor Parry-Giles, "Collective Memory, Political Nostalgia, and the Rhetorical Presidency: Bill Clinton's Commemoration of the March on Washington, August 28, 1998," *Quarterly Journal of Speech* 86 (2000): 430.

60. See W. Lance Bennett, *News: The Politics of Illusion*, 2nd edition (New York: Longman, 1988); Michael Parenti, *Inventing the Politics of News Media Reality*, 2nd edition (New York: St. Martin's Press, 1993); and Stephen D. Reese, "The News Paradigm and the Ideology of Objectivity: A Socialist at *The Wall Street Journal*," *Critical Studies in Mass Communication* 7 (1990): 390–409.

61. See Chapter 1 and Trevor Parry-Giles, and Shawn J. Parry-Giles, "Political Scopophilia, Presidential Campaigning, and the Intimacy of American Politics," *Communication Studies* 47 (1996): 191–205.

62. Hart, *Seducing America*.

63. Windt, "Presidential Rhetoric."

Chapter Three

Political Nostalgia, Hyperreal History, and the 1996 Presidential Campaign

As they approached their summer national convention in August 1996, the Democrats had a problem. How would they make sure that the television networks covered both their convention in Chicago and their anointed candidate, President Bill Clinton? The major television networks had already soured on conventions after years of covering these party "infomercials" where news was scarce and costs were high. Ted Koppel had, in fact, taken his *Nightline* crew and departed the 1996 Republican San Diego convention in a snit, claiming that these political spectacles generated no news anymore.[1] So how could the Democrats appease a hostile media and a bored public? How could they make certain that the nation's attention was on their candidate and their convention at the same time?

The answer: a train—the *21st Century Express*. By putting President Clinton on a train, winding its way through the heartland of America toward the Chicago convention, with citizens lining the route and waving their greetings, the Democrats guaranteed that the television networks covered both their convention and their candidate. The idea came from Clinton friend and television producer Harry Thomason (the creator of *The Man from Hope*), and its simplicity and showiness were masterful in the contemporary hyperreal atmosphere of presidential politics. The news networks believed that they must cover the conventions, despite Koppel's protestations, which meant that coverage of the Chicago convention was guaranteed. And placing the president of the United States on a train assured coverage for the candidate, forcing the networks to double their coverage of the Democrats. After all, not only did the train motif provide great visuals for the television news cameras, it also hearkened back to an American past that was powerfully resonant. "There's something about a train," Thomason said, "that seems to represent a better time in our lives."[2]

Clinton's use of the *21st Century Express* and its nostalgic appeal to carry him to Chicago is emblematic of the dominant thematic tension of the 1996 presidential campaign. Perhaps it was the respective ages of the candidates, or just that there was not a pressing national crisis or problem to galvanize the voting public, but the 1996 campaign was primarily a clash between the past and the future. The economy was sound though still uncertain, the furor of the national health care debate was over, and there were no major international crises facing the nation. Furthermore, the Dole campaign opted against directly highlighting "character" as its main campaign message against President Clinton. As such, the 1996 campaign was waged primarily on competing thematic grounds about the overall direction for the United States.

Bob Dole's bid for the presidency was a call to the past, as the candidate repeatedly emphasized his ability to restore virtue and integrity to government, and to bring moral foundation and rectitude back to the nation. As he said in his acceptance speech to the 1996 GOP convention, "Age has its advantages. Let me be the bridge to an America that only the unknowing call myth. Let me be the bridge to a time of tranquility, faith, and confidence in action. To those who say it was never so, that America has not been better, I say, you're wrong, and I know, because I was there. I have seen it. I remember."[3] Though quite powerful and thoroughly nostalgic, Dole's rhetoric sent the politically counterproductive message that he was old, and that the past that he valorized and represented was the 1930s and 1940s—complete with the Great Depression and World War II.

Bill Clinton's approach to the 1996 campaign was more nuanced and skillfully played, featuring the powerful cultural and symbolic themes of nostalgia for the past *and* a hope for the future. Clinton speechwriter Michael Waldman writes that as he watched Dole's speech to the GOP convention, he "leapt out of my chair." The Dole speech cemented the theme for the Democrats: "Dole wants to build a bridge to the past; Clinton would build a bridge to the future." This theme, Waldman notes, capitalized on the truism in American politics "that the more optimistic candidate always wins."[4]

But Clinton's reelection campaign was waged on both a nostalgic rendering of an optimistic American past and a forward-looking hope for a better future. As Clinton told the delegates at the Democratic convention, "I love and revere the rich and proud history of America. And I am determined to take our best traditions into the future. But with all respect, we do not need to build a bridge to the past. We need to build a bridge to the future."[5] Not only did Clinton orient his campaign around the oft-quoted "bridge" theme, but he also frequently referenced a specific nostalgia that valorized the Progressivism of Theodore Roosevelt, arguing that the Progressive period was the past most analogous to America in 1996, in contradistinction to Dole's nostalgia for the World War II era.

Clinton's 1996 campaign strategy evidences the capacity of collective memory to function politically and nostalgically for electoral success. Our focus in this chapter is on Clinton's ability to evoke nostalgia as a justification for his reelection, and how his views of the past are reflective of the hyperreality of the political culture in which Clinton operated. Specifically, we analyze Clinton's 1996 book *Between Hope and History* and the untitled campaign video presented at the 1996 Democratic convention immediately prior to the president's acceptance speech. Both texts evidence Clinton's use of a nostalgic, hyperreal history to secure electoral success. In addition, Clinton's political nostalgia in these texts is of both a personal and a national quality. That is, Clinton not only offers a nostalgic rendition of the nation's history; he also presents a nostalgic retelling of his personal history to convince voters that he should have another four years in office. Clinton's 1996 strategy, as with the other texts constructing this president's image, expresses the tensions at work in his persona—specifically tensions between the past and the future and between his public and his private lives.

Collective Memory, Political Nostalgia, and Hyperreal History

Museums and monuments, history classes, and Hollywood films are just a few of the means by which members of a community come to understand and share collective memory.[6] From our earliest childhood, we learn the past in particular ways that are consistent with a shared pattern of meaning or comprehension. As Barbie Zelizer defines it, collective memory "refers to the recollections that are instantiated beyond the individual by and for the collective."[7] This collective consciousness—our collective memory—is combined with individual remembrances to provide what Maurice Halbwachs calls a "handier and surer grip" on the events of the past.[8]

Collective memory is, by definition, partial and material in its communication and demarcation of the past. In this sense, our collective memory is "pieced together like a mosaic," with some memories having greater or lesser resonance than others.[9] Those memories, moreover, have material consequences as they are expressed by narratives and embodied in particular individuals or objects.[10] Unlike individual memory, which is often only present in thought or confined to documents reserved for private consumption, collective memory is public and it is the publicity of collective memory that establishes its political/rhetorical power.

The public articulation of collective memory reveals how history and politics are fundamentally connected.[11] Stephen Browne reveals that "public memory gets performed within contexts of power and aspirations so routinely that its political character cannot be missed."[12] Ideologically, collective memory is integral to the formation of power and influence that constitute social interactions and involvements. Strategically, collective memory becomes a powerful tool in the rhetorical repertoire of leaders striving for electoral and political ascendancy. Collective memory works as an interpretive strategy for the definition of political image, as political actors seek to link their character to familiar and secure markers of collective identity drawn from the community's shared past. Bill Clinton's 1996 campaign reveals precisely how appeals to and definitions of collective memory, uttered as political nostalgia, operate as powerful rhetorical devices for political leaders, especially for those attempting to influence their own rhetorical images for political success.

Political Images and Collective Memory

Politics in the United States, especially in this postmodern time of media proliferation and imaged candidates, is primarily a rhetorical phenomenon.[13] In the rhetorical campaign for the presidency, epideictic oratory is a dominant rhetorical form[14]—a genre of rhetoric particularly conducive to transmitting collective memory and highly useful in campaign settings where images predominate and in-depth policy discussions are fairly limited.[15] The preponderance of epideictic oratory emanating from presidential candidates does not delegitimize rhetoric's role in public debate or policy formation.[16] Quite the opposite is true. To say that presidential campaign rhetoric is exclusively, or primarily, epideictic is to suggest that our contemporary rhetorical politics is fundamentally concerned with the formation and demarcation of

American values—the cultural ideology that defines the very ontological nature of the community. When a presidential candidate, or a president in office, announces a position or justifies a policy, such announcements, Dan Hahn alleges, "function less to argue about the efficacy of the decision in solving problems than in reestablishing the legitimacy of government by 'proving' that the decisions fit the prevailing value preferences of the electorate."[17]

As presidential candidates effectively and epideictically express the community's values in the service of politics, decision, or policy, they often invoke historically derived arguments, examples, commonplaces, or *topoi*—employing collective memory to convince and persuade.[18] In so doing, campaigns come to occupy a central role in the struggle to define collective memory. By utilizing collective memories for political purposes, presidential candidates offer an interpretation or understanding of that collective memory that carries considerable authority and legitimacy in U.S. culture.

In this role, the campaign process reveals two of the primary characteristics of collective memory and its rhetorical expression—its partiality and its usability.[19] Events are never expressed in their entirety because it would be impossible for a candidate to do so. Instead, the offered interpretation of the collective past is partial and, in Bill Clinton's hands at least, selfish in the construction of his political image. The partial use of collective memory in the service of political image speaks to the larger postmodern quality of American political culture—a culture where images dominate and political meaning is fluid and malleable.[20]

When campaigns invoke collective memory for their electoral or political goals, they demonstrate the usability of collective memory as a rhetorical tool. Collective memory functions as a device of the rhetorical campaign to "make connections—to each other over time and space, and to ourselves."[21] Those connections reinforce and stabilize political traditions and institutions, maintaining existing power relationships and preserving order and social cohesion. After all, as Zelizer concludes, "Political traditions are validated through some sense of a stable past."[22] This is precisely why constructions of public, collective memory are "never given, but always managed." Through such management, Browne asserts, collective memory is "constructed in ways designed to accrue to the advantages of the constructors."[23] Thus, the presidential candidate uses his or her vision of the past to preserve political power publicly and to ensure the survival of enduring social systems.

Because collective memory is limited in its representation of the past, it easily succumbs to political manipulation and exploitation and is smoothly transformed into political nostalgia. *Political nostalgia is the limited, distorted narrative of the past-in-memory that argumentatively resurrects and glorifies bygone times and is communicated to achieve an emotional response in the service of a political or electoral goal.* As such, it is a particular manifestation of collective memory; it is a hermeneutic expression of that memory in all of its partiality and the exploitative use of that memory for discrete and singular political purposes.

Political Nostalgia and Bill Clinton's 1996 Campaign

Nostalgia is a psychological construct that explains a longing for the past—a "yearning for yesterday," according to sociologist Fred Davis.[24] The term relates to the German *Heimweh*, or homesickness, and nostalgia was incipiently used to describe a condition faced by Swiss soldiers who became so debilitated by their longing for home that they were unable to function in the military. Nostalgia, according to psychologists, is a latent part of the human psyche.[25] It is a phenomenon of human experience that "is not a substitute for a wish but is an experience of the past that is recalled, normally or pathologically, for itself."[26]

Just as memory is distinct from history, so too is nostalgia distinct from memory. History is a record of events, while collective memory is the "depository of traditions" where a culture or a community comes to understand the events of the past.[27] Distinctively, nostalgia *distorts the past for the sake of affect and for the sake of the present* and is more culturally specific and normative. It is, as Davis concludes, "the means for holding onto and reaffirming identities which had been badly bruised by the turmoil of the times."[28]

Nostalgia is a powerful political/rhetorical appeal because of its emotional resonance with an audience and because of the identification it creates between political leaders and their audiences.[29] The rhetorical use of nostalgia invokes an idealized, mythologized past to "find/construct sources of identity, agency, or community, that are felt to be lacking [in the present]."[30] For political leaders and presidents, nostalgia offers an almost irresistible rhetorical tool, given its highly affective and effective rhetorical consequences. Nostalgia becomes a means for the political rhetor to affiliate their image and character to a distorted, yet memorialized aspect of the community's heritage.[31]

Political Nostalgia in *Between Hope and History*

As he had done in 1992, with *Putting People First*, Bill Clinton published a book-length manifesto of his policy positions and vision for the country in 1996 entitled *Between Hope and History*.[32] In general, the book was fairly conventional in its communication of the accomplishments of the first Clinton term and in its programmatic discussion of what the president hoped to achieve with a second term. Clinton organized the book around three central themes—opportunity, responsibility, community—that were recurrent in the Clinton rhetoric of 1996.[33] He offered a detailed rendering of the economic, social, and foreign policy achievements of his first term, highlighting the fiscal turnaround of the nation and peace that was restored throughout the world. Clinton's discussion of the future was also straightforward, with specific, largely small-scale solutions to persistent problems that reflected the "triangulation" strategy he employed in the 1996 campaign.[34]

What made *Between Hope and History* interesting, though, was Clinton's use of his own version of history—a decidedly hyperreal, nostalgic version of history—to justify his successes and his proposals. This use of history in the book was indicated immediately by its title. Derived from the Irish playwright Seamus Heaney, the title symbolized for Clinton that "there are moments in history when people's hopes are more likely to be fulfilled."[35] But the title is more loaded with meaning than that given it by the president. The "hope" theme that dominated the 1992 campaign was maintained in the selection of this title, speaking as it did to Clinton's idealism, his birthplace, and his constructed linkages with John F. Kennedy. The book's title positioned Clinton (and by extension, the nation) in 1996 at a tenuous and uncertain point, between the idealistic roots of his youth and the verdict of "history" as it will judge his presidential accomplishments. The past and the future were interwoven with Clinton's image, as were the public and the private. On the one hand there is the "hope" of rural Arkansas and the Clinton narrative of his childhood and youth in small-town America—a childhood that leads to the mythic handshake with the martyred, mythic president.[36] On the other hand is the very public sense of "history" with its futuristic orientations toward legacies and lasting accomplishments. Once again, the persistence of these dualities emerged from Clinton's discourse, figuring how his vision of America was to be viewed and interpreted.

Between Hope and History frequently referenced Clinton's childhood (the metaphorical "hope" so dominant in Clinton's campaign rhetoric) during the 1950s to justify specific policy proposals and visions for America in the 1990s. This strategy reflects the truism that nostalgia is most effective as a personal, material telling of the past, that it works best politically when it comes in the form of personal recollection.[37] To justify his commitment to personal responsibility, for instance, Clinton wrote,

> When I was growing up, Americans could pretty much walk down the street of any city without fear of violent crime. Having children out of wedlock was rare and a source of shame. . . . In neighborhoods all across America, people could say what President Lyndon Johnson said when he left Washington to go back to his small hometown in Texas, "People know when you're sick and care when you die." For too many young people growing up today, that world exists only in black-and-white reruns on television."[38]

The president referenced Hope and Hot Springs as "tight-knit communities" when he was a child, where the "fabric of community life was strong and whole."[39] He recalled the importance of the GI Bill that helped create "unparalleled prosperity in the postwar period."[40] And even as he noted the presence of learned racism and prejudice in a segregated Arkansas, Clinton called the era of his childhood "a time of great hope, as people rebuilt their lives here at home and as our nation committed itself to rebuilding the war-ravaged economies of Europe and Asia."[41]

Bill Clinton's nostalgia for the 1950s in *Between Hope and History* demonstrates how political nostalgia accomplishes its characterological mission of fusing national goals and public policy with the persona of a particular political leader. Clinton painted an optimistic view of life in postwar Arkansas, and that constructed vision worked to justify his contemporary vision of the United States in the 1990s. But Clinton's view of that time was constructed through his vantage point, as a middle-class, white, male youth who saw before him a time of limitless possibilities. His vision of the 1950s in Arkansas, as a warrant for the policies offered for his second term, manufactured a constricted narrative of that time and ignored the multiplicity of perspectives that shape other renditions of the past. The safety of small-town life in Hot Springs, Arkansas, the tight-knit nature of community then, the concern and neighborly regard that Clinton remembers are fictions of his personal memory—pure, though powerful, nostalgia. But they come to be fused, because of his status as a powerful agent of collective memory, with a political vision for contemporary public policy. And that is where the potentially distorting power of political nostalgia is most evident. The voters are urged by this rhetoric to see the past not only as a justification for the present and future, but to limit their view of the past to the perspective put forth by the political agent, in this case Bill Clinton.

The dangers of political nostalgia are most evident in Clinton's renditions of segregation in 1950s Arkansas. He wrote in *Between Hope and History* that

> In Hope, Arkansas, the streets in the black neighborhoods near where my grandfather had his store were the only ones in town that weren't paved. The movie house was segregated. The high school from which I graduated was segregated. Thirty years ago it was rare to see women or people of color as police officers or firefighters or doctors or lawyers or college professors or even, believe it or not, sports figures.[42]

Of course, Clinton was sensitive to racial issues in ways that elude many presidents and public policymakers.[43] But his fond recollections of the wonders of small-town life in Arkansas decades ago seem incongruous with the segregation he has described so dramatically. Rather than providing his reader with a vision of the past through the eyes of the victims of segregation (or sexism, or homophobia, or any of countless prejudices and discriminations that shaped the 1950s), the president seemed blissfully content to note in passing the degradation of segregation and racism and to subvert that historical memory to the more idyllic vision of the wholesome small Arkansas town that shaped his vision of America. Moreover, he used this rendition of Arkansas' segregated past to justify his lukewarm endorsement of Affirmative Action ("mend it, don't end it") and to self-congratulate his administration's record on diverse executive appointments. No mention of substantive policy solutions to meaningful and persistent problems of racism and discrimination emerged from Clinton's discussion of segregation in his childhood.

Not content to rely only on the nostalgia of his upbringing in Ike's America, Bill Clinton also justified his record and proposals on the basis of nostalgic renditions of other periods in American history, notably the Progressive era and the time of the Founders. A powerful aspect of political nostalgia is its ability to distort and blur distinctions in time. "Nostalgia presents itself as a special moment of remembering," notes Eugene Daniels, "one in which there is a commingling of past become present, even future manifesting itself in the present as already past."[44] This blurring of distinctions for affective impact is central to Clinton's use of the Progressives and the Founders for his own political purposes. In the president's nostalgic vision, he is the inheritor of the Progressives' sense of social justice and the Founders' foresighted wisdom. The nostalgia, in these cases, is more associational than characterological, as Clinton sought to capture the ethos and stature of historical heroes to achieve his own political and electoral ends.

Noting that the United States in the 1990s "has an instructive parallel in the not-too-distant past,"[45] Clinton likened contemporary circumstances in 1996 to the Progressive Era at the turn of the twentieth century. Similar pressures of urbanization, community erosion, workplace change, technological advancement, and economic disruption faced the Progressives just as they confronted America in 1996, Clinton wrote. And just as those challenges brought forth new leadership, so too would today's challenges occasion Clinton's leadership for the nation:

> [The Progressive Movement] was given voice and direction by Theodore Roosevelt, a president who was committed to ensuring that the free market worked for all Americans, protecting them from the abuses of the Industrial Age, conserving the nation's natural resources, reforming government, and asserting America's leadership in the world.
> Theodore Roosevelt, and later Woodrow Wilson, went beyond the conventional thinking of both their parties. They were determined to use the power of the United States government to ensure that America secured the benefits of the new age so that our identity as a nation, our character as a people, the ideals expressed in the Declaration of Independence and the Constitution would be enhanced in the new era. . . . That same shared vision guides us today.[46]

Progressivism provides the model, Clinton maintained, for political leadership. The nation turned to national leaders for help in solving national problems then, and "so too today it takes national leadership to frame the issues, point the way, and mobilize people to work to resolve them."[47]

Clinton's rhetorical maneuver here is clever. Drawing historical parallels with a time that most voters would only know through history and myth, as opposed to lived experience, allowed Clinton to shape his rendition of that time nostalgically for political purposes. As such, he becomes, in this discourse, the successor to Theodore Roosevelt's mythological mantle. He borrowed the crusading ethos of the hero of San Juan Hill, fighting big industry to help consumers, working to preserve America's natural heritage. This nostalgic portrait of Theodore Roosevelt also allowed Clinton to avoid some of TR's less savory characteristics—his rather overt racism, sexism, and imperialism do not figure into Clinton's hagiography.

The president also used the mythology of Roosevelt and Wilson to justify his own political centrism. The maverick nature of TR's and Wilson's historical legacy were grafted onto Clinton, who like them, goes beyond the "conventional thinking" of his own party to achieve the national good. Clinton, like so many other politicians before him, recognized the power of political nostalgia and presidential mythology, and worked skillfully and cunningly to achieve associational status with America's legendary political heroes.

By co-opting Progressivism in *Beyond Hope and History*, Clinton nostalgically distorted the Progressive Era to achieve his mythological parallel with Theodore Roosevelt. The United States in 1996 was quite different from the United States in 1896, or 1900, and those differences may be more meaningful than the similarities. The president's construction of the Progressive Era neglected most of those differences in favor of the myth of Progressivism that molds our view of that time in particular, self-serving ways. The vast changes in population, technology, diversity, and the ever-expanding size of government could not possibly have been imagined in the Progressive Era. Their rhetorics of "antimonopolism . . . social bonds and the social nature of human beings, and . . . the language of social efficiency"[48] would make little sense to contemporary America, where corporate mergers are commonplace, and social union and efficiency are assaulted by the spread of identity politics and the inefficiencies of government. In short, Clinton's appropriation of Progressivism achieved associational goals for political success rather than provide historically analogous reasoning to justify policy proposals or a public vision.

The associational function of Clinton's political nostalgia for the Progressive Era figured as well into this use of the nation's Founders to argue for his thematic approach to governance. At each thematic moment in *Between Hope and History*, as the president argued for his ideals of opportunity, responsibility, and community, he invoked the Founders. As with his use of Progressivism and the 1950s, this nostalgia legitimated Clinton's political goals rather than offering historical argument for his ideals.

Clinton planted his idealistic themes for twenty-first century America firmly in the grounds of the nation's nostalgic history. As he wrote in the introduction of *Between Hope and History*:

> It wouldn't hurt for each of us to keep our Declaration of Independence, Constitution, and Bill of Rights handy and look them over from time to time. The promise embedded in our founding documents is clear: America promises liberty, but demands civic responsibility. America promises opportunity to pursue happiness, but does not guarantee it. To make good on those promises, we must provide the conditions and tools which give all citizens willing to work hard and play by the rules the chance to make the most of their God-given potential.[49]

This nostalgic distortion of the Founders' documents is astounding. The aristocratic men who drafted these documents would scarcely recognize in them the values that Clinton finds there. These slave holding, well-educated men of the American colonies feared the rabble, constructed a government that minimized popular democracy, and labored to maintain the institutions and class distinctions existent in their time in order to preserve their own well-heeled way of life. That Clinton so freely tapped into schoolbook mythologies of the Founders for his political purposes reveals his political ends quite clearly. Of course, such values can be located interpretatively, but Clinton's nostalgic vision is so certain, so absolute.

This same nostalgia for the Founders resurfaced in *Between Hope and History* when Clinton discussed his commitment to greater "responsibility." "Our Founders," the president penned, ". . . understood very clearly something many Americans forget: freedom works only when it is exercised with responsibility."[50] The certainty of Clinton's nostalgia is noteworthy here. Nowhere in any of the documents that Clinton referenced in the introduction of the book is there written a commitment to the responsible exercise of freedom. Nowhere do the Founders say, as Clinton extrapolated, that Americans must "speak civilly, . . . [and] be truthful, accurate, and fair [in exercising freedom of the press]."[51] Yet the president so forcefully and certainly declared his interpretation of the Founders' thoughts and motivations to be the correct version of that memory and, once again, *Between Hope and History* evidenced political nostalgia's power as a tool of political rhetoric, a means of associational authority for contemporary political leadership.

The early history of the United States also figured into Clinton's justification for the value of "community," as the president used Alexis de Tocqueville's observations about America to refute Robert Putnam's fears concerning the decline of social capital and trust in contemporary public life.[52] Tocqueville "marveled at our eagerness to form associations and called it perhaps our most distinctive characteristic as a nation," the president wrote.[53] Despite Putnam's warnings, for Clinton America's sense of community "is growing again."[54] Growth of community, according to the president, depended upon the development of the modern parallel to Jefferson's "yeoman farmer," the American family. For Clinton, this Jeffersonian construct evidenced the point "that democracy would rise or fall not on the strength of some political elite, but on the strength of ordinary people who hold a stake in, and take responsibility for, how our society works."[55] In short, Bill Clinton justified his calls for welfare reform, school uniforms, and all the other "triangulating" strategies of the 1996 campaign on his nostalgic appropriations of Tocqueville and Jefferson.

The parallel between Jefferson's "farmer" and contemporary families is illuminating as it reveals the somewhat extraordinary lengths that Clinton pursued to make his arguments fit with his historical renditions. It reveals, quite starkly, how political nostalgia is a sought after and frequently used tool of political leadership. As with Clinton's appropriation of the Progressives, his construction of families in 1996 as analogous with Jefferson's farmer again highlights similarities more than differences. Eliding those differences for the sake of political expediency, Clinton revealed the deft use of memory and nostalgia that so defined his 1996 reelection bid.

Cultural critic Stuart Tannock observes that via its distortive and emotive capabilities, nostalgia ultimately functions as an appeal for stability and structure.[56] In so doing, nostalgic rhetoric may also, as rhetorician Stephen Depoe concludes, provide a community with a positive and therapeutic healing of divisions.[57] Not surprisingly, Bill Clinton employed nostalgia to seek reelection and to articulate his campaign themes of opportunity, responsibility, and community—

themes that are fundamentally concerned with stability and structure. Clinton's use of nostalgia was adroit, as he wove together powerful allusions to the nation's founding, to Progressivism at the turn of the twentieth century, and to his own childhood in the 1950s. The use of his childhood memories also worked to fuse his national policy goals with his own perspective on the past, performing a commanding use of nostalgia that beckoned a fusion of larger public memories with the president's personal past. And in the wake of the searing partisan divisions of 1995 and 1996, with government shutdowns, intensifying investigations, and fervent reactionary rhetoric from emboldened congressional Republicans,[58] Clinton's use of nostalgia can be seen for its therapeutic and healing qualities, reminding Americans, as presidents are supposed to do, of our glorious past and its triumphs. By locating his proposals and his persona within the sweep of history, and by using familiar and soothing nostalgic visions of that history, the president assured the voting public that even as the Republicans were fixated on the here and now, his vision was grander and more lasting.

Perhaps more than anything, Bill Clinton's political nostalgia in *Between Hope and History* revealed his own struggling with questions of presidential legacy, lasting impact, and the proverbial "verdict of history." Clinton went to great effort in this work to position his presidency and our moment in American history within a larger panorama of the American narrative. The president personified history when he claimed that it "has a habit of testing us . . . a habit of demanding that we choose between our hopes and fears, between our vision of how things ought to be and an acceptance of things as they are."[59] Our particular historical test is "immense," Clinton warned, as "we move from the Industrial Age into the Information Age, from the Cold War to the global village."[60] And at the conclusion of the book, Clinton likened 1996 as "another moment for Americans to decide," not unlike, he maintained, the declaration of national independence, the Civil War, the Progressive Era, the Great Depression, and the Cold War.[61] In this formulation of America's collective memory, Clinton nostalgically defined the past and validated his vision of the future. His values are the values rooted in American history. And his policies for the twenty-first century, based as they are in the values of the nation, are the best to carry the mythology of America into the future, his campaign narrative maintained.

The message at every turn in *Between Hope and History* is the placement of Bill Clinton at the center of American national life and, more significantly, as the focus of this moment in American history. His hyperreal, nostalgic vision of history, where knowing what the entirety of the past is indistinguishable from believing Clinton's version of the past, demonstrates political nostalgia's influence in the service of political image-making. It functioned for Bill Clinton, at least, as one means of reinvigorating his presidency, of articulating the relevance of his leadership to a nation being asked to offer its verdict on that leadership in 1996 and to select a vision for the remaining four years of the twentieth century.

**Annulling Memory with a Love Story:
Bill Clinton's 1996 Convention Film**

Clinton's dedication of *Between Hope and History* to his immediate family is revealing. On the dedication page, the president wrote: "To Hillary, whose love, support, and example have made my work possible and life joyful, and to Chelsea, whose love and life remind me every day of what all this work is for."[62] The dedication is instructive because it calls the reader's attention to another dimension of Bill Clinton's image and persona—and it speaks to the president's attempt to use his family again as a means of securing electoral support from the voting public. This strategy was even more evident from the 1996 convention film presented to the assembled delegates (and some television viewers) in Chicago immediately prior to Clinton's acceptance speech. This film highlighted Clinton's ability to not only apply political nostalgia to justify public policy and a national vision, but also to reconstruct and reimage his marriage and his family for political purposes.

As in 1992, Clinton turned to his friends Linda Bloodworth-Thomason and Harry Thomason in 1996 and asked them to craft his convention film. The untitled 1996 film, consistent with Clinton's incumbent status, offered a new rationale for his candidacy. Rooted in the accomplishments of his first four years, the 1996 film was noteworthy for its presidentiality—or its attempt to define Clinton *as president*.[63] The film also employed political nostalgia skillfully and successfully in the construction of the president's persona. What makes the film remarkable, though, is its use of nostalgia at both the private and the public levels. That is, the 1996 film not only offered Bill Clinton's vision of America at the dawn of the new century that was firmly planted in his telling of the past, it also used nostalgia to reinscribe an image of Bill Clinton as husband and father.

Recasting Clinton's personal, private image in 1996 was, in part, an inoculation against expected Republican attacks on his character. The use of nostalgia in the film to offer a particular vision of his marriage and family life also fulfilled what rhetorical critic Jeff D. Bass has termed the "symbolic annulment of history." A rhetoric that hearkens to a nostalgic past may work, Bass suggests, because of "its ability to relieve a form of temporal anxiety that results not so much from the fear of the uncertainties of the future, but from the guilt regarding the irreversibility of the consequences of past actions."[64] The rhetor becomes the past, in a sense, and the nostalgic vision offered in the rhetoric is the accepted version of events that annuls oppositional histories.

In 1992, *The Man from Hope* put forth a vision of Clinton's life story that was undoubtedly nostalgic and heavily reliant on a distorted version of his life and upbringing. But from the perspective of the voting public, there was precious little shared understanding of Clinton's biography—*The Man from Hope* was among the first of several rhetorics to *initially* define Clinton for millions of Americans. The task in 1992 was to annul the tabloid persona of Bill Clinton and to fill in the constructed contours of his personal story. At the time of its airing, there was little specific history of Clinton available for voters to weigh against *The Man from Hope*.[65] By 1996, though, Clinton's life story was well known; opinions about him and his family were well established. As such, the 1996 film in its use of a personal nostalgia about the Clintons' family life worked to symbolically annul the past, to reimage that family life in the face of four years of tabloid rumors, incessant investigations, and repeated allegations from all quarters that challenged its legitimacy.[66]

Beginning with the date "January 20, 1993" on a black screen, the 1996 convention film immediately historicized Bill Clinton. We hear Clinton reciting the presidential oath of office, and see a shot of the Clintons and the Gores on the steps of the Lincoln Memorial during their inaugural celebrations, reminiscent of Ronald Reagan's famous 1984 convention film, *A New Beginning*. Each of these public moments featured Hillary Clinton prominently—holding the Bible at the inauguration and Bill Clinton's hand at the Lincoln Memorial. But the public focus of the film's narrative immediately shifted to the private as it proceeded to a personal interview with the president. As if to magnify the more personal focus of the film, Clinton was visually "feminized" in the interview portions. That is, his dress was casual and relaxed as was his posture. He was placed on a beige sofa in what appears to be a sitting room. Behind him were flowers; bright sunlight streamed in from a window. The film seamlessly juxtaposed the more masculine and formal inauguration ritual with the more "feminine" and personal interview, naturalizing their simultaneous performance by Bill Clinton and beckoning the voter into the private lives of the presidency.

Clinton's personal recollections were entirely nostalgic in the 1996 film, fusing his persona with American heroes and images and offering a emotional rendition of his family life and his memories of the first Clinton term. The "interview" began with Clinton reminiscing about his departure from Arkansas in 1993. Filled with "mixed emotions," the president recalled how leaving Arkansas "reminded him of a little speech that Abraham Lincoln made from the train when he left Illinois for the last time to go to Washington." Immediately, the nostalgia was evident, as Clinton wove together his personal memories of the beginning of his presidency with the Lincoln mythology. Again, as in *Between Hope and History*, the voter was invited to view the first Clinton term through Clinton's memory, remembering it nostalgically as Clinton did, and to associate this president with Abraham Lincoln. Coupled with the visual a few seconds earlier of Clinton at the majestic Lincoln Memorial, the nostalgic tone of the film was set.

Hillary and Chelsea Clinton were overtly featured in the president's remembrance of his departure from Arkansas as well. Both were highlighted in visual images, one of Hillary speaking at the lectern in Little Rock as they prepared to leave, and another of Chelsea crying as she embraced a woman in the airport hangar. Hillary Clinton reemerged as central to the president's nostalgia as the film moved to its next theme—the palpable presence of death and tragedy in Clinton's first term. As Clinton listed the people who died during his first term (including his mother, father-in-law, Vince Foster, and Ron Brown), the film displayed visual images of Hillary and Bill Clinton at funerals. Clinton noted that all of the funerals "had a profound effect on me, and on Hillary, and on the work that we're doing." Interestingly, their "work" was joined in this statement, and visually reinforced by showing Hillary at the various funerals. The remark was reminiscent of Clinton's assertion in 1992 that were he elected, the American public would get two for one because Hillary Clinton would also be in the White House.

At the outset of the film, at least, Hillary Clinton was a prominent player in the nostalgic retelling of the Clinton first term as president.

The First Lady's image and role dominated the first third of the 1996 film. As if to answer the president's remark about the First Couple's "work" during the first term, the 1996 film abruptly switched its focus to the Clintons' family life and the strength of their marriage. In this segment, what emerged most compellingly was the nostalgic rereading of the Clinton marriage. Their marriage was, of course, thoroughly hyperreal—it was impossible to distinguish reality from image in its depiction. But the 1996 film responded to a host of competing images circulating in the political culture, many of them negative. In many quarters, from late-night comedy to the virulent right-wing talk radio shows, Hillary Clinton was depicted as pushy and domineering; the president was caricatured as a serial philanderer and sexual harasser. Moreover, the First Lady's political role in the administration's failed effort to reform health care positioned her as a political figure, in contradistinction to more traditional images of First Ladies.[67] The 1996 convention film seemed determined, both verbally and visually, to nostalgically reconstruct the Clintons' marriage as a genuine love story, in much the same manner as *The Man from Hope* nostalgically rendered Bill Clinton's childhood as a story of the American Dream.

To a series of endearing and moving still photographs of Bill Clinton, the 1996 film featured a lengthy testimonial by Hillary Clinton attesting to the president's abilities in office. She certified Bill Clinton's "extraordinary compassion as well as competence," and remarked that "Every day that goes by, I see him doing more and more to try and fulfill his vision of the kind of country that he wants for our daughter and for all children, and I just think we're very lucky to have him at this point in our *history*." Humorously, the First Lady concluded, "And I say that as a totally objective observer."

As Hillary Clinton offered these observations, the film displayed Bill Clinton in situations and poses that reinforced her conclusions. The president was shown greeting an African American child in a wheelchair and hugging a bald female cancer victim at the same time that the First Lady discussed his compassion. Visuals also punctuated her observations about his competence, showing him in a Cabinet meeting, and with Vice President Gore, and amidst a group of veterans as Hillary Clinton mentioned his ability to perform his job.

This weaving of visual imagery with Hillary Clinton's verbal authentication of President Clinton's ability and character worked on two ideological levels. First, as in *The Man from Hope*, the 1996 film employed women, primarily, to testify to Clinton's character. Hillary Clinton not only concluded that the president possessed the skills to be the nation's chief executive, but that he cared about people compassionately. As if to further establish the historical importance of Bill Clinton, the First Lady even established his importance for "this point in our history." Furthermore, the visual images reinforced the First Lady's conclusions. Lest there be any doubt as to the veracity of her testimony, the film offered visual evidence of Hillary Clinton's conclusions. There was an intimacy and an authenticity to the still images that propped up the First Lady's thoughts and made real her conclusions. The voter should not question Hillary Clinton's judgment of her husband, these images suggested, because that judgment was supported by the president's photographed actions.

Second, this portion of the 1996 film reduced Hillary Clinton to a supportive and sincere wife, anxious to convince the world that her husband was the best man to be president. The First Lady did not discuss their "work" together, or her role in the administration's political efforts, or her efforts spearheading health care reform. She instead invited the viewer to see Bill Clinton through her eyes as his wife who "stands by her man," and bears witness to his compassion and care for children. In this sense, the photographs that accompanied Hillary Clinton's remarks functioned almost as a family album, with the First Lady beckoning our gaze at the "real" Bill Clinton as he displayed the compassion and competence she witnessed so frequently. Indeed, by reducing Hillary Clinton to the role of supportive wife, the 1996 film set the stage for its next narrative segment, where the Clintons' marriage was nostalgically reconstructed.

Reimaging the Clinton's marriage was the task given to Dorothy Rodham, the president's mother-in-law. While Rodham appeared briefly in *The Man from Hope*, she was prominently featured in 1996, giving testimony to the strength of the "First marriage," and, by extension, to the character of the candidate. Her mere presence here is instructive as to the gravity of her task—testifying about the Clintons' marriage and family life. Clearly, the Clinton campaign felt this to be an important dimension of the film's message.

Rodham began her comments with a humorous attempt to establish credibility: "Everybody knows that there's only one person in the world that can really tell the truth about a man, and that's his mother-in-law." After admitting that she admired Bill Clinton, she remarked:

> But I love him for the way that he defended and loved my daughter. I would love to have had, while I had a really good marriage, I would love to have had the kind of intellectual partner that I could bounce off these great ideas and the independence of thought, the sharing of experience, and the kind of good-natured ribbing and fun that they have with each other. Because they're both very complicated people, but their relationship is not—they just simply love each other.

Rodham elevated the Clintons' marriage beyond the mundane in her comments, which were punctuated by numerous still images of Bill and Hillary Clinton in very complementary and intimate poses. Many of the images are black and white, and they almost all feature the First Couple smiling warmly at each other, or embracing, or sharing a private moment. Again, the visuals authenticated, within the grammar of the film, the testimony offered by Rodham.

Rodham's remarks again highlight the ideological dimensions of the 1996 film, and the attempts it made to rehabilitate the Clintons' marriage from the popular stereotypical conceptions of it. Read carefully, her words were disjointed—Bill Clinton is her daughter's defender and intellectual partner. The Clintons engage in good-natured fun and "ribbing," according to Rodham, but they also can bounce ideas back and forth. Indeed, by the end of her statement, Rodham seemed to have lost sight of the point, so she returned to the key theme and asserted that despite their complicated personalities, Bill and Hillary Clinton "simply love each other." Later in the film, Rodham returned to defend the First Couple from the "personal attacks" they faced. She concluded, "They know who they are. They've been really grounded and have faith in themselves." Again, the film featured numerous intimate photographs of the Clintons hugging, laughing, talking, or simply being with one another.[68]

Rodham essentially situated Bill Clinton back into the ideologically comfortable and popular role of loving husband and father. As if to answer the critical appraisals of the Clintons, Rodham redefined their marriage in a nostalgic manner so as to not only diminish or annul the memory of Hillary Clinton's political activism, but also to erase the collective memory of Bill Clinton's alleged philandering. Theirs is a story of love, according to Rodham, and all the unflattering or negative images of Bill and Hillary Clinton that exist in the collective memory as a result of investigations and political attacks were erased in Rodham's depiction of their partnership. Her rendition sought an emotional reaction, and as such, it slanted and shaped the tale of the Clintons' marriage to achieve that response. Rodham even dismissed all of the criticisms of the Clintons as mere "personal attacks" that do little to harm the First Couple who, according to Rodham, "have the truth on their side." Moreover, the visual images that accompanied her words were powerful confirmations of the nostalgic love story she told about the marriage.

After a discussion of Chelsea Clinton's role in the White House, the film then turned to a segment that nostalgically hearkened back to memories of Camelot and the Kennedy mythology. Moving from the death and despair of the funerals from the first term, Clinton next discussed the future as personified by his two nephews. The nephews functioned, in a sense, as the bridge in the film, between the past and the future. They worked within the film's narrative to testify to a larger sense of purpose for the Clinton presidency. Toward that end, the president stated:

> It's an incredible thing for me to look at Tyler and it reminds me so much of Mother, every time I look at him I think of Mother. It's a wonderful way of still having her here. It also is a real reality check for me. Even if I'm having a bad day, if I can see one of them, or even look at their pictures, it kind of connects me to what I'm really doing here.

As Clinton said these words, the film featured several images, moving and still, of both Bill and Hillary Clinton with the children. One image, in particular, was nostalgic. It showed Tyler Clinton, the president's toddler nephew running into the Oval Office to greet his uncle. The video clip also displayed Clinton playing with Tyler, showing him the statues on the credenza behind the president's desk. Of course, this segment was powerfully reminiscent of the famous photographs featuring John F. Kennedy and his small children playing in the Oval Office. Past became future, and future remembered the past in Clinton's nostalgic rendering of his "purpose" as president.

Ultimately, the early portions of the 1996 convention film were an exercise in nostalgia, a reconstruction and rehabilitation of the Clinton personal saga that mightily tried to rescue it from the clutches of investigations, rumors, exposés, and tabloids. In the Clintons' version, this story is one of loss and grief for the loved ones who died, love and care in a marriage that is strong and resilient, and hopeful because of the new life and promise offered by the family's children. This version sought to annul the memory of Gennifer Flowers, to subvert the recollections of Hillary Clinton's political activities, and to elevate an almost JFK-like visage for Bill Clinton. It was, in sum, a carefully crafted, highly nostalgic exercise in presidential image-making that significantly blurred distinctions between public and private and the past and future.

Using Hyperreal History: The Reelection of Bill Clinton

Politically speaking, there was high degree of uncertainty festering in U.S. political culture in 1996. As with much of the 1990s, ambivalences and anxieties were everywhere, from trouble spots around the world, to increased partisanship at home. The president of the United States was accused in a sexual harassment lawsuit, and numerous investigations probed the ethics of his administration. In his reelection bid, Bill Clinton used political nostalgia to provide catharsis and to lessen anxiety, both about his personal character and his presidential leadership. He constructed, as such, a presidentiality that relied on a hyperreal history, a telling of the past infused with his image and designed to place him at the center of American history in the 1990s.

Nostalgic narratives, literature scholar Nicholas Dames reveals, are "the set of sites and temporal processes that reflect, and manage, *dislocation*—experiences of dissonance, disconnection, separation from past spaces and certainties."[69] Dames concludes that a nostalgia that looks backward also looks forward, is "a dilution and disconnection of the past in the service of an encroaching future."[70] Clinton answered the dislocation of the 1990s with a nostalgic justification for his reelection and continued leadership. In *Between Hope and History*, Clinton placed his presidential and policy values firmly within a vision of American history, a vision that distorted the past for emotionally derived justifications of policy positions in the present. In so doing, Bill Clinton used the past to serve his hope for the future. As with all of Bill Clinton's imaging, however, his telling of history in *Between Hope and History* was hyperreal—there was no sense of Clinton's overtly political use of history. His historical voice was authoritative and his use of historical analogy was presented so as to seem above the politics that motivated it. In short, the political imaging under way with Clinton's nostalgia was hidden and suppressed.

Bill Clinton's personal narrative also occasioned dislocation, dissonance, and a separation from certainty. Was he the kind and compassionate president, or was he the sexual harasser and interloper described by his enemies? In response, the 1996 convention film nostalgically retold the Clinton story, restoring certainty and eliminating dissonance by recasting the "two-for-one" political narrative of the Clintons' marriage into an old-fashioned love story of care and devotion. Children, family, and love surrounded Clinton in this narrative, and its nostalgic rendering of his personal story was in stark distinction to the circulating rumors and gossip that defined him for many Americans.

Again, though, this version of the Clinton story was thoroughly hyperreal such that the voter consuming it had no way of knowing what actually happened in Clinton's life and marriage and what was simply constructed for the sake of political image. In fact, as Bill Clinton shot the 1996 film, at the same time that his mother-in-law testified to the love and truth of the Clintons' marriage, the president was also engaging in an "inappropriate relationship" with a young White House intern named Monica Lewinsky.

Nowhere was Bill Clinton's use of political nostalgia and his construction of a hyperreal history more powerfully on display than at the conclusion of the 1996 convention film. After testimonials from Al Gore and a discussion of Clinton's efforts on behalf of world peace, the film concluded with a nostalgic romp through America's past. The content of the segment is mostly visual, with rapidly edited photographs that iconically represent American history. These images included numerous shots of the Statue of Liberty, film of immigrants arriving on boats, Ellis Island, a Dust Bowl farmer, shots of Pearl Harbor and D-Day, and V-E Day and V-J Day celebrations. Disembodied voices of scratchy oratory extolling American virtue and perseverance were heard as the images continued. The images then slowed to a still of Coretta Scott King and her children, in mourning, as Robert F. Kennedy's voice was played on the sound track. After the King family image, a visual montage occurred, with a series of film and still photographs that, again, were an iconic photo album of American history. This montage included: soldiers consoling each other in battle, the Dorothea Lange 1936 photograph "Migrant Mother," a veteran kneeling at the Vietnam Veterans Memorial, Henry Ford with a Model T, the Kitty Hawk flight of the Wright Brothers, Amelia Earhart, astronauts on the moon, Jesse Owens at the 1936 Olympics, Elvis Presley performing, Bob Hope entertaining troops, Theodore Roosevelt giving an impassioned speech, Franklin Roosevelt with Eleanor Roosevelt, Caroline Kennedy's wedding picture outside of Hyannisport, Michael Jordan dunking a basketball, Martin Luther King, Jr. giving the "I Have a Dream" speech, Cal Ripken, Jr. greeting a crowd, and the flag-raising on Iwo Jima.[71]

Many, if not all, of these photographs were familiar and immediately occasioned nostalgic remembrance. Additionally, the selection of images contrasted death, pain, and suffering, with hope and optimism for a brighter future. Certainly the Depression era images spoke to painful memories, but they were followed by hopeful and optimistic visions of the nation celebrating its triumph over fascism at the end of World War II. The heartache of the Vietnam War and the assassinations of Martin Luther King, Jr. and Robert F. Kennedy are juxtaposed with depictions of American triumph, from Henry Ford and the Wright Brothers to Michael Jordan and Cal Ripken, Jr. This collision of images represented a phenomenon of media communication wherein not so obvious rearrangement of images creates new understanding and a specific persuasive slant. Paul Messaris notes that this may be the "most prominent form of visual manipulation that exists."[72]

The montage was nostalgic, therefore, in its tone and emphasis, capturing thematically the ideals at the basis of the Clinton reelection campaign. Missing, of course, are many of the unflattering episodes from America's twentieth century: the internment of Japanese Americans during World War II, the rise of the Ku Klux Klan in the early twentieth century, the segregation and lynching so characteristic of Jim Crow, the plight of the Latino farm workers, the forced displacement of Native Americans, the persistent violence and discrimination against gay men and lesbians, the persistence of patriarchy and sex-based discrimination.

The president's narrative accompaniment to the photographic montage was also nostalgic, highlighting only those aspects of the twentieth century American experience that were positive and optimistic for the future. As he said:

> As we look back on the twentieth century, it can be said that we Americans have been in the arena. There is much to be proud of. But there is also still

much to do. I've learned all over again that what Alexis de Tocqueville said is still true; America is great because America is good. Most of the people in this country are just good people, and they share a common love of freedom, and they love their families, and they desperately want to work, and they deserve, they deserve, a leadership and a direction in this country that will keep opportunity alive for all of them in the twenty-first century, and that will bring us together instead of taking us apart.

Once again, as in *Between Hope and History*, the voters' understanding of the past was filtered and defined by Bill Clinton's vision of the past. The film's narration asked its viewers to believe, with Clinton, in America's greatness because of what Bill Clinton has "learned all over again." In this way, by refracting the past through Clinton, the voter has no option but to accept the president's reading, to believe in the optimism and values that were validated by his nostalgic rendering of the past.

Additionally, the president's rendition of America's optimistic past annulled its less savory historical episodes, opting instead for a sanitized optimism. Such is the power of political nostalgia. Within contemporary political discourse, uses of the past cannot be self-reflective. *Mythos* and nostalgia must reign, because to do otherwise would be to associate a candidacy with negativity and risk charges of "un-Americanism." Political nostalgia eliminates the possibility of using history in a more complete manner and fails to account for the complexities of history and memory, opting instead for compelling and safe renditions of that memory. Distortion and affectivity is a necessity, not a by-product, of contemporary political culture in the United States.

Toward this end, then, the final moment of the 1996 campaign film made sense. Reminiscent of *The Man from Hope*, the 1996 film ended with Bill Clinton saying: "I still believe these things are possible. I still believe in the promise of tomorrow. And I still believe in a place called America." These statements were uttered as the film visually showed Bill Clinton shaking hands with an African American Boys' Nation delegate in front of a large, framed photograph of the famous Clinton-Kennedy handshake from 1963. This final moment invoked all of the Kennedy mythology, all of the Clinton-Kennedy connections, and all of the power of Clinton's charisma. It was both nostalgic and future focused, bringing into collusion for political purposes the myth of JFK and the promise of racial reconciliation. It was a powerful and emotional climax to the film.

It was also a classic example of the power of political nostalgia in contemporary discourse. The scene lacked context, elided a series of contradictory and difficult collective memories of John F. Kennedy, and glossed over the problems of racism and discrimination that are significantly more than symbolic in the lived experiences of real Americans. But the scene quickly and rashly affiliated Bill Clinton with a nostalgia that was unifying and hopeful, that resolved the dislocations of 1996 by referencing Camelot and the "passing of the torch" from one generation to the other. It was, thus, hyperreal history at its most politically effective, distorting the past for political purposes and creating emotions about that past that envision a positive and optimistic future.

Notes

1. See Robert D. Loevy, *The Manipulated Path to the White House, 1996* (Lanham, MD: University Press of America, 1998), 242. Roger Simon notes that Koppel was probably naïve to expect a surprise or any kind of news at the convention: "Koppel was *expecting* a surprise? That's why he flew to San Diego in the first place? What kind of surprise? That Dole would withdraw in favor of Elizabeth? In the news business, surprises and wishful thinking should never be confused." See Roger Simon, *Show Time: The American Political Circus and the Race for the White House* (New York: Times Books, 1998), 228, emphasis in original.

2. Quoted in Simon, *Show Time*, 229.

3. "Full Text of Bob Dole's Speech," available at http://www.usatoday.com/elect/ec/ecr/ecr126.htm. Georgine Hodgkinson and Chris M. Leland conclude that the dominant metaphor for the Dole campaign, evident in his debate performances, was of Dole as a historian and keeper of tradition. See Georgine Hodgkinson and Chris M. Leland, "Metaphors in the 1996 Presidential Debates: An Analysis of Themes," in *The Electronic Election: Perspectives on the 1996 Campaign Communication*, edited by Lynda Lee Kaid and Dianne G. Bystrom (Mahwah, NJ: Lawrence Erlbaum, 1999), 153–4. See also William L. Benoit, "Framing Through Temporal Metaphor: 'Bridges' of Bob Dole and Bill Clinton in their 1996 Acceptance Addresses," *Communication Studies* 52 (2001): 70–84.

4. Michael Waldman, *POTUS Speaks: Finding the Words That Defined the Clinton Presidency* (New York: Simon & Schuster, 2000), 131. For an analysis of the "bridge" metaphor, see Todd S. Purdum, "Bridges for Both Parties: Requiem for a Metaphor Too Far," *New York Times*, September 8, 1996, sec. 4, p. 5.

5. "President Bill Clinton," transcript of 1996 Acceptance Speech, available at http://cgi.cnn.com/ALLPOLITICS/1996/news/9608/30/clinton.speech/clinton.shtml.

6. See Carole Blair, Marsha S. Jeppeson, and Enrico Pucci, Jr., "Public Memorializing in Postmodernity: The Vietnam Veterans Memorial as Prototype," *Quarterly Journal of Speech* 77 (1991): 263–88; Greg Dickinson, "Memories for Sale: Nostalgia and the Construction of Identity in Old Pasadena," *Quarterly Journal of Speech* 83 (1997): 1–27; Cheryl R. Jorgensen-Earp and Lori A. Lanzilotti, "Public Memory and Private Grief: The Construction of Shrines at the Sites of Public Tragedy," *Quarterly Journal of Speech* 84 (1998): 150–70; and Tamar Katriel, "Sites of Memory: Discourses of the Past in Israeli Pioneering Settlement Museums," *Quarterly Journal of Speech* 80 (1994): 1–20.

7. Barbie Zelizer, "Reading the Past Against the Grain: The Shape of Memory Studies," *Critical Studies in Mass Communication* 12 (1995): 214. See also Steven

Knapp, "Collective Memory and the Actual Past," *Representations* 26 (1989): 123–49; and Barbie Zelizer, *Covering the Body: The Kennedy Assassination, the Media, and the Shaping of Collective Memory* (Chicago: University of Chicago Press, 1992).

8. Maurice Halbwachs, *The Collective Memory* (New York: Harper Colophon Books, 1980), 59.

9. Zelizer, "Reading the Past," 224–5.

10. Zelizer, "Reading the Past," 232.

11. Richard Johnson, Gregor McLennan, Bill Schwartz, and David Sutton, *Making Histories: Studies in History-Writing and Politics* (Minneapolis: University of Minnesota Press, 1982), 8.

12. Stephen H. Browne, "Reading Public Memory in Daniel Webster's *Plymouth Rock Oration*," *Western Journal of Communication* 57 (1993): 466. For more on the role of memory in political argument, see J. Robert Cox, "Memory, Critical Theory, and the Argument from History," *Argumentation & Advocacy* 27 (1990): 1–13. Browne has further explored the power of public memory to "fashion the past to partisan and selective ends" in Stephen H. Browne, "Remembering Crispus Attucks: Race, Rhetoric, and the Politics of Commemoration," *Quarterly Journal of Speech* 85 (1999): 169–87.

13. Of course, the highly rhetorical nature of political campaigning has translated into a rhetorical mode of governing. This is most clearly seen in the development in the twentieth century of the "rhetorical presidency." See, for instance, Richard J. Ellis, ed. *Speaking to the People: The Rhetorical Presidency in Historical Perspective* (Amherst: University of Massachusetts Press, 1998); Wayne Fields, *Union of Words: A History of Presidential Eloquence* (New York: Free Press, 1996); Carol Gelderman, *All the Presidents' Words: The Bully Pulpit and the Creation of the Virtual Presidency* (New York: Walker and Company, 1997); Martin J. Medhurst, ed., *Beyond the Rhetorical Presidency* (College Station: Texas A&M University Press, 1996); Mary Stuckey and Frederick J. Antczak, "The Rhetorical Presidency: Deepening Vision, Widening Exchange," *Communication Yearbook* 21 (1998): 405–41; and Jeffrey Tulis, *The Rhetorical Presidency* (Princeton, NJ: Princeton University Press, 1987).

14. Dan Hahn, "The Media and the Presidency: Ten Propositions," *Communication Quarterly* 35 (1987): 260. Hahn specifically addresses presidential oratory, and not campaign oratory, but many of his propositions apply to presidential campaigning as well as governing. However, we believe Hahn goes too far when he states that *all* presidential oratory is epideictic. This may have been true with some presidents (Reagan comes to mind), but is too broad to accurately reflect all presidential

rhetoric. Much of President Clinton's public discourse is highly deliberative and/or forensic. Indeed, Hahn even acknowledges the presence of non-ceremonial presidential speeches, though he believes that such oratory is always crisis-centered.

15. Browne, "Reading Public Memory," 465.

16. Celeste Condit commented persuasively about the varied functions and powers of epideictic oratory. See Celeste Condit, "The Functions of Epideictic: The Boston Massacre Orations as Exemplar," *Communication Quarterly* 33 (1985): 284–98.

17. Hahn, "The Media and the Presidency," 260.

18. G. Thomas Goodnight's examination of Ronald Reagan's justifications for U.S. intervention in Central America demonstrates how history and historical narratives are implicated in the justification of policy. See G. Thomas Goodnight, "Reagan, Vietnam, and Central America: Public Memory and the Politics of Fragmentation," in *Beyond the Rhetorical Presidency*, edited by Martin J. Medhurst (College Station: Texas A&M University Press, 1996), 122–52. Depoe is similarly concerned with the use of nostalgic appeals for political and policy purposes. See Stephen P. Depoe, "Requiem for Liberalism: The Therapeutic and Deliberative Functions of Nostalgic Appeals in Edward Kennedy's Address to the 1980 Democratic National Convention," *Southern Communication Journal* 55 (1990): 175–92. Additionally, as Karlyn Kohrs Campbell and Kathleen Hall Jamieson conclude, "*memoria*, or recollection of a shared past, becomes an exceptionally important resource for epideictic speeches." See Karlyn Kohrs Campbell and Kathleen Hall Jamieson, "Form and Genre in Rhetorical Criticism: An Introduction," in *Form and Genre: Shaping Rhetorical Action*, edited by Karlyn Kohrs Campbell and Kathleen Hall Jamieson (Falls Church, VA: Speech Communication Association, 1978), 10.

19. See Zelizer, "Reading the Past," 224–30.

20. For a discussion of the power and evolution of image-based communication, see Mitchell Stephens, *the rise of the image the fall of the word* (New York: Oxford University Press, 1998).

21. Zelizer, "Reading the Past," 226. Nora reflects on the competing uses of memory and history, with memory working as a "perpetually actual phenomenon, a bond tying us to the external present," and history functioning as a "representation of the past." See Pierre Nora, "Between Memory and History: *Les Lieux de Mémoire*," *Representations* 26 (1989): 8.

22. Zelizer, "Reading the Past," 227. In the British context, the construction of political consequence through performances of popular memory is discussed in Popular Memory Group, "Popular Memory: Theory, Politics, Method," in *Making Histories: Studies in History-Writing and Politics*, edited by Richard Johnson, Gregor

McLennan, Bill Schwartz, and David Sutton (Minneapolis: University of Minnesota Press, 1982), 205–52.

23. Browne, "Reading Public Memory," 465.

24. Fred Davis, *Yearning for Yesterday: A Sociology of Nostalgia* (New York: Free Press, 1979). Another good introduction to the concept of nostalgia is Stuart Tannock, "Nostalgia Critique," *Cultural Studies* 9 (1995): 453–64. A review of nostalgia that locates its development in progressive ideology is offered in Kimberly K. Smith, "Mere Nostalgia: Notes on a Progressive Paratheory," *Rhetoric & Public Affairs* 3 (2000): 505–27.

25. The psychological and psychoanalytic dimensions of nostalgia are explained in Eugene B. Daniels, "Nostalgia and Hidden Meaning," *American Imago* 42 (1985): 371–83; Janice Doane and Devon Hodges, *Nostalgia and Sexual Difference* (New York and London: Methuen, 1987); Mario Jacoby, *The Longing for Paradise: Psychological Perspectives on an Archetype*, translated by Myron B. Gubitz (Boston: Sigo Press, 1985); and David S. Werman, "Normal and Pathological Nostalgia," *Journal of the American Psychoanalytic Association* 25 (1977): 387–98. Renato Rosaldo disputes the idea that nostalgia is a latent or natural human characteristic when he notes that it is a peculiarly Western concept. He concludes that the absence of nostalgia as a concept in other cultures undermines claims that this psychological attribute is "natural or pan-human." See Renato Rosaldo, "Imperialist Nostalgia," *Representations* 26 (1989): 109. The Westernness of nostalgia is also noted in Malcolm Chase and Christopher Shaw, "The Dimensions of Nostalgia," in *The Imagined Past: History and Nostalgia*, edited by Christopher Shaw and Malcolm Chase (Manchester and New York: Manchester University Press, 1989), 1–17.

26. Werman "Normal and Pathological Nostalgia," 393.

27. Halbwachs, *The Collective Memory*, 83.

28. Fred Davis, "Nostalgia, Identity, and the Current Nostalgia Wave," *Journal of Popular Culture* 11 (1977): 422. For a discussion of the perils of nostalgia from a feminist perspective, see Doane and Hodges, *Nostalgia and Sexual Difference*; and Gayle Greene, "Feminist Fiction and the Uses of Memory," *Signs* 16 (1991): 290–321.

29. Depoe, "Requiem for Liberalism," 179. The political nature of nostalgia is also the subject of Wendy Wheeler, "Nostalgia Isn't Nasty: The Postmodernising of Parliamentary Democracy," in *Altered States: Postmodernism, Politics, Culture*, edited by Mark Perryman (London: Lawrence & Wishart, 1994), 94–112.

30. Tannock, "Nostalgia Critique," 454. See also David Lowenthal, *The Past Is a Foreign Country* (Cambridge: Cambridge University Press, 1985).

31. Ronald Reagan, for instance, skillfully fused his political persona with a nostalgic manipulation of America's history. Reagan's sense of myth, nostalgia, and narrative are well documented and often criticized. As David Lowenthal concludes, "Reagan's invention of the American past, as of his own, was a necessary myth, part of the age-old American need to deny sin and escape history. His fantasies were acceptable because both he and his people genuinely held them." See David Lowenthal, "Nostalgia Tells It Like It Wasn't," in *The Imagined Past: History and Nostalgia*, edited by Christopher Shaw and Malcolm Chase (Manchester and New York: Manchester University Press, 1989), 26. See also James Combs, *The Reagan Range: The Nostalgic Myth in American Politics* (Bowling Green, OH: Bowling Green State University Press, 1993); Walter R. Fisher, "Romantic Democracy, Ronald Reagan, and Presidential Heroes," *Western Journal of Speech Communication* 46 (1982): 299–310; Sara Russell Hankins, "Archetypal Alloy: Reagan's Rhetorical Image," *Central States Speech Journal* 34 (1983): 33–43; Haynes Johnson, *Sleepwalking Through History: America in the Reagan Years* (New York: W. W. Norton, 1991); William F. Lewis, "Telling America's Story: Narrative Form and the Reagan Presidency," *Quarterly Journal of Speech* 73 (1987): 267–79; Michael Paul Rogin, *Ronald Reagan the Movie: And Other Episodes in Political Demonology* (Berkeley: University of California Press, 1987); and Garry Wills, *Reagan's America* (New York: Doubleday, 1987).

32. President Bill Clinton, *Between Hope and History: Meeting America's Challenges for the 21st Century* (New York: Times Books, 1996). It is worth noting that Clinton acknowledges the help of a William E. Nothdurft, who "was primarily responsible for helping to draft this book." As Clinton admitted to Brian Lamb in an appearance on C-Span's *Booknotes*, Nothdurft was essentially a ghostwriter for the book, though Clinton goes to great lengths to stress his personal involvement in composing the work: "And then he [Nothdurft] did a proposed outline for me and I changed it and said, 'This is the way I want it.' And then he did some drafts and I changed it. And then he did another draft. And then I took it off to Wyoming and essentially substantially rewrote it the way I wanted it to be. But he did a fabulous job. He really understood exactly what needed to be done after we'd talked. And I think it would have taken me probably two or three times as long to do it if he hadn't been involved in helping me write it." See *"Booknotes* Transcript," available at http://www.booknotes.org/transcripts/50037.htm. Nothdurft is described by Clinton as a "writer and a man who cares about public policy."

33. Clinton revealed to Brian Lamb that much of the second inaugural address is found in *Between Hope and History*. See *"Booknotes* Transcript."

34. For more on the "triangulation" strategy of the 1996 Clinton campaign, see James W. Ceaser and Andrew E. Busch, *Losing to Win: The 1996 Elections and American*

Politics (Lanham, MD: Rowman & Littlefield, 1997); Dick Morris, *Behind the Oval Office: Getting Reelected Against All Odds* (Los Angeles: Renaissance Books, 1999); and Gerald M. Pomper, Walter Dean Burnham, Anthony Corrado, Marjorie Randon Hershey, Marion R. Just, Scott Keeter, Wilson Carey McWilliams, and William F. Mayer, *The Election of 1996: Reports and Interpretations* (Chatham, NJ: Chatham House, 1997). Rachel Holloway offers a compelling discussion of how this strategy played itself out in Clinton's rhetoric during the campaign. See Rachel L. Holloway, "Taking the Middle Ground: Clinton's Rhetoric of Conjoined Values," in *The 1996 Presidential Campaign: A Communication Perspective*, edited by Robert E. Denton, Jr. (New York: Praeger, 1998), 123–42.

35. "*Booknotes* Transcript."

36. See Chapter One.

37. Davis, "Nostalgia, Identity, and the Current Nostalgia Wave," 415.

38. Clinton, *Between Hope and History*, 63–4.

39. Clinton, *Between Hope and History*, 118.

40. Clinton, *Between Hope and History*, 46.

41. Clinton, *Between Hope and History*, 130, 142.

42. Clinton, *Between Hope and History*, 131–2. There is something tacitly stereotypical in the last sentence of this passage, where Clinton acknowledged the contemporary preponderance of people of color in professional athletics. Of course, there still are not many women or people of color in the other professions listed.

43. For discussions of Clinton's record on racial matters, see James MacGregor Burns and Georgia J. Sorenson, *Dead Center: Clinton-Gore Leadership and the Perils of Moderation* (New York: Scribner, 1999); Virginia Sapiro and David T. Canon, "Race, Gender, and the Clinton Presidency," in *The Clinton Legacy*, edited by Colin Campbell and Bert A. Rockman (New York: Chatham House, 2000); and Sharon D. Wright, "Clinton and Racial Politics," in *The Postmodern Presidency: Bill Clinton's Legacy in U.S. Politics*, edited by Steven E. Schier (Pittsburgh: University of Pittsburgh Press, 2000).

44. Daniels, "Nostalgia and Hidden Meaning," 379.

45. Clinton, *Between Hope and History*, 13.

46. Clinton, *Between Hope and History*, 14–15. Burns and Sorenson note "For young Clinton, Wilson and the two Roosevelts were role models in courageous leadership."

See Burns and Sorenson, *Dead Center*, 22.

47. Clinton, *Beyond Hope and History*, 124. After this rousing call for leadership, Clinton proceeded to discuss the importance of the V-chip to curb television violence.

48. Daniel T. Rodgers, "In Search of Progressivism," *Reviews in American History* 10 (1982): 123. See also Barry D. Karl, *The Uneasy State* (Chicago: University of Chicago Press, 1983).

49. Clinton, *Between Hope and History*, 18.

50. Clinton, *Between Hope and History*, 61–2.

51. Clinton, *Between Hope and History*, 62.

52. See Robert Putnam, *Bowling Alone: The Collapse and Revival of American Community* (New York: Simon & Schuster, 2000). Joseph Turow suggests that a competing reason for the increased fragmentation of citizens in the U.S. is the persistent and powerful marketing techniques of contemporary advertisers. See Joseph Turow, *Breaking Up America: Advertisers and the New Media World* (Chicago: University of Chicago Press, 1997).

53. Clinton, *Between Hope and History*, 115.

54. Clinton, *Between Hope and History*, 116.

55. Clinton, *Between Hope and History*, 127.

56. Tannock, "Nostalgia Critique," 455.

57. See Depoe, "Requiem for Liberalism," 179.

58. For more on the divisiveness leading up to the 1996 elections, see Elizabeth Drew, *Showdown: The Struggle Between the Gingrich Congress and the Clinton White House* (New York: Simon & Schuster, 1996); David Maraniss and Michael Weisskopf, *"Tell Newt to Shut Up!"* (New York: Touchstone Books, 1996); and Evan Thomas, Karen Breslau, Debra Rosenberg, Leslie Kaufman, and Andrew Murr, *Back from the Dead: How Clinton Survived the Republican Revolution* (New York: The Atlantic Monthly Press, 1997).

59. Clinton, *Between Hope and History*, 3.

60. Clinton, *Between Hope and History*, 10–11.

61. Clinton, *Between Hope and History*, 171.

62. Clinton, *Between Hope and History*, n.p.

63. We note the different characterological strategies emergent from various convention films in our analysis of Reagan's 1984 film, Bush's 1992 film, and *The Man from Hope*. Clinton's 1996 film was reminiscent of Reagan's 1984 film in that it focused on Clinton's presidential persona, an incumbent strategy that Bush failed to exploit to maximum effect in 1992. See Trevor Parry-Giles and Shawn J. Parry-Giles, "Political Scopophilia, Presidential Campaigning, and the Intimacy of American Politics," *Communication Studies* 47 (1996): 191–205. See also Bruce E. Gronbeck, "Characterological Argument in Bush's and Clinton's Convention Films," in *Argument and the Postmodern Challenge: Proceedings of the Eighth SCA/AFA Conference on Argumentation*, edited by Raymie E. McKerrow (Annandale, VA: Speech Communication Association, 1993), 392–7.

64. Jeff D. Bass, "Becoming the Past: The Rationale of Renewal and the Annulment of History," in *Argument in Transition: Proceedings of the Third Summer Conference on Argumentation*, edited by David Zarefsky, Malcolm O. Sillars, and Jack Rhodes (Annandale, VA: Speech Communication Association, 1983), 305.

65. Janet Novak argues for the similarity of the two films, rooting her conclusions in their stylistic affinities and the fact that Linda Bloodworth-Thomason and Harry Thomason produced them both. The differences that Novak isolates are more strategic than stylistic. Novak's main conclusion is that the 1996 film replaced the "Hope" theme of *The Man from Hope* with "America." See Janet Novak, "Hope Springs Eternal: The Reinvention of America in Bill Clinton's 1996 Campaign Biography Video," *American Behavioral Scientist* 40 (1997): 1048–57. This shift was also noted in newspaper coverage of the film. See, for instance, Bill Nichols, "Clinton Puts Focus on Future: Says He'll Lead into 21st Century," *USA Today*, August 30, 1996, p. 3A.

66. The press coverage that even commented on the film paid particular attention to its portrayal of the Clintons' marriage. Martin Fletcher wrote in *The Times* [London] that "a principal goal of the video was to portray the Clintons as an intensely loving couple." *Newsday*'s coverage inaccurately reported that the film "consisted largely of a montage of playful and tender moments in the Clintons' marriage." And the *Los Angeles Times* said that the film's "chief visual point appeared to be the strength of the marriage between the president and First Lady Hillary Rodham Clinton." See John M. Broder, "Clinton Declares 'Hope Is Back,'" *Los Angeles Times*, August 30, 1996, p. 1; Martin Fletcher, "Illicit Romance Eclipses the President's Own Love Story," *The Times* [London], August 31, 1996, available at http://www.lexis-nexis.com/.; and Jonathan Schell, "Jonathan Schell's Campaign '96," *Newsday*, September 1, 1996, p. A43. Coverage of the film was slight. Perhaps the news media shared Syracuse University professor Robert Thompson's cynical appraisal that the

conventions had become essentially infomercials complete with "shameless promotional films." See Robert Siegel, "Analysts Take Aim at Convention Media Coverage," *National Public Radio Weekly Edition*, August 31, 1996, available at http://www.lexis-nexis.com/.

67. For discussions of the health care reform efforts of the Clinton administration, see Burns and Sorenson, *Dead Center*; Rachel L. Holloway, "The Clintons and the Health Care Crisis: Opportunity Lost, Promise Unfulfilled," in *The Clinton Presidency: Images, Issues, and Communication Strategies*, edited by Robert E. Denton, Jr., and Rachel L. Holloway (Westport, CT: Praeger, 1996); and Gil Troy, *Mr. & Mrs. President: From the Trumans to the Clintons* (Lawrence: University Press of Kansas, 2000).

68. Many of these photographs are black and white images from Robert McNeely, the official White House photographer. A collection of his pictures from his time at the White House is available in *The Clinton Years: The Photographs of Robert McNeely* (New York: Callaway, 2000).

69. Nicholas Dames, *Amnesiac Selves: Nostalgia, Forgetting, and British Fiction, 1810–1870* (New York: Oxford University Press, 2001), 12.

70. Dames, *Amnesiac Selves*, 236.

71. This list is not exhaustive. The montage is extensive and includes over 40 images.

72. Paul Messaris, "'Visual Manipulation': Visual Means of Affecting Responses to Images," *Communication* 13 (1992): 189.

Chapter Four

Primary Colors and the Hyperreal Authentication of Bill Clinton

On a cold day at the end of January in 1996, President Bill Clinton welcomed to the White House Russian prime minister Viktor Chernomyrdin. At the time of Chernomyrdin's visit, battles were raging in Chechnya, anti-reform efforts were pressuring the Yeltsin government in Moscow, Boris Yeltsin was seriously ill, and Clinton was preparing for a trip to Russia in just four months. Ignoring the geopolitical implications of Chernomyrdin's visit and the complexities of U.S.-Russo relations in 1996, however, a reporter present at the customary photo opportunity following the meeting rose and asked President Clinton a rather unusual question: "Who do you think wrote *Primary Colors*?" In pure Clintonian fashion, the president remarked that he did not know who had written the novel and that he had not read it. He then chided the gathered reporters: "you all find out everything in the wide world. The least you could do is tell all of us who wrote that book."[1]

This was a revealing moment. A news reporter, facing the president of the United States and the prime minister of Russia, decided to use this rare opportunity with the leaders of two quite powerful nations to inquire as to the authorship of an anonymous novel about Washington politics. And the president of the United States felt compelled to reply. Put simply, the exchange reveals the importance of *Primary Colors* as a critical rhetorical incident in the construction of Bill Clinton and his meaning for U.S. political culture in the 1990s. This novel attracted considerable attention, at least partly because its author was "Anonymous" and because it offered a portrait of Clinton that was only thinly disguised by its fiction. As it put forth a compelling and controversial vision of Clinton, *Primary Colors* contributed to the persistent mystery and uncertainty about the "real" Bill Clinton. Its claim to accuracy and validity, furthermore, was powerfully enhanced by the perceived fact that its author was allegedly hiding behind the

"Anonymous" moniker out of fear of political retribution because of the accuracy of the fiction's characterizations. These factors combined to make *Primary Colors* the subject of one reporter's inquiry at a photo opportunity and, more significantly, a signature moment of the Clinton years.

Primary Colors and the ensuing public controversy about the authorship of the work speaks to the power of hyperreality and image-making in contemporary political culture. Faced with increasingly hyperreal portraits of political leaders, the political culture and its participants generate discourses that ostensibly erode the image and attempt to uncover the authentic or the real. Journalists, thus, offer voters a plethora of behind-the-scenes accounts of political activity, and politicians provide the access necessary for such accounts. Voters consume tabloid accounts of political scandals, read "tell all" biographies of political leaders, and access insider Internet information about politicians and their private lives and activities.

Perpetually searching for the real, the authentic, is ultimately a futile task in a political culture dominated by hyperreal images. This search for the real that is behind the image, Sanford Schram concludes, "ends in the imagery of those appearances themselves" and is finally a frustrating exercise.[2] The ironic result, of course, is that all the actors in contemporary political life participate in this quest for the authentic, even as they generate rhetorics of image and persona that are highly crafted and significantly hyperreal in their presentation of political character. *Primary Colors* was yet another attempt by the political culture to find, amidst the hyperreality, an authentic portrait or rendering of Bill Clinton.

Primary Colors also reflected the persistent duality between the public and the private that is characteristic of Bill Clinton's constructed persona and that is a source of so much attention in contemporary politics. This relentless tension between public and private results from several factors. Media sources continue to proliferate, with an ever-increasing demand for news and information as the inevitable result. "Mainstream news outlets," argues Larry Sabato and his colleagues, "no longer serve as almost exclusive gatekeepers of information about those who hold or seek elected office."[3] As such, previous systems of control and access are lessened giving just about anyone the ability to find and publish information and rumor about the private lives of political leaders.

Political leaders become, in this new information overloaded, hyper-technologized climate, a form of cultural celebrity.[4] Information about them, their families, and their private lives, once held in private out of respect for governmental institutions or basic propriety, now are the stuff of tabloid journalism and celebrity gossip together with the lives of film stars and television personalities. Alongside policy news and discussion of political strategy and electioneering are reports of scandalous behaviors, unsubstantiated rumors, and family gossip. Such news is not new,[5] but its spread and growth accompanies the proliferation of media forms and outlets in the contemporary media climate. And political leaders participate in this process; Bill Clinton dignified the press conference question about *Primary Colors* with a pithy and quick answer, suggesting that the president knew the relative importance of the novel for U.S. political culture.

These same political leaders, furthermore, contribute to the collusion of public and private. Often they seek to exploit and manipulate personal, private information for electoral gain while simultaneously condemning the exposure of information that would tarnish their carefully constructed images or depress votes. For instance, Bill and Hillary Clinton featured their daughter Chelsea in *The Man from Hope* and other campaign discourses with some frequency, using her to demonstrate their familial bonds and strong commitment to children. Yet the Clintons also demanded that news and information about their daughter not be broadcast publicly to give her the possibility of a "normal" childhood. The Bushes have followed this same pattern. Both Presidents Bush highlighted and magnified their familial connections and bonds to appear more palatable and electable to a scrutinizing public, yet both sought to keep unpleasantries about their relatives out of the public spotlight.[6]

The search for political authenticity and the tension between public and private typify contemporary constructions of presidentiality. In the midst of all this discourse, voters are seeking information of relevance to their decision making and sorting through an ever-increasing myriad of data about political leaders. Contemporary voters are conditioned by their culture to expect the private and the personal and yet to shun gossip and rumor as somehow inappropriate and unseemly. These same voters, living as they do at the cusp between modernism and postmodernism, sophisticatedly consume hyperreal political images while longing for the authentic and the real in their political leadership. Voters, and their journalistic surrogates, are trapped in a hyperreality in which discerning the authentic is virtually impossible. Yet that same hyperreality creates a powerful desire among voters and the media to crave and seek out the illusive authenticity that holds, the mythology tells us, the key to political "reality."

Our concern here is with *Primary Colors* as it functioned culturally and discursively as an authenticating text in the image construction of Bill Clinton. The novel was published in early 1996, as Bill Clinton commenced his campaign for reelection.[7] As we have indicated thus far, the community's conception of Clinton was so thoroughly hyperreal by this point that determining the authenticity of perceptions about him was difficult at best for the American public. *Primary Colors* offered a portrayal of Clinton that seemed to peel away the veneer of political image construction to offer a truly "behind-the-scenes" vision of the Clinton persona. The novel and the film both reflected the cultural and political tensions present in Clinton's constructed image. *Primary Colors*' edifying resonance as a text of political image and authentication is significant as an avenue to further understand the power of these tensions for political life in the 1990s. Of course, while *Primary Colors* put forth portrayals of Bill Clinton that appeared authentic, they were fundamentally just additional images of this highly complex, thoroughly hyperreal political figure. In this sense, *Primary Colors* became yet another in the series of rhetorics that defined and shaped the constantly changing public image of Bill Clinton.

Authentication and the Hyperreal Political Culture

The political and cultural search for authenticity is a phenomenon that predates our postmodern, hyperreal age and that is rooted in significant existential and metaphysical questions about human agency and being. Persistent concerns about authenticity linger and are renewed by the rush of contemporary culture toward hyper-mediation and the rise of image-based communication systems and discourses. Those same questions are made even more relevant in the political realm by the increased professionalization of political conduct and discourse and the intense reliance of politics on channels of communication that privilege the image in the pursuit of political success.[8] Before turning to the authenticating power of *Primary Colors*, therefore, we must first discuss the development of political authenticity as a cultural and discursive force in contemporary political culture.

Political authenticity has its roots in the philosophical musings of the ancient Greeks.[9] It was Plato, after all, who crafted the now famous cave parable wherein the inauthentic and unreal images deluded those who were metaphorically trapped and unable to view or dispute alternative conceptions of reality.[10] And it was Plato's theory of forms that articulated the virtue of authenticity where "nothing fake can be good and nothing good can be fake."[11] Loathing and anxiety about the unreal, the inauthentic, emerged from these early Platonic understandings, such that the inauthentic became unethical and virtue was conjoined with authenticity to define the appropriate standards of human behavior and communication.

Authenticity acquired a decidedly moral relevance in the eighteenth century, when thinkers and theorists began to question the disengaged rationality of Cartesian dualism and started to ponder the moral obligation of the individual to his or her community. Finding the authentic self became a moral pursuit, and this quest was rooted in the assumption that humans possessed an innate moral sense or bearing. The truly important process of human development was the discovery of that authentic moral center. Extracting the meaning of this new modernist search for authenticity from Jean-Jacques Rousseau, philosopher Charles Taylor notes that "Our moral salvation comes from recovering authentic moral contact with ourselves."[12] Again, authenticity is something of importance, a valued and relevant quality to be achieved and discovered through thoughtful introspection and reasoned evaluation.

In the contemporary postmodern context, replete with its continuous images and hyperreality, the search for authenticity acquires even more legitimacy and credence. Because our culture is not fully free of its modernist predilections, there continues to linger a persistent fear of deception and fraud. As images and media continue to proliferate, these fears become more intense, leading to the enduring worry that all meaning is lost and that referents and reality are no longer significant constructs governing human understanding and behavior. In short, those who worry about the inauthenticity of contemporary culture fear that we are trapped in Plato's cave, forever destined to see more and more of the distorted shadows on the televisual wall of our own making.[13]

Indeed, the tension between a culture of imitation and a culture of authenticity is the defining "category of American civilization," claims cultural critic Miles Orvell. Grounded in an aesthetic shift at the end of the nineteenth and the beginning of the twentieth centuries, this tension orders virtually all layers of American cultural life.[14] Along with a powerful economic and industrial shift occasioned by the Industrial

Revolution, American culture was also dominated by a fascination for the imitative, Orvell claims, and this fascination manifested itself in the fondness of elite Americans for photography and photographic images. As that fascination waned, however, other economic and social forces moved the culture toward a quest of authenticity. Rapid industrialization and the enhanced stratification of American life, as well as the infusion of immigrants into the American community created a condition where the U.S. community "sought to reconnect the worker and the thing made. . . . It would affirm social values that allowed the individual his or her own development while affirming also a community of individuals."[15] Authenticity, or the quest to know the real and the genuine, became a source of personal fulfillment and communal obligation.

Other media forms and channels overtook photography in dominance in U.S. culture, and with the advent of television and new media came renewed concerns for the location of the authentic. The growth and development of media, however, failed to engage the larger philosophical questions about authenticity—what it means to know the "real," how we know what the "real" is, etc. Instead, as communication theorist Hanno Hardt suggests, the progress of communication technologies "tends to solidify the ambiguity of chatter and curiosity, and therefore, entrench media controlled forms of social and political authority." The result, Hardt concludes, is the "further alienation of the individual."[16] Of course, as communication technology continues to expand and change, so too will the concerns that the discursive products of that technology are fundamentally inauthentic. As communication moves more rapidly toward the virtual, Steven Jones notes, "our very notions of authenticity" are called into question.[17]

The search for authenticity is both a philosophical yearning for a true sense of moral bearing and a discursive attempt to pierce the image and the façade for a glimpse of the real. This search is also a political exploration, affecting how power is exercised and manipulated in an increasingly complex political culture. Reflecting on the political turmoil of the 1930s and the 1960s, Marshall Berman concluded in 1970 that "the desire for authenticity has emerged in modern society as one of the most politically explosive of human impulses."[18] Writing in the wake of 1968, with the tumult of the Vietnam War still raging, Berman reflected the political angst of his time that still shapes our political quest for authenticity today. Add to this mix the political betrayal of Watergate and the desire for an authentic politics is easily understood.

In fact, much of the political culture of the late twentieth century was defined by a quest for political authenticity. This search, Doug Rossinow argues, "lay at the heart of the New Left," and defined many of the most prominent political struggles and campaigns since the end of World War II.[19] Decades of discrimination and segregation motivated millions of Americans to seek real civil rights and authentic, activist leadership in the search for social justice on behalf of Americans of African descent. The fears of cover-up and conspiracy concerning the assassination of President John F. Kennedy and the accompanying disillusionment with the Johnson administration energized the protests of the New Left that sought a more authentic politics. Government duplicity in the Vietnam War and the Watergate scandal resulted in an even more intense desire for a return to an authentic politics, personified in 1976 in the person of Jimmy Carter.[20] The manipulations of the Reagan years, culminating in the perfidy of the Iran-Contra scandal and the increasing distrust of government, fueled a growing sense of inauthenticity in politics and government. And, of course, Bill Clinton represented for many Americans the epitome of inauthentic politics—a politics governed by artifice and polls with a singular concern for communication and image, not governance and rectitude.[21]

Voters in the late twentieth century, thus, absorbed three powerful political discourses that confirmed a persistent cultural sense of inauthenticity about U.S. politics. The first was a cultural discourse that questioned truth, undermined certainty, and challenged conventional norms and discourse—what might be called the postmodern turn. Of course, our concern with this particular discursive shift in U.S. politics is the manner in which postmodernity manifested the increased hyperreality of U.S. politics. The second was the series of mishaps, lies, mistakes, and cover-ups committed by the U.S. government. The third was the perpetually cynical, almost fatalistic journalism that repeatedly emphasized the inauthenticity and unreality of politics and politicians.[22] Bolstered by the haughty criticisms of their academic experts, journalists covering politics and government reflected a decidedly "antipolitics" orientation. This "antipolitics" bias of the news media, Thomas Patterson reveals, is rooted in the Progressive era, but came to full fruition following the Vietnam War and Watergate. The result, Patterson warns, is the continuing erosion of public legitimacy for government and political action.[23] Ignoring what politics and government do accomplish, forgetting the good men and women who work hard to achieve good things for their constituents, and highlighting only the scandals, deceptions, and mistakes committed by government and public officials deepens a feeling, a sense among the public, that politics is somehow fake, unreal, inauthentic.[24]

The search for political authenticity, the never-ending quest to find the real leader and the true person behind the crafted image became a dominant *telos* of American political discourse. On one level, political authenticity is "a symbolic, mediated, interactional, and highly contested process by which political candidates attempt to 'make real' a vision of self and political character within the public sphere."[25] It involves all of the various campaign discourses whereby candidates and campaigns put forth images of persona and character. On another level, political authenticity also references the continual cultural search to uncover and unmask the "real" political leader or the "true" actions of government. *Primary Colors* was one attempt to offer an authentic version of the 1992 Clinton campaign and of Clinton himself. By 1996, the inauthenticity of Bill Clinton was completely ensconced in public discourse, and the desire to uncover and find the real Bill Clinton was a cultural preoccupation.

Bill Clinton and the Search for Political Authenticity

Bill Clinton personified all of the different philosophical, cultural, discursive, and political strands present in the perpetual quest of authenticity. First, Clinton was a political figure with an indiscernible moral core. Clinton supporters saw a compassionate, empathic leader who had risen from humble middle-class roots to the pinnacles of power and success because of hard work and intelligence. He overcame the hardships of a broken home, domestic abuse, and alcoholism, and he brought to his political leadership an ability to "feel the pain" of the average American. Clinton opponents, conversely, believed him to be a usurper, someone who manipulated, lied, and schemed his way into power. Investing literally millions of dollars, Clinton-haters sought to uncover the "truth" about Bill Clinton as they saw it, from the supposed conspiracy to kill Vince Foster to his alleged drug running activities during his tenure as Arkansas' governor. Of course, the culminating attempts to discover the "truth" about Clinton were the investigations into the Whitewater real estate development, the Paula Jones sexual harassment lawsuit, and the Independent Counsel's investigations of the

Monica Lewinsky affair that led to the impeachment and trial of Bill Clinton.[26] The result of all the images of Clinton and all the investigations of this president was a murky sense of this president's moral core—the authenticity of his character.

Uncovering Clinton's authentic moral character was complicated by his use of new media and the alternative sites he used to communicate with the voting public. Clinton was the first virtual president with an image constructed well outside of the traditional political venues of major network television and the national newspapers and news magazines. Clinton often bypassed much of the traditional news media to reach voters via *Larry King Live*, MTV, and via local news outlets.[27] In 1992, especially, this communication strategy was new and risky for a major presidential candidate. The risk came from the existing political bias in favor of dominant and traditional news media outlets. When the entrenched media establishment covered a candidate, he or she acquired legitimacy and authenticity. It is the *New York Times*, *Time* magazine, and other major organs of mainstream news in the United States that have for decades controlled the flow and composition of political news.

When Bill Clinton sought to reach new and different voters on MTV or by appearing on the *Arsenio Hall Show*, he challenged existing orthodoxies of political news. In the process, he revealed his past experiences with marijuana, discussed issues and concerns normally outside of typical campaign news, and increased suspicions about his legitimacy and character. Much of the information he communicated was of a private, interpersonal nature, and these characterological data, when woven together with his policy positions, manifested his sincere and personal commitment to his positions.[28] In addition, the initial defining scandal of the Clinton campaign, the Gennifer Flowers episode, was driven largely by tabloid journalism, with the initial accusations appearing in the supermarket tabloid *The Star*.

Voters expect politics and politicians to appear in their newspapers and in the news magazines that come to the house every week. They are accustomed to finding political news on the nightly network newscasts or on cable news channels. But in 1992, political news appeared on talk shows, in supermarkets, on talk radio, and on alternative television outlets in new and startling ways, driven largely by the Clinton campaign's efforts to reach new voters. And with all the added exposure came concerns about the candidate's authenticity. What was real and what was artifice? Washington-based journalists (the "boys on the bus"[29]) generally provided the answers and now they were often bypassed in favor of a satellite interview with local news anchors or a sit-down chat with an MTV veejay.

Bill Clinton also personified many of the challenges to political authenticity that characterized most of the late twentieth century in the United States. As the first baby-boomer presidential candidate, Clinton resurrected the very controversies and scandals that defined his generation. When it was discovered that Clinton successfully avoided the Vietnam draft by seeking deferments and special privileges, the nightmares of that war and the forced conscription of so many Americans resurfaced. Clinton's involvement in anti–Vietnam War protests, his political rise on the heels of the Watergate scandal, and even his marriage to an independent, powerful, and forthright career professional brought forth all of the uncertainties and ambivalences of the 1960s and 1970s. Indeed, Clinton not only confronted existing orthodoxies about the conduct of political campaigns, he manifested the larger cultural challenges to powerful ideological orthodoxies of patriotism and patriarchy. In this way, Clinton came to mean so much to those who shared his experiences with the uncertain exciting past of the 1960s and 1970s, while he simultaneously represented all that was evil and uncertain about that turbulent time for his opponents.

Authenticating Bill Clinton in *Primary Colors*

Primary Colors was first published in early 1996.[30] Written by "Anonymous," the novel told the story of a young African American politico named Henry Burton who is hired as the "body man" for a southern governor (Jack Stanton) seeking the Democratic nomination for president. Through Burton's eyes and via his first-person narration, the reader becomes privy to all of the controversies, personalities, and political machinations involved in a primary campaign for president. *Primary Colors* spent thirty-one weeks on the bestseller list in 1996 and was ranked eighth on the top ten hardcover fiction bestseller list for all of 1996.

The story was a satire. As with all satire, *Primary Colors* appeared to be an attack on others, a broadly drawn rendition of the vagaries and flaws of the American political system. At the same time, the novel satirically was self-reflexive of the same politics that it attacked. It fulfilled, to paraphrase Kenneth Burke, the satirical function of highlighting the weaknesses and temptations that exist in the larger cultural and political milieu.[31] Thus, while *Primary Colors* might appear on the surface to simply skewer Bill Clinton and those associated with politics in the 1992 Clinton campaign, it was also a telling commentary on the nature of contemporary political culture. It was an uncomfortable satirical prism that commented on U.S. politics precisely because it offered "new contexts . . . for analyzing existing models of political and social phenomena [and] . . . new models in the form of imagined characters, situations, and worlds."[32]

Uncovering and Authenticating "Anonymous"

Nothing contributed more to the notoriety and to the sense that *Primary Colors* was an authentic rendering of the 1992 Clinton campaign than the author's decision to remain anonymous. Upon publication of the novel, pundits and journalists immediately commenced speculating as to its source. The novel's portrayal of scandal and its sense of insider knowledge of the Clinton campaign fueled the speculation, and lists of likely suspects quickly appeared. It was a skilled marketing ploy as well, allowing Random House, the novel's publisher, to capitalize on the mystery of the book's author for publicity purposes.

The quest to identify "Anonymous" began almost immediately upon the publication of *Primary Colors*. Conjecture swept through Washington, DC, and appeared on the national airwaves as the news media spread this "inside the Beltway" fascination to the entire country. For instance, in a January 17, 1996, installment of *Primetime Live*, ABC's Sam Donaldson interviewed numerous "inner circle" members of the Clinton campaign about the authorship of the novel. Mark Halperin speculated to Donaldson that the book was written by "an insider, either a journalist who covered the campaign every day, or by someone who was very close to the Clintons." Sidney Blumenthal, another Clinton "insider," countered with the theory that *Primary Colors* was authored by "somebody who knew somebody who might have been in the inner circle."[33]

Finding the identity of Anonymous spread beyond Washington and seeped into the national culture. Likening the search of Anonymous' identity to the hunt for Deep Throat, CNN's *Showbiz Today* program fingered George Stephanopoulos, Paul Begala, and Dee Dee Meyers as possible authors.[34] Larry King devoted an entire hour-long program to a discussion of the author's identity, conducting extended interviews with Random House's president and publisher, Harold Evans, and an array of Clinton insiders and journalists including Begala, Mandy Grunwald, Roger Altman, and Mark Miller.[35] Even more venerable news sources, including PBS's *The NewsHour with Jim Lehrer*, devoted interview segments and air time to the guessing game under way about Anonymous' identity.[36]

By late February, Anonymous' identity was revealed. It was Joe Klein, a columnist for *Newsweek* magazine, identified by an English professor from Vassar College who confirmed Klein's identity through computer writing analysis.[37] For several months, Klein maintained that he did not author *Primary Colors* even when confronted with Foster's evidence. Only after *The Washington Post* retained a handwriting expert to confirm Klein's authorship in July was he compelled to admit the truth.[38] His revelation unleashed a torrent of commentary about the proper role of journalists and the uneasy divide between the truth and fiction that *Primary Colors* represented. Roundly condemned by his colleagues, Klein continued to collect the royalties, film rights, and international rights from *Primary Colors*, reported to be at least $6 million.[39] Klein even authored a *Primary Colors* spin-off novel entitled *The Running Mate* that focused on a character from the original work, Senator Charlie Martin, who was clearly patterned after former Nebraska senator Bob Kerrey.[40]

The search for the real author of *Primary Colors* was significant not so much for the mystery itself as for what it revealed about the importance and relevance of authenticity in U.S. political culture. Consumers of political discourse in the United States are accustomed to knowing the source of such discourse. It generally emanates from journalists or politicians and the knowledge of source is relevant to the credibility and believability of the information communicated. This is particularly true in cases where such discourse is of a backstage or insider nature, because to know the author is to know the relative truth value of the account provided.

Primary Colors confounded this grammar of contemporary politics. It offered readers a thinly disguised insider account of the 1992 Clinton campaign, but refused to acknowledge its source. Numerous reviewers and commentators noted that the real interest value of the novel was not its literary quality or its status as a ground-breaking novel, but because it offered a glimpse of the true nature of political campaigns. *People*

Magazine's book critic, Kristin McMurran, concluded that *Primary Colors* was "too authentic in terms of the flavor of *The War Room* and some of the language and the dialogue to have been written without some kind of access to the inner sanctum."[41] And the appeal of *Primary Colors*, Gene Lyons wrote, is "its Peeping Tom aspect; the real lowdown on 'Jack and Susan Stanton's most intimate secrets."[42] Indeed, because the novel was so intimate, and because the characterizations were so lightly masked, its source and the accuracy of its rendition came to occupy primary importance. The insider and humorous look of the novel, wrote *New York Times* reviewer Michiko Kakutani, was "underscored by the decision of the author, presumably a political operative or reporter, to keep his or her name a secret."[43] In other words, the anonymity of the author made the account he provided all the more real and truthful of the actual Clinton campaign.[44]

When a major national newspaper hires a handwriting expert to identify the author of an anonymous novel, when an English professor devotes hours of labor to uncovering that same author, and when countless column inches and hours of airtime are devoted to the search for his identity, something important is happening in U.S. political culture. The cultural search for authentication in the case of *Primary Colors* said that the novel was compelling for its portrait of Bill Clinton, for what it purported to reveal about this illusive political figure. And it spoke to the power of authenticity for a political culture awash in image and façade.

Fundamentally, the months of effort to identify "Anonymous" laid bare the tension between the public and the private at work in U.S. political life.[45] *Primary Colors* was a very "private" book. That is, it offered a rendering of politics that went behind the artifice and revealed the inner emotions and private conversations in ways that conventional journalism could not and does not offer.[46] Only a novel can display political leaders in this way. Yet the work was also very public given that it concerned the sitting president of the United States and that its fiction was so slight. By revealing the source of this private account of Bill Clinton, the political culture legitimated this account of Clinton's campaign and his personal life. The identification of "Anonymous," therefore, was an attempt to give power and authority to the private discourse of *Primary Colors*—discourse that would normally remain hidden from view. The search for "Anonymous," thus, made public and real that which was presented as private and fictional.

Jack Stanton as the "Real" Bill Clinton

If the tension between public and private defined the search for "Anonymous," the tensions between masculine/feminine and black/white characterize *Primary Colors'* narrative authentication of Bill Clinton. The novel clearly positioned its candidate, Jack Stanton, firmly within the ambivalences of the baby-boomer generation, particularly as Stanton confronted issues of sex and gender relations and as he dealt with persistent problems of racial division. In this way, Stanton represented his real life alter ego, reflecting the difficulties and triumphs that Bill Clinton faced concerning both of these questions. Stanton epitomized, thus, these dualities of Bill Clinton, and this characterization of Clinton occurred in stark terms, made possible by the alleged fictionality of *Primary Colors*.

In his exposé of Klein's identity, Vassar professor Donald Foster speculated that *Primary Colors* was written by a woman-hating gay male preoccupied by questions of race.[47] Jacob Weisberg, writing in the same issue of *New York*, concluded that the novel was vintage Klein, "bitter about Clinton, obsessive about race."[48] Not surprisingly, Klein is generationally linked to Clinton. Both men are representative of the so-called baby-boomer generation, coming of age in the 1960s, conflicted about the Vietnam War, made cynical by Watergate, and achieving midlife success in the postmodern 1980s and 1990s when new patterns of discourse and fresh communication technologies challenged everything known to be secure and certain. As such, Klein's portrait of Clinton in *Primary Colors*, confronting as Jack Stanton does difficult questions about race and gender, was consistent with the baby-boomer angst that defined their generation. And this portrait reflected Klein's anxiety about Bill Clinton's role as the political representative of baby-boomer success and achievement.

One dimension of baby-boomer politics, emergent from the civil rights movements of the 1960s and 1970s, is a concern for identity, a search to find the authenticity of individual persona. Such concerns, Doug Rossinow reveals, compelled "individuals to define their politics along lines of race, gender, ethnicity, and sexual identity, in part to make themselves feel rooted, real, solid." As a political trend, Rossinow concludes, identity politics "expresses a quest for authenticity."[49] In addition, the civil rights movement "quickened the desire of young, white, middle-class Americans to transcend alienation and achieve authenticity." They could achieve that authentication through the activism of the civil rights movement, a movement that "crystallized into nodes of liberal political dissidence" for many young, white, activist males of the baby-boomer generation.[50]

The focus on identity politics as a marker of authenticity is powerfully evident in *Primary Colors'* characterization of Jack Stanton/Bill Clinton. Told in the voice of Henry Burton, the African American grandson of a slain civil rights leader, the novel was highly race reflexive. Indeed, the very first paragraph of *Primary Colors* highlighted the preoccupation of the novel with questions of race and identity: "He was a big fellow, looking seriously pale on the streets of Harlem in deep summer. I am small and not so dark, not very threatening to Caucasians; I do not strut my stuff."[51] Jack Stanton was demarcated immediately to the reader as "pale," in contrast with the book's narrator with whom the reader is invited to sympathize. Stanton was placed squarely within a center of African American identity in the United States—Harlem. Furthermore, Stanton was defined as comfortable in his surroundings, enjoying the interactions with potential voters, and caring deeply about the adult literacy program he was visiting. Though his identity was characterized clearly as "white" at the outset of *Primary Colors*, Jack Stanton was able to transcend and embrace racial divisions.

Indeed, Burton reflected on the various capacities of white Americans to deal with African Americans, offering yet another characterization of Stanton's racial consciousness in the process:

> The thing I loved about Richard [Jemmons, a political strategist] was, he was overtly race-conscious. I took it as a piece of performance art, a running commentary on the mortal prissiness of most white people.
>
> Most white people do this patronizing number: They never disagree with you, even when you are talking the worst sort of garbage. It is near impossible to have a decent, human conversation with them. They are all so busy trying *not* to say anything offensive—so busy trying to prove they aren't prejudiced—that they freeze up, get all constricted, formal. They never just talk. This may be more true in the political community, where everyone is hyperconscious of perceived offenses and consequences, than it is in real life. But it is hard to be black, and in politics, and not disdain these fools.
>
> There are two subgroups, however, that are tolerable: There are those who are truly color-blind—like Jack, and to a lesser extent, Susan. They will argue with you, yell at you, treat you like a human. And then there are the occasional miracles like Richard Jemmons, who just lay it all out there.[52]

As if to prove this characterization, Burton revealed how Stanton introduced him to the deputy attorney general of Alabama, William Johnson, an old law school classmate of Stanton's. During the visit, Burton saw an old photograph on the attorney general's wall of a young Stanton talking with Johnson:

> "Law school," Johnson explained, noticing my interest. "What were we arguing about, Jack? Send the North Vietnamese guns or bandages?"
> "Naww, you were pissed off at me for asking your sister out," Stanton said.
> "Susan was pissed at you 'bout that," Johnson replied. "I thought Cyrilla'd teach you some manners, 'specially 'bout not eating off other folks' plates. You remember what we really were talking about?"
> Stanton nodded. "What we always talked about: white folks. Dr. King had just died—"
> "No, it was months later—it was Bobby," Johnson said. "We were in finals. You were about to go off to work for him. Remember, you were trying to get Professor Screechy—whatsisname . . . "
> "Markowitz."
> "Yeah, Markowitz—to reschedule torts, or let you take it long-distance, so you could be out there on primary night?"
> "Yeah, I remember," Stanton said softly.
> "You figured you would've spotted Sirhan."
> "And you were ready to pick up a gun, or somethin'."
> "Right," Johnson said, turning to me. "This asshole talked me out of it. I was ready to walk out of law school. I mean, what was law? Who gave a shit about law with all our guys gettin' capped? But he said we had to stick with it, stick with the program. I had to think about my responsibility to the kids, the message I'd be sending if I walked."[53]

In their interaction, Stanton displayed an easiness that illustrated his "color-blind" qualities, proving to the reader that this character, at least, embraced and conquered the problem of race in American politics. The character of Jack Stanton was also placed squarely by this exchange in the midst of the turmoil of 1968 and the civil rights movement. He was validated and authenticated as a product of that time, as someone who fought for racial justice via his political activities, and who lived his commitment to racial equality in his personal relationships, befriending an African American and seeking to date his sister. In this sense, Jack Stanton clearly represented Bill Clinton, an individual able to secure high levels of African American support and to work comfortably with people of all races and ethnicities striving to achieve racial and social justice.[54]

But this exchange also reveals the complexities of race in the United States, especially for that transitional generation of Americans who witnessed the end of segregation. In this moment from *Primary Colors*, Stanton was the responsible agent of reason and rationality. Johnson sought to validate his racially charged rage at the assassinations of King and Kennedy by leaving law school and resorting to violence; it was Stanton who kept him within the system, fighting for change incrementally and peacefully.

> "Now look, tell me 'bout my favorite program. If I'm gonna try it, you'd better have made it happen." He [Stanton] turned to me: "Dr. Johnson over here has been lifting driver licenses off of kids who are truant in three counties for the past year."
>
> "Attendance up twenty percent," Johnson said. "Dropout rates down ten percent."
>
> Stanton whistled. "Now aren't you glad I talked you out of pickin' up the gun?"[55]

Black anger was sublimated in this narrative and that sublimation was validated by the achievement of public policy success. Moreover, black anger and frustration, however righteous, was only expressed in this incident through threats of violence, fostering powerful cultural stereotypes about African Americans. Of course, the narrative also created a clear hierarchy where Stanton was the agent of prudence and responsibility, and he was positioned by the novel as the white, southern governor seeking the presidency and assisted by African American underlings. So just as in the larger culture, *Primary Colors* reflected both the advancements made in the United States regarding race and the continued power and status of "whiteness" in the political world.

Indeed, as with all of the dualities of Bill Clinton, the question of race and racial justice was murky and ambivalent, and *Primary Colors* authenticated its depiction of Clinton (Stanton) by embracing that murkiness and uncertainty. There can be no denying Clinton's commitment to ending racism and fighting for racial justice. But Clinton's pragmatism often mitigated the strength and power of his ideals. We have already discussed the 1992 campaign's treatment of Jesse Jackson and Sister Souljah (Introduction). Additionally, in Clinton's first term, little was accomplished on racial issues beyond the symbolic, and despite high profile nominees, Clinton quickly retracted the nomination of Lani Guinier to head the Justice Department's Office of Civil Rights when she was attacked for her "radical" viewpoints.

In like manner, Jack Stanton was also portrayed as at ease with people of different races. Stanton was "truly color-blind" and engendered the support and respect of Burton as someone who was genuine and committed to helping real people of all races. And Stanton, unlike Clinton, appointed an African American to a high level position in his campaign organization. At the same time, *Primary Colors* problematized the Stanton character and the question of race. We are reminded of Stanton's southernness when Burton was refused admittance to the governor's office because of suspicions by the security guard.[56] Stanton was accused at one point in the novel of using a racial epithet in describing a character that resembled Jesse Jackson.[57] And, in what became a pivotal moment in the narrative, the candidate was accused of fathering the child of his African American teenage babysitter. When Stanton asked Burton to deal with the girl's father and smooth over the situation, another racially ambivalent moment occurred, indicating again the uncertainty created by the novel concerning Jack Stanton and questions of race:

> "Tomorrow, I want you and Howard to go over there, to Fat Willie's, and lean on him a little," the governor said. "Not really *lean* on him—but tell him we have to resolve this thing, establish paternity. Tell him we want the girl to have an amniocentesis. Explain what that means, in detail. Tell him it's a long needle through the belly button. Tell him to explain that to Loretta. Henry, these aren't sophisticated people. They're good people, but not sophisticated. I think you present this to them, tell them that I am insisting on it, that I had my blood pulled already. Chances are, the girl will back off her claim."
>
> "Why me?" I said, shivering. "Is it because I'm—"
>
> "It's because Willie chose you," he said. "*I* didn't. I can't help it if he can't see past skin color."[58]

Immediately subsequent to this episode, Burton was told by Stanton's mother how "Jackie" almost single-handedly brought about integration in the fictional southern town of Grace Junction by hiring an African American restaurant owner to cater the senior prom.[59] Again, *Primary Colors* authenticated Jack Stanton as a rendition of Bill Clinton through the prism of race. Burton's uncertainty about Stanton expressed the nation's uncertainty about Clinton on matters of race. Are these characters in our political life reformed southerners who have transcended the evils of racism or are they merely rednecks skilled at hiding what is a regionally prescribed loathing and disrespect for people of color? The answer to this question from *Primary Colors* was unclear, and the novel gave its readers no unambiguous answer about Jack Stanton. As such, *Primary Colors* reflected the ambivalence of larger cultural questions about Bill Clinton and authenticated Stanton as a valid and accurate rendition of Clinton.

Race functioned as but one mode of authentication in *Primary Colors*. The other means that Klein used to match his Jack Stanton with our Bill Clinton was the novel's preoccupation with sex and its concerns with gender relations. As with race, questions of sex and gender infused baby-boomer politics and the quest for political authenticity amongst members of that generation. To be authentically engaged and active in the 1960s and 1970s was to be masculine and the equation of political authenticity and masculinity, Rossinow reveals, "not only became pervasive but also acquired a tone of urgency—even hysteria." The result was a view that saw "aggressive male sexuality" as a marker of political authenticity, a sign of active engagement.[60] Indeed, this fusion of activism, authenticity, sexuality, and masculinity may have contributed to the development and rise of the feminist movement, given that "women who also sought authenticity and social change had to contend with this legion of men in search of their manhood."[61] All too often, women were relegated to the sidelines or the periphery in the New Left movements of the 1960s and 1970s, and sought with the women's movement to argue for the equality of sexes in much the same manner as the civil rights movement sought equality for people of color.[62] But the blending of baby-boomer activism with prevailing and dominant notions of masculinity informed the demarcation of authenticity that emerged from the 1960s and 1970s.

Primary Colors' Jack Stanton is nothing if not aggressively sexual and hyper-masculine. This character behaved in a manner that confirmed and matched the popularly held conception of Bill Clinton, and thus the portrayal of his sexuality in the novel authenticated the character as a version of the president. For instance, right after Burton's commentary about the racial dimensions of Stanton's visit to Harlem at the beginning of the novel was an episode that revealed the candidate's aggressive sexuality. Burton was called to a New York hotel room to discuss his role with the campaign when he encountered the candidate:

> Stanton cracked open the door to the bedroom behind me; he was buttoning his shirt over a hairless, pink chest; he was the color of a medium-rare steak just off the grill, steaming a little. I had heard about this. He opened the door wider. "You remember Ms. Baum," he said.
>
> The librarian. I hoped I didn't gasp. She was . . . arranging herself. She seemed a bit dazed. She whacked her shoulder on the bedroom door, trying to squeeze past him. "Ow," she yipped. He leaned into her, put his arm on her. "You all right, darlin'?" She stiffened, desperately attempting to maintain the appearance of propriety. He was—well, he was entirely unembarrassed, as if he'd just sneezed, or scratched himself, or yawned, or done any of those semiprivate physical things normal people are willing to do in front of strangers.
>
> "Well, Governor," she said, "it was good to have . . . this . . ."
>
> He saved her, or tried to. "Henry," he said, turning to me. "Don't you think Ms. Baum runs just a great program?"
>
> I said something.[63]

From the very outset of *Primary Colors*, then, there's a demarcation of Stanton as a character of considerable sexual appetites, and this character definition continued over the course of the novel. Such a characterization, of course, was consistent with the culturally held perceptions of Bill Clinton, firmly in place by 1996 and derived from the Gennifer Flowers episode and from the sexual harassment lawsuit of Paula Corbin Jones that was pending against Clinton. This characterization, furthermore, reflected the linkages at work between the sexually expressed masculinity of the baby-boomer generation and the authenticity that such masculinity connoted. In this way, the Stanton character behaved as the reader thinks he should given the obvious parallel to Clinton and the ideological structuring of sex in the larger popular culture as a sign of masculine achievement.

The authentication of this portrait of Bill Clinton found in *Primary Colors* was furthered when a librarian from Harlem who runs an adult literacy program filed a libel lawsuit against Klein and Random House for the defamation of her character in the novel. Daria Carter-Clark maintained in 1997 that *Primary Colors'* depiction of the sexual liaison between Stanton and the librarian at the beginning of the novel damaged her reputation and caused her "extreme mental anguish, embarrassment and humiliation." She sought $120 million in damages.[64] Again, the lines that were drawn between the historical 1992 Clinton campaign and the fiction of *Primary Colors* were blurred further when Klein admitted that he had visited an adult literacy program in Harlem with Clinton in 1991, but that the sexual liaison suggested in the novel was fictitious. Interestingly, it was Carter-Clark who insisted that *her* reputation was libeled, and there was little in the coverage of her lawsuit to suggest that Clinton's sexual behavior, as reflected by Jack Stanton's conduct in this particular incident in *Primary Colors*, was inconsistent with reality.

Primary Colors also recounted the Gennifer Flowers incident from the 1992 campaign, when the former lounge singer came forward in the tabloid magazine *The Star* and asserted a long-standing affair with Bill Clinton. In the novel, the woman was a hairdresser named Cashmere McLeod and the entire episode recalled the Flowers incident, coming in the midst of the New Hampshire primary and nearly derailing the Stanton campaign. The novel even replicated Flowers's New York City press conference where she played supposed "love tapes" of conversations she had had with Clinton. And it featured a *60 Minutes*-like interview with both Jack and Susan Stanton that echoed the Clintons' *60 Minutes* installment from January 1992. But the parallels are less interesting than how this episode further authenticated its rendition of Bill Clinton through the character of Jack Stanton.

As the McLeod situation unfolded in *Primary Colors*, the novel took its readers backstage into the truly private realm of a political campaign dealing with an embarrassing public scandal. Libby Holden (a character based on Betsey Wright, a Clinton confidant and former chief of staff in Arkansas) informed Burton at the outset of the McLeod incident that "Our Jackie has done some pretty stupid things in his life. He's poked his pecker in some sorry trash bins." Stanton's aggressive sexuality was obvious as the campaign staff sought to learn as much as possible about future scandals that might hurt the candidate, and there was much conversation among the staffers that the reader was privy to about the possibilities and consequences of sexual scandals for the campaign. When it was revealed in *Primary Colors* that the McLeod character has tapes of Stanton and her conversing suggestively, the novel allowed its readers to see the personal impact of such a revelation when Burton tells the Governor and Mrs. Stanton about the tapes:

> I did not try to finesse it. "Governor," I said, "I was just on the phone with Libby. She says that Cashmere McLeod has tape recordings of you and her talking on the phone, and she's going to play them at a press conference tomorrow."
>
> Susan hauled off and slapped him right across the face. It was a perfect shot, a resonant *splat*—God, she was even good at that. His cheek flushed

immediate pink, his chin dropped, his hand rose—not against her—but to massage himself. Neither of them said anything at first. She turned away, faced the plate-glass window, sun streaming in.
    Then he said, "I'm sorry."
    "How bad?" she asked. Him? Me? I wasn't sure.
    "Don't know," he said.
    "Did you tell her you . . ." She looked over at me. "Henry, could you excuse us, please?"
    Oh, absolutely.[65]

Burton's awkwardness is the reader's ambivalence when confronted with the intensely private and personal. *Primary Colors* took the sexuality of its candidate and used it as a means to allow its readers to see the impact of scandal on politics and political leaders. As such, the novel authenticated this vision of Bill Clinton by confirming the aggressive and reckless sexuality familiar to all who followed Clinton's political career and by taking us into the truly backstage, private realms where the consequences of that recklessness were made real and powerful. Only through its fiction could *Primary Colors* envision the interactions between Stanton and his wife when confronted with this news. Only in its fiction could this novel give its readers an insider's glimpse into campaign machinations as scandal and controversy threatened it. And only in fiction could a consumer of political discourse actually witness such conversations and interactions.

    Primary Colors, thus, authenticated its portrayal of Bill Clinton via Jack Stanton in highly specific and important ways. The novel was specifically fixated on questions of race and sex in much the same way that such concerns dominated the 1992 campaign and the first years of the Clinton presidency. But read in a larger cultural context, *Primary Colors*' preoccupation with these issues was also a function of the search for authenticity at work in U.S. political culture—a search that was generational and emergent from decades of political uncertainty and cynicism. We believed, in other words, that Jack Stanton was a close approximation of Bill Clinton because he behaved in ways that Bill Clinton did, particularly concerning race and sex. Stanton struggled with race and confronted his own southernness in much the same manner as Clinton and he faced sex scandals and behaved in a sexually aggressive manner in much the same manner as the prevailing portrait of Clinton suggested that this president behaved. The authentication of Clinton via Stanton was furthered by the book's proclivity for the private. *Primary*

Colors became a look at what "really" happened during the 1992 primary because it placed its barely fictionalized characters in intensely private situations and because its author protected himself with the cloak of anonymity.

The fact that *Primary Colors* was originally a written, not a visual, discourse enhanced its authenticity. Because there were no pictures, and because the plot and characterizations were so lightly disguised, the reader was almost beckoned to affiliate their reading of Jack Stanton with their knowledge and images of Bill Clinton. The fusion of constructed fictional image and "real" persona was made complete in the imagination of the reader, who was further asked to believe that this image of Clinton was more real because of its insider focus. As such, the novel invited the belief that it offered a real portrait of Bill Clinton via its marketing, its narrative, and its form.[66] In this sense, *Primary Colors* was yet another hyperreal contribution to the lexicon of images about Bill Clinton. It pretended to break through the artifice of politics but only offered another, slightly different, ostensibly more personal, and clearly more unflattering image of Clinton for the U.S. political culture—an image made possible and significantly more interesting by its status as a political novel.

John Travolta and the Visual Inauthentication of Bill Clinton

"The reason I want to film the novel," film director Mike Nichols allegedly told Joe Klein, "is that it's about honor, and that's the thing very good movies are about."[67] Add to that sentiment $1.5 million for the filming rights, and Nichols received the task of translating Klein's political vision in *Primary Colors* to the big screen. In so doing, he created a film that simultaneously furthered the authentication at work in the novel and undermined it through its characterization of Jack Stanton by John Travolta. Because the film's plot so closely adhered to the novel's, the same authenticating behaviors—the quests for sexual dominance and the ambivalence toward race—and the same obvious similarities with Bill Clinton remained. But because the film was visual, because there was a living physical presence to Jack Stanton rather than a vision in the mind of a reader, the authentication of Stanton as Clinton was weakened. No longer could the consumer of *Primary Colors*' account of the 1992 campaign imagine Jack Stanton as Bill Clinton; in the film, John Travolta intervened as an actor *playing* Jack Stanton *and* imitating Bill Clinton. Thus, the intensified hyperreality of *Primary Colors* the novel, dependent as it was on the reader's mental fusion of Stanton with Clinton, was disrupted as this character was given a material form that called attention to its mimesis, that made real its performativity.

Released on March 20, 1998, *Primary Colors* achieved an even broader public audience than would have occurred had the story remained simply a novel.[68] The film was a major studio production, released by Universal Pictures, adapted for the screen by Elaine May and directed by Nichols. It starred Travolta in the Stanton role, and also featured Emma Thompson, Kathy Bates, Billy Bob Thornton, and Adrian Lester. Costing over $65 million to make, the film version of *Primary Colors* only grossed $38.966 million in the United States and fared poorly overseas.[69] The film's unfortunate coincident timing with the Monica Lewinsky scandal may have affected its popularity at the box office.

The release of *Primary Colors* occasioned considerable coverage in the press and numerous profiles of the actors and filmmakers involved in the film. Most notable was *Time* magazine's cover of March 16, 1998, featuring a full headshot of John Travolta as Jack Stanton with the headline: "Lights! Camera! Clinton!" The captions read, "John Travolta—Yep, he's Bill" and "*Primary Colors* is an uncanny tale of his relationships with women, the truth and America." On the inside spread, the magazine worked hard to keep the hyperreality of *Primary Colors* front and center. The photograph accompanying the main story was of the right side of Travolta's face and the left side of Clinton's face side-by-side, with the headline "Tale of Two Bills." *Time* worked hard to deny the fictionality of *Primary Colors* and it fused together the Travolta performance of Stanton with the larger public perception of Clinton. The magazine's efforts spoke to both the authenticity of Travolta's portrayal and its capacity to erode the hyperreality of Jack Stanton as an image of Bill Clinton. Clearly, Travolta's rendition of Stanton evoked Clinton and prompted *Time*'s comparison. At the same time, *Time* felt a need and made the choice to front the similarities, to make clear the fusion of persona and character. In so doing, *Time* called attention to the imitative quality of Travolta's depiction, making clear that a copy rather than the original was on display in *Primary Colors*.

John Travolta's interpretation of Jack Stanton was heavily dependent upon his physical imitation of Bill Clinton. Travolta made clear his intention to model the character after Clinton in several interviews. In *Premiere*, the actor noted, "I decided Clinton was as good a model as any for the role. I studied tapes of him. I was familiar with the speeches. We had a similar voice register, similar body type, similar facial features. It wasn't difficult to move into his zone. He's more raspy than me, and he has a southern accent, but I had done that before in *Urban Cowboy*."[70] Travolta succeeded in capturing Clinton physically and vocally. His height and weight were consistent with Clinton's and his hair was styled and colored to resemble the president's. Travolta translated his *Urban Cowboy* accent in *Primary Colors* and captured a Clintonesque southernness in speech and diction. Travolta was especially successful at reflecting specific and often subtle Clinton mannerisms or character traits. At one point in the film, during a political debate with his primary opponents, Travolta as Stanton gestured in a manner highly reminiscent of Clinton. And near the end of the movie, Stanton laughed in way that is eerily Clintonian. Indeed, more than any other character in *Primary Colors*, Travolta's Stanton was modeled clearly after a real-life counterpart. Emma Thompson, who played Susan Stanton, did not mimic Hillary Clinton in hair, speech, or mannerism. The same was true of the other characters, including the George Stephanopoulos character of Henry Burton, who was African American; only Travolta sought the complete transformation of his character into Bill Clinton.

In terms of physicality and vocal performance, then, the film version of *Primary Colors* beckoned its viewers to see Jack Stanton as Bill Clinton. Aided by the efforts of *Time* magazine, and confirmed by the testimony of the actor portraying the character, the movie cemented its image of Bill Clinton via its characterization of Jack Stanton. The moviegoer encountered another image of Clinton, another rendition of his private affairs and personal interactions. And everything was done to capitalize and to magnify this rather obvious comparison. All of the intimacies and plot elements that made *Primary Colors* an authentication of Bill Clinton were given a physical presence and a visual power in the film version of the story.

But those same moviegoers also clearly knew that Travolta's Stanton was not Bill Clinton. In this sense, the physical manifestation of Stanton in the film version of *Primary Colors* undermined the hyperreality of the novel's depiction because it fronted the comparison and made it obvious. To be truly hyperreal, an image and its referent must merge completely, such that distinctions between them disappear and they become one and the same. In the novel, this was possible. Reading the novel, the reader was invited to merge Stanton and Clinton together. To further this hyperreality, the same novel reader was bombarded with messages making the comparison clear, and suggesting that the author of the novel possessed unique insider access to the Clintons. Not so with the film version of *Primary Colors*. Here the viewer was given a physical being in the form of Travolta playing Stanton. While the character was clearly patterned after Clinton, it was also an imitation, even a caricature, and not the "real thing." The fusion of image and referent was thus ruptured, because the ontological existence of the image as image was made apparent. And extra-textually, the message to the filmgoer was not that they would be viewing an accurate depiction of Bill Clinton in *Primary Colors*, but rather that John Travolta had imitatively and successfully captured the physical persona of Clinton in a movie.[71]

Primary Colors the movie also undermined the hyperreality of the story's depiction of Bill Clinton on another level. Unlike some political films (e.g., *The Candidate*, *Bob Roberts*, *Tanner '88*) that were filmed as faux documentaries to give the illusion of "reality," *Primary Colors* was very much a feature film, presented in a visual manner that highlighted its fictional qualities. Unlike the novel, where the reader was invited into the action by the first-person account of the insider campaign operative, the film positioned its viewers as spectators to the action under way in its narrative. The camera in the film was positioned repeatedly as outside of the action looking in, as in the first scene in the adult literacy program at the library. Here, the camera swooped the viewer in from the corner of the room and then circled the table repeatedly as the students told their stories and Stanton listened. Several edited cuts gave the viewer reaction shots from other characters, but the positioning of the camera clearly presented the action from a spectator's orientation rather than from a participant's. There were frequent maneuverings in the film that highlighted its highly crafted and scripted quality as a major studio feature film. The smoothness of the editing in *Primary Colors* contrasted powerfully with the rough *cinéma vérité* of *The War Room* and *Primary Colors*' vantage point and construction of its audience defied the subject positioning evident in both *The Man from Hope* and the 1996 convention film. In the only depiction of Stanton in a debate, for instance, the camera positioned the viewer as a television viewer, with the campaign aides, watching the debate on a monitor. Then, suddenly, the film cut to the actual debate and the illusion of watching it on television was broken.

Indeed, there were numerous stylistic features of the filming of *Primary Colors* (e.g., long sweep shots, long approach shots, rapid editing, frequent reaction shots, foreshadowing shots) that are conventional for major feature fiction films. At one point, as campaign staffers discussed the likely entrance of Orlando Ozio (Mario Cuomo) into the presidential race, the film rapidly cut from one face to another, revealing the large number of cameras that were used in the shooting of the sequence and the careful editing of the film. Another example of the "Hollywood" nature of the film's presentation happened during its depiction of the New Hampshire primary. As campaign staffers pondered the future of their efforts, Burton tried to locate the candidate, only to be told he was at a Krispy Kreme store across the street from the hotel. The camera then slowly moved toward the Krispy Kreme store, at the same pace as Henry, walking toward its entrance. When Burton arrived at the donut store, the camera took the viewer through the door with the character, and over to a seat next to Stanton. The cleverness of this filming was apparent and self-indulgent, reminding the audience that they were clearly watching a feature film presentation of a fictional narrative. Moreover, it was clearly an example of product placement, a common Hollywood phenomenon often seen in feature films. Given that *Primary Colors* was a major studio release and a feature fiction film, the presence of such camera work is not surprising. But the novel offered its readers something else, an insider's vision of the Clinton presidential campaign. It constructed and marketed that vision in a manner that clearly capitalized on the similarities to the Clinton campaign present in the narrative. It encouraged the hyperreality of its image of Bill Clinton.

The film version of *Primary Colors* did just the opposite. In much the same manner as other overtly fictionalized versions of real presidents (e.g., *Saturday Night Live* parodies, Rich Little imitations, Comedy Central's *That's My Bush* program), the imitation of Bill Clinton in *Primary Colors* the movie was made obvious and apparent. Coming as it did in a feature film, with all of the trappings involved in that genre, from camera angles to marketing strategies, the imitation was further magnified and self-reflexively revealed to be an imitation and not something more, not something hyperreal. In this way, the filming of *Primary Colors* took the hyperreal teeth out of the novel, revealing the story for what it was—a fiction. As Klein wrote in an author's note at the beginning of the novel, "Several well-known people—journalists, mostly—make cameo appearances in these pages, but this is a work of fiction and the usual rules apply. None of the other characters are real. None of these events ever happened."[72] No one believed that when the novel was published. But *Primary Colors'* asserted fictionality became much more plausible when John Travolta transformed Jack Stanton from the "real" Bill Clinton into simply a well-done caricature.

Primary Colors and Political Authenticity

At the end of *Primary Colors*, Henry Burton, our narrator, has offered his resignation to Jack Stanton. Burton has become so distressed and demoralized by the Stanton campaign and the electoral process that he sought a more fulfilling means of public service. As Stanton pleaded with Burton to stay, Burton reflected on the power of the governor:

> "Henry, come on," Stanton said, stretching his arms out across the desk toward me. His voice caught slightly. His eye narrowed, burrowing deep, searching my consciousness, desperate to make a stronger connection. His brow, his nostrils, the veins on his neck, his arms, his fingers—everything was reaching out, everything was focused on me. I knew this moment so well; I had seen him do it so many times. He could talk all he wanted about an eternity of "false" smiles; his power came from the exact opposite direction, from the *authenticity* of his appeal, from the stark ferocity of his hunger. There was very little artifice to him. He was truly needy. And now he truly needed me.[73]

The novel left us hanging; we never learned if Henry acceded to Stanton's entreaties or if he baled on the campaign for more moral and decent pursuits. But the novel could leave us hanging, because it had already fulfilled its purpose. *Primary Colors* existed in U.S. political culture as another moment in the construction of Bill Clinton. It offered that culture a vision of this president rooted in Henry's final impressions; Stanton/Clinton was a consummate politician, a man who needed to be needed and loved, with immense power and with a reality, an authenticity, that drew others to his midst and his service.

This fictionalized vision of Bill Clinton achieved cultural and political legitimacy through careful marketing strategies and specific narrative constructions. Klein's decision to conceal his identity not only created considerable buzz about *Primary Colors*, and undoubtedly contributed to increased sales, it also manufactured an air of authenticity to the narrative. The novel was too revealing, too real, too true about those in political power, Klein's anonymity maintained, that he needed protection and secrecy. Moreover, Klein's decision to construct his vision of Stanton/Clinton as a philandering, sexually aggressive, racially ambivalent, consummate politician also contributed to the novel's authentication of Bill Clinton. Klein's Stanton was not a caricature, but an all too realistic and familiar character. Deriving its power from the cultural and political milieu of the 1990s and drawing upon the political sensibilities of the baby-boomer generation to depict its presidential candidate, *Primary Colors* invited, almost commanded, its readers to see Jack Stanton as Bill Clinton.

When screening audiences saw the first version of *Primary Colors*, the movie, though, they did not like the ending. Finishing just as the novel did, the film refused to resolve for its audiences Henry's ambivalence. That did not work for America's movie going public. Nichols was forced, as a result, to film a final scene of Jack and Susan Stanton dancing at an inaugural ball and meeting a smiling Henry Burton who hailed Stanton with the greeting "Mr. President." This new ending confirmed what director Nichols saw as the primary message of the movie: "It's still two cheers for democracy. There's nothing better."[74]

The film's ending, in contrast to the novel's, left no ambiguity. Such was the message of the film version of *Primary Colors*. Though the plot was similar and its staging was effective, the film robbed the novel of its authenticating strength. The hyperreal fusion of Stanton and Clinton that occurred in the novel was broken by the mimetic portrayal of Stanton by John Travolta. Despite *Time* magazine's promotional attempts, John Travolta's Stanton was not Bill Clinton, but a fairly good, and thoroughly obvious, imitation of Bill Clinton.

Beyond its portrayals of Bill Clinton, *Primary Colors* also spoke to the nature of hyperreal image-making in contemporary U.S. political culture. Though there is a long history of U.S. political fiction, both in literature and on film,[75] *Primary Colors* was unique. Unlike other fictional depictions of presidents, *Primary Colors* offered citizens a conflicted and often unflattering vision of the actual, sitting American president. In addition, *Primary Colors* also critiqued in its fiction the campaign that elected that sitting president. As such, the story not only magnified the palpable uncertainties about Bill Clinton but it undermined the legitimacy of the campaign process that elected him to the office in the first place.

The vision of Clinton and the 1992 campaign put forth in *Primary Colors* was only slightly disguised, and its thin fiction did little to undermine the credibility and authenticity of the depiction, especially given the anonymity of its creator. Voters were encouraged, motivated, invited, and even directly told to believe that Jack Stanton was Bill Clinton and that they should make the connection between fiction and truth in their reading of *Primary Colors*.

As such, *Primary Colors* further complicated an already confusing political culture in the United States, where "true" political news and the authentic reality of political leadership is more and more elusive. Voters are increasingly confronted with a much wider array of political discourse offering commentary about the character and nature of political leadership than ever before. It comes at them from television, newspapers, at their bookstores, and on the movie screens of the local cineplex. Genres and forms are blurred as voters recognize their president in fictional characters, see him in television commercials, find him on the news, and form him in their minds from all of these sources. *Primary Colors* reflected this increasingly complex political environment.

On a front-page of *Primary Colors*, immediately prior to the author's note asserting the fictionality of the novel, Klein included a quotation from Machiavelli: "Men as a whole judge more with their eyes than with their hands."[76] Unintentionally perhaps, Klein has commented on the nature of political authenticity in the contemporary, hyperreal political environment. Political judgment is not a tactile process any longer, but a sensory one, a process replete with competing, confusing images and uncertain, unclear realities. And the voters making those judgments continue to wade through the images, searching for the "real," and finding even more and more images, from new and different sources, creating increasing levels of hyperreal confusion and dizzying complexities of political intensity.

Notes

1. "Remarks by the President and Prime Minister Chernomyrdin in Photo Opportunity," January 30, 1996, available at http://www.clinton.nara.gov/public_papers/public_papers.html.

2. Sanford Schram, "The Post-Modern Presidency and the Grammar of Electronic Electioneering," *Critical Studies in Mass Communication* 8 (1991): 213.

3. Larry J. Sabato, Mark Stencel, and S. Robert Lichter, *Peepshow: Media and Politics in an Age of Scandal* (Lanham, MD: Rowman & Littlefield, 2000), xi. For a critical assessment of this development, see Michael Janeway, *Republic of Denial: Press, Politics and Public Life* (New Haven, CT: Yale University Press, 1999).

4. See P. David Marshall, *Celebrity and Power: Fame in Contemporary Culture* (Minneapolis: University of Minnesota Press, 1997); and Neal Gabler, *Life: The Movie* (New York: Vintage Books, 1998). James Jasinski sees a danger in focusing on the "who" of politics rather than on the "what" or what he calls the "politics of intimacy." See James Jasinski, "(Re)constituting Communication Through Narrative Argument: *Eros* and *Philia* in *The Big Chill*," *Quarterly Journal of Speech* 79 (1993): 467–86.

5. Michael Schudson details the history of political reporting and its concern with scandal and personal intrigue. See Michael Schudson, *The Good Citizen: A History of American Civic Life* (New York: Martin Kessler Books, 1998). See also John B. Thompson, *Political Scandal: Power and Visibility in the Media Age* (Cambridge, UK: Polity Press, 2000), 41–59.

6. For a discussion of President George H. W. Bush's use of family to achieve electoral success, see Trevor Parry-Giles and Shawn J. Parry-Giles, "Political Scopophilia, Presidential Campaigning, and the Intimacy of American Politics," *Communication Studies* 47 (1996): 191–205. This same President Bush sought to reduce the damage from revelations about his son Neil's involvement with a failed savings and loan venture. George W. Bush's own use of his children was evident in the 2000 convention film, where the candidate choked up when discussing the birth of his twin daughters. When those same daughters were cited by Texas police for illegally obtaining alcoholic beverages, White House press secretary Ari Fleischer said this in response to a reporter's query: "The President views this as a family matter, a private matter, and he will treat it as such." See "Press Briefing by Ari Fleischer," May 31, 2001, available at http://www.whitehouse.gov/news/briefings/20010531.html.

7. For more on the Clinton image construction efforts during the 1996 campaign, see Chapter Three. Accounts of the 1996 presidential campaign include Roger Simon, *Show Time: The American Political Circus and the Race for the White House* (New York: Times Books, 1998); Evan Thomas, Karen Breslau, Debra Rosenberg, Leslie Kaufman, and Andrew Murr, *Back from the Dead: How Clinton Survived the Republican Revolution* (New York: The Atlantic Monthly Press, 1997); and Bob Woodward, *The Choice* (New York: Simon & Schuster, 1996). Interestingly, the film version of *Primary Colors* was released in March 1998—another moment of reassessment concerning Bill Clinton.

8. These concurrent phenomena of contemporary political life are noted and discussed in W. Lance Bennett and Robert M. Entman, "Mediated Politics: An Introduction," in *Mediated Politics: Communication in the Future of Democracy*, edited by W. Lance Bennett and Robert M. Entman (Cambridge, UK: Cambridge University Press, 2001), 1–17.

9. As Lionel Trilling reveals, the meaning of the word "authenticity" is etymologically rooted in the Latin word *sincerus* meaning clean, pure, or sound. Trilling remarks that the word originally applied to things, not persons, but has come to mean "the absence of dissimulation or feigning or pretence." See Lionel Trilling, *Sincerity and Authenticity* (Cambridge, MA: Harvard University Press, 1972), 12–13. An alternative definition of authenticity, that recognizes its philosophical moorings in the eighteenth century, sees it as the "effort to act on the basis of one's own understanding." See Imants Barušs, *Authentic Knowing: The Convergence of Science and Spiritual Aspiration* (West Lafayette, IN: Purdue University Press, 1996), 152.

10. Plato, *The Republic*, Book VII.

11. Alexander Nehamas, *Virtues of Authenticity* (Princeton, NJ: Princeton University Press, 1996), xxxiv.

12. Charles Taylor, *The Ethics of Authenticity* (Cambridge, MA: Harvard University Press, 1992), 27. See also Alessandro Ferrara, *Modernity and Authenticity: A Study of the Social and Ethical Thought of Jean-Jacques Rousseau* (Albany: State University of New York Press, 1993).

13. An interesting example comes from a study of the visual and verbal conventions of television news. This analysis indicates how the artifice of journalism can be manipulated and exploited and the devices used to create a perception of reality and immediacy. See Sharon Goodman and Paul Manners, "Making It 'Real': Words and Pictures in Television News," *Language & Communication* 17 (1997): 53–66.

14. Miles Orvell, *The Real Thing: Imitation and Authenticity in American Culture, 1880–1940* (Chapel Hill: University of North Carolina Press, 1989), xv.

15. Orvell, *The Real Thing*, 155.

16. Hanno Hardt, "Authenticity, Communication, and Critical Theory," *Critical Studies in Mass Communication* 10 (1993): 51. While not concerned with individual alienation per se, E. Deidre Pribram also notes the increasingly inauthentic quality of contemporary image-based discourse. She concludes that "in our culture of information and the mass media, we are inundated with an abundance of images and signs that no longer have referential value but, instead, interact solely with other signs. This marks the advent of simulation." See E. Deidre Pribram, "Seduction, Control, and the Search for Authenticity," in *The Madonna Connection: Representational Politics, Subcultural Identities, and Cultural Theory*, edited by Cathy Schwichtenberg (Boulder, CO: Westview Press, 1993), 201.

17. Steven Jones, "A Sense of Space: Virtual Reality, Authenticity, and the Aural," *Critical Studies in Mass Communication* 10 (1993): 238. In his discussion of the advent and explosion of "new video," communication historian and theorist Mitchell Stephens also addresses significant questions about the evolving nature of "reality" and the impact of communication on our understanding of "reality." See Mitchell Stephens, *the rise of the image the fall of the word* (New York: Oxford University Press, 1998).

18. Marshall Berman, *The Politics of Authenticity: Radical Individualism and the Emergence of Modern Society* (New York: Atheneum, 1970), xix.

19. Doug Rossinow, *The Politics of Authenticity: Liberalism, Christianity, and the New Left in America* (New York: Columbia University Press, 1998), 4.

20. By 1979, Carter would warn America of its "crisis of confidence," widely translated in the media to mean malaise. See Stephen Paul Miller, *The Seventies Now: Culture as Surveillance* (Durham, NC: Duke University Press, 1999), 63–4; David Brian Robertson, ed., *Loss of Confidence: Politics and Policy in the 1970s* (University Park: The Pennsylvania State University Press, 1998); and Bruce J. Schulman, *The Seventies: The Great Shift in American Culture, Society, and Politics* (New York: Free Press, 2001), 140–3.

21. See George C. Edwards III, "Campaigning Is Not Governing: Bill Clinton's Rhetorical Presidency," in *The Clinton Legacy*, edited by Colin Campbell and Bert A. Rockman (New York: Chatham House, 2000).

22. J. Michael Hogan labeled this phenomenon "media nihilism" in his reading of the 1988 presidential debates. See J. Michael Hogan, "Media Nihilism and the Presidential Debates," *Argumentation & Advocacy* 25 (1989): 220–5.

23. Thomas Patterson, *Out of Order* (New York: Alfred A. Knopf, 1993).

24. We have previously commented on the dangers and shortsightedness of seeing political communication in an overly cynical and fatalistic way. See Trevor Parry-Giles and Shawn J. Parry-Giles, "Reassessing the State of Political Communication in the United States," *Argumentation & Advocacy* 37 (2001): 158–70. For a compelling and refreshingly optimistic reading of the role of cynicism in American political culture, see William Chaloupka, *Everybody Knows: Cynicism in America* (Minneapolis: University of Minnesota Press, 1999).

25. Shawn J. Parry-Giles, "Political Authenticity, Television News, and Hillary Rodham Clinton," in *Politics, Discourse and American Society: New Agendas*, edited by Roderick P. Hart and Bartholomew Sparrow (Lanham, MD: Rowman & Littlefield Publishers, 2001).

26. Various accounts of the investigations of Bill and Hillary Clinton include Joe Conason and Gene Lyons, *The Hunting of the President: The Ten-Year Campaign to Destroy Bill and Hillary Clinton* (New York: St. Martin's Press, 2000); Michael Isikoff, *Uncovering Clinton: A Reporter's Story* (New York: Crown, 1999); Gene Lyons, *Fools for Scandal: How the Media Invented Whitewater* (New York: Harper's Magazine Foundation, 1996); Richard A. Posner, *An Affair of State: The Investigation, Impeachment, and Trial of President Clinton* (Cambridge, MA: Harvard University Press, 1999); James D. Retter, *Anatomy of a Scandal: An Investigation into the Campaign to Undermine the Clinton Presidency* (Santa Monica, CA: General Publishing, 1998); and Susan Schmidt and Michael Weisskopf, *Truth at Any Cost: Ken Starr and the Unmaking of Bill Clinton* (New York: HarperCollins, 2000).

27. Clinton was also available to the traditional news media outlets, but was not as dependent upon them as typically was the case for a major party presidential candidate. For a discussion of the power of new media in American politics see Richard Davis and Diana Owen, *New Media and American Politics* (New York: Oxford University Press, 1998). Specific discussions of Clinton's use of new media and alternative media channels can be found in Edwin Diamond and Robert A. Silverman, *White House to Your House: Media and Politics in Virtual America* (Cambridge, MA: MIT Press, 1995); Robert E. Denton, Jr., and Rachel L. Holloway, "Clinton and Town Hall Meetings: Mediated Conversation and the Risk of Being 'In Touch,'" in *The Clinton Presidency: Images, Issues, and Communication Strategies*, edited by Robert E. Denton, Jr., and Rachel L. Holloway (Westport, CT: Praeger, 1996); and Kenneth L. Hacker, "Virtual Democracy: A Critique of the Clinton Administration Citizen-White House Electronic Mail System," in *The Clinton Presidency: Images, Issues, and Communication Strategies*, edited by Robert E. Denton, Jr., and Rachel L. Holloway (Westport, CT: Praeger, 1996).

28. This was perhaps most famously evident in Clinton's answer in the 1992 Richmond Presidential Debate when an audience questioner asked the candidates about the personal impact of the national debt on them: "Well, I've been governor of a small state for 12 years. I'll tell you how it's affected me. Every year Congress and the

president sign laws that make us do more things and gives us less money to do it with. I see people in my state, middle class people—their taxes have gone up in Washington and their services have gone down while the wealthy have gotten tax cuts. I have seen what's happened in this last four years when—in my state, when people lose their jobs there's a good chance I'll know them by their names. When a factory closes, I know the people who ran it. When the businesses go bankrupt, I know them." See "The Second 1992 Presidential Debate," available at http://park.org/Events/Debates/presdeb3.html#ques9.

29. This reference, of course, comes from Timothy Crouse, *The Boys on the Bus* (New York: Random House, 1973).

30. [Joe Klein], *Primary Colors: A Novel of Politics* (New York: Random House, 1996).

31. See Kenneth Burke, *Attitudes Toward History* (Berkeley and Los Angeles: University of California Press, 1984), 49–52.

32. Lee Sigelman, "Taking Popular Fiction Seriously," in *Reading Political Stories: Representations of Politics in Novels and Pictures*, edited by Maureen Whitebrook (Lanham, MD: Rowman & Littlefield, 1992), 160.

33. *Primetime Live*, ABC, January 17, 1996, available at http://www.lexis-nexis.com/.

34. *Showbiz Today*, CNN, February 12, 1996, available at http://www.lexis-nexis.com/. Many noted the same Deep Throat parallel, including David Jackson who called the search for Anonymous "the biggest whodunit since Deep Throat." See David Jackson, "Anonymous Creates Novel Intrigue in D.C. Authorship Is Biggest Mystery Since Deep Throat," *Dallas Morning News*, January 31, 1996, p. 1C.

35. *Larry King Live*, CNN, January 30, 1996, available at http://www.lexis-nexis.com/.

36. *The Newshour with Jim Lehrer*, PBS, February 5, 1996, available at http://www.lexis-nexis.com/.

37. See Donald Foster, "Who Is Anonymous?" *New York*, February 26, 1996, p. 50. Foster later wrote a book chronicling his efforts at authorship detection. See Donald Foster, *Author Unknown: On the Trail of Anonymous* (New York: Henry Holt & Company, 2000).

38. See David Streitfeld, "'Anonymous' Undone by His Own Hand?" *The Washington Post*, July 17, 1996, p. A1. Klein's insider access to the Clinton campaign is confirmed by George Stephanopoulos, who notes that during the campaign, he and Klein "talked openly and often, either on the phone or when he hooked up with us on the road." Stephanopoulos also reveals that Klein was "either smitten with Clinton or doing a smooth job of spinning me." See George Stephanopoulos, *All Too Human: A Political Education* (Boston: Little, Brown, 1999), 52. An interesting

profile of Klein is found in Howard Kurtz, "True Colors: The Man Behind Anonymous; Joe Klein Made a Name for Himself as a Crusading Reporter," *The Washington Post*, August 8, 1996, p. C1. Klein reflects on his variable relationship with Bill Clinton in his interview/article about Clinton's legacy in *The New Yorker*. In the article, Klein defends *Primary Colors* as not an attack on Clinton, but as a "paean to political roguery." Interestingly, Clinton granted Klein considerable time and access for this lengthy analysis of the Clinton legacy. See Joe Klein, "Eight Years," *The New Yorker*, October 16 & 23, 2000, pp. 188–217. Kurtz attacks the Clinton "propaganda" machine for their castigations of Klein as an "asshole" after the publication of *Primary Colors*, noting, "the White House had never quite figured out that Klein cared deeply about policy." See Howard Kurtz, *Spin Cycle: Inside the Clinton Propaganda Machine* (New York: Free Press, 1998), 148.

39. Streitfeld, "'Anonymous' Undone," p. A1.

40. Joe Klein, *The Running Mate* (New York: The Dial Press, 2000). And just as *Primary Colors* confronts persistent baby-boomer issues of race, sex, morality in politics, etc., so too does *The Running Mate* deal directly with the ongoing cultural anxieties about the Vietnam War.

41. *News*, CNN, February 4, 1996, available at http://www.lexis-nexis.com/.

42. Gene Lyons, "'Anonymous' Author Is Unmasked; Computer Sniffs Out Quintessential Joe," *Arkansas Democrat-Gazette*, February 28, 1996, p. 9B.

43. Michiko Kakutani, "Books of the Times," *New York Times*, January 19, 1996, p. C29.

44. For a discussion of the role of anonymity in the communication of sensitive information, see [Craig R. Scott], "To Reveal or Not to Reveal: A Theoretical Model of Anonymous Communication," *Communication Theory* 8 (1998): 381–407. Also of relevance here is Barthes's notion of exnomination, wherein an anonymous or exnominated voice is often more influential or powerful because it comes to be taken for granted and its truthfulness assumed. See Roland Barthes, *Mythologies*, translated by Annette Lavers (New York: Hill and Wang, 1972). See also John Fiske, *Television Culture* (London: Methuen, 1987).

45. A discussion of the theoretical underpinnings of the differences between public and private communication is found in William K. Rawlins, "Theorizing Public and Private Domains and Practices of Communication: Introductory Concerns," *Communication Theory* 8 (1998): 369–80. A full treatment of the public/private distinction in political and sociological theory is offered by Maurizio Passerin d'Entrèves and Ursula Vogel, eds., *Public & Private: Legal, Political and Philosophical Perspectives* (London: Routledge, 2000); and Jeff Weintraub and

Krishan Kumar, eds., *Public and Private in Thought and Practice: Perspectives on a Grand Dichotomy* (Chicago: University of Chicago Press, 1997).

46. Gunther Kress discusses the uses of language in the media to construct public and private domains of action differently. See Gunther Kress, "Language in the Media: The Construction of the Domains of Public and Private," *Media, Culture, and Society* 8 (1986): 395–419.

47. Foster, "Who Is Anonymous?" p. 50.

48. Jacob Weisberg, "Revenge Fantasy," *New York*, February 26, 1996, p. 50.

49. Rossinow, *The Politics of Authenticity*, 343.

50. Rossinow, *The Politics of Authenticity*, 85, 339.

51. [Klein], *Primary Colors*, 3.

52. [Klein], *Primary Colors*, 27.

53. [Klein], *Primary Colors*, 35–6.

54. Clinton's commitment to racial justice and an end to discrimination is noted in several sources. Clinton's former aide, and the alleged model for the Burton character in *Primary Colors*, George Stephanopoulos, wrote that "Bill Clinton inspired me most when he spoke about race." See Stephanopoulos, *All Too Human*, 362. A more nuanced and psychologically rooted account of Clinton's commitment is offered by James MacGregor Burns and Gloria Sorenson, who note that "deep in his heart Bill Clinton always had a passionate desire for justice and equality, particularly for black Americans. That desire he would not moderate or ignore. It was etched in his soul, his music, his friendships, his marriage, and his early life experiences." See James MacGregor Burns and Gloria J. Sorenson, *Dead Center: Clinton-Gore Leadership and the Perils of Moderation* (New York: Scribner, 1999), 242.

55. [Klein], *Primary Colors*, 37.

56. [Klein], *Primary Colors*, 66–7.

57. [Klein], *Primary Colors*, 170–5.

58. [Klein], *Primary Colors*, 192.

59. [Klein], *Primary Colors*, 197.

60. Rossinow, *The Politics of Authenticity*, 299.

61. Rossinow, *The Politics of Authenticity*, 301.

62. See Charlotte G. O'Kelly, *Women and Men in Society* (New York: D. Van Nostrand Co., 1980); Rossinow, *The Politics of Authenticity*.

63. [Klein], *Primary Colors*, 13–14.

64. See Brett Pulley, "Librarian Speaks Out on 'Primary Colors' Suit," *New York Times*, February 19, 1997, p. 3B; and David Streitfeld, "Seeing Red Over 'Primary Colors'; Librarian Says Portrayal Libels Her," *Washington Post*, February 19, 1997, p. C1.

65. [Klein], *Primary Colors*, 122.

66. Paul Begala, a Clinton loyalist and former campaign worker, summed up the power of *Primary Colors* well in *George* magazine. He said, "The book sold because it suggested that it told a larger truth, and because the author hid his identity so as to suggest that someone who actually knew these people, and knew them well had written it. The whole thing was savage." See Josh Young, "Bill Clinton's Grand Seduction," *George*, March 1998, p. 109.

67. Richard Corliss, "True Colors," *Time*, March 16, 1998, pp. 67, 69.

68. Interestingly, only 3% of moviegoers, according to Universal Studio's surveys, had read *Primary Colors* as a novel, and at one screening, only 1% of the audience noted similarities with the scandals taking place in the White House in early 1998. Nichols reported that one focus group respondent commented about the film version of *Primary Colors*, "Hilarious, thought-provoking, touching. Reminds me of the Clintons." See Corliss, "True Colors," p. 70.

69. Box office gross information was obtained from the Internet Movie Database, available at http://www.imdb.com/.

70. Peter Biskind, "Compromising Positions," *Premiere*, April, 1998, pp. 100–1. There was also reporting that suggested Clinton's collusion in the formation of Travolta's Stanton. Josh Young reported in *George* that Clinton had expressed sympathy with Travolta's quest to ease German restrictions on Scientology, and that in return, Travolta softened his portrayal of Stanton in the film. See Young, "Bill Clinton's Grand Seduction."

71. The imitative power of Travolta's performance is noted by Ernest Giglio, *Here's Looking at You: Hollywood, Film, and Politics* (New York: Peter Lang, 2000), 2–3, 99.

72. [Klein], *Primary Colors*, n.p.

73. [Klein], *Primary Colors*, 366, emphasis in original.

74. Biskind, "Compromising Positions," p. 101.

75. See Terry Christensen, *Reel Politics: American Political Movies from* Birth of a Nation *to* Platoon (New York: Basil Blackwell, 1987); James E. Combs, *American Political Movies: An Annotated Filmography of Feature Films* (New York: Garland, 1990); Phillip L. Gianos, *Politics and Politicians in American Film* (New York: Praeger, 1998); Giglio, *Here's Looking at You*; Irving Howe, *Politics and the Novel* (New York: Horizon Press, 1957); and Maureen Whitebrook, ed., *Reading Political Stories: Representations of Politics in Novels and Pictures* (Lanham, MD: Rowman & Littlefield, 1992).

76. [Klein], *Primary Colors*, n.p.

Chapter Five

Bill Clinton's Hyperreal Legacy

On August 17, 1998, President Bill Clinton delivered an unprecedented live message from the Map Room of the White House, where he finally acknowledged that he "did have a relationship with Ms. Lewinsky that was not appropriate." For Clinton, the issue did not so much center on his relationship with the twenty-something intern; rather, the matter most evidenced the need "to stop the pursuit of personal destruction and the prying into private lives."[1] As Bill Clinton became more conciliatory, he continued his fight against the intrusion into private life over the ensuing weeks. Simultaneously, he flexed his military muscle by ordering a retaliatory attack against factions of Sudanese and Afghan terrorists who were allegedly responsible for the embassy bombings in Kenya and Tanzania. And, he commemorated the thirty-fifth anniversary of Martin Luther King, Jr.'s March on Washington, offering an ode to nonviolence and an epideictic to such civil rights leaders as King, John Lewis, and Nelson Mandela.[2]

The events that swirled around Bill Clinton in 1998 and 1999 epitomized the same ideological tensions that persisted throughout his 1992 and 1996 presidential campaigns. During this period, Clinton fought to preserve a level of presidential privacy while continuing to wage an all-out public image campaign to salvage his position and his legacy. He continued to articulate an antiviolence message as he used violence as a means to solve foreign policy problems. He persisted in championing women's issues as public attention focused mostly on his inappropriate relationships with women and his repeated perpetuation of masculine heroism. Clinton fostered a black identity through his reverence to such leaders as King and Mandela as he performed whiteness with his predominantly white "war room" and inner presidential circle, and his scant policy attention to issues affecting the lived experience for persons of color (e.g., racial profiling). And finally, Clinton used the past as an image-making strategy and worked to build the bridge to the twenty-first century. The ideological ambivalence that epitomized Clinton's 1998 and 1999 reaction to the scandals he confronted, though, reflected larger social tensions and new presidentialities defining the presidency in the late 1990s.

The Clinton presidency, of course, was situated within a constructed presidentiality, containing the institution's history as well as the practices of those who occupied the position. More broadly, the Clinton presidency was part of a postmodern presidentiality—a context that arguably transformed the institution,[3] especially in the aftermath of the Kennedy assassination, the Vietnam War, Watergate, and the Iran-Contra situation.[4] The postmodern turn coincided with recent presidential controversies and scandals and with a growing commitment to adversarial journalism to produce a cynical U.S. public that is hyper-suspicious of the officeholder's character and even critical of its past presidential heroes (e.g., slave-owning Washington and Jefferson, philandering FDR and JFK).[5] Richard W. Waterman et al. contend, for example, "There are indeed serious problems with the state of the presidency as we come to the end of the twentieth century."[6]

The ambivalences that defined presidentiality during the 1990s helped frame the Clinton presidency even before candidate Clinton began his hyperreal imaged campaign. As Richard Bradley explains, it was Bill Clinton "who experienced the full impact of the ghosts of Nixon, Johnson and JFK."[7] Clinton, thus, embodied the angst not only related to the presidency but to larger cultural anxieties inherent in his generation. Steven E. Schier highlights Clinton's status as the "first baby-boomer president," who was forced to deal with the "ambiguity, confusion, and irony" associated with such issues as "the Vietnam draft . . . drugs . . . sex outside of marriage."[8] Thus, even as Clinton uttered his first words on the campaign trail, even as he took the oath of office, his bid for the presidency as well as his performance in office were shaped by the ideological dissonances of the larger political culture.

Clinton's hyperreal imaging was likewise situated in the cultural yearnings that surrounded a societal search for a hero replacement and the lost hope that died with JFK. John Hellmann calls this search for the new hero a "dream of resurrection," which has been visible in the "ceaseless attempts to place Kennedy once again in the White House."[9] While Robert Kennedy, Ted Kennedy, and even Gary Hart were possible successors, only Bill Clinton represented Kennedy's most probable surrogate to the "nation's thwarted hopes,"[10] an image that was reified with the unending broadcast of the Kennedy-Clinton handshake.

The handshake and Clinton's fusion of his image with Kennedy's accentuated the salience of political images[11] and reinforced the idea that he "was the first member of the cohort that came of age after the Kennedy assassination to hold the presidency."[12] James MacGregor Burns and Georgia J. Sorenson portend that "it was JFK's youthful élan and glittering style that Bill Clinton most wanted to emulate."[13]

As Clinton neared the end of his second term in office, the scandal surrounding his impeachment pitted the aura of hope that framed his presidency against a sentiment of despair, expressed most clearly by his impeachment trial. This ideological uncertainty, however, transcended Bill Clinton's presidency and was a persistent part of the cultural parlance over presidentiality pervasive from the time of JFK's assassination and Nixon's resignation to the climaxing event of Clinton's impeachment. Stephen Paul Miller characterizes the time period of Bill Clinton's presidency by referencing the American public's need "to return to the 'real.'"[14] In response to this moment of presidential crisis, numerous texts emerged that searched for that "real" and tried to make sense of Bill Clinton's presidency and his presidential legacy. This chapter, in part, examines the ways in which two different cultural artifacts addressed the presidential exigency of the impeachment through constructions of Clinton's image, framing that image in similar messages of hope. The examination of such legacy-centered texts likewise offers a glimpse into the overall impact of Bill Clinton's hyperreal imaging from the beginning of the 1992 campaign through the end of his presidency.

Our first text is MTV's *BIOrhythm*, which is a television series that presents the "lives of our favorite artists as they've never been seen—or heard—before" by showcasing fast-paced imagery complete with captions set to period music. *BIOrhythm* is an unusual documentary form, more similar to a music video than to conventional documentary. MTV's website declared that the Clinton episode, which debuted in its current form on February 23, 1999, only eleven days following the U.S. Senate's not guilty verdict in the president's impeachment trial, represented "the personal journey of a man who dreamed of uniting America, and who now presides over a country divided." With an unusual focus on a political leader, *BIOrhythm* promised to "capture the spirit of who Bill Clinton really is" by addressing the following three questions: "How did this boy who shook hands with President Kennedy realize his own dream of becoming president?" "What was the price for that ambition?" And "[W]hat is it about Bill Clinton that inspires such passionate feelings—both for and against—among Americans?"[15]

A second text that grappled with the impact of the Clinton impeachment was PBS's 1999 series *The American President*, narrated by Hugh Sidey, and produced and directed by Philip B. Kunhardt, Jr., Philip B. Kunhardt III, and Peter W. Kunhardt.[16] As Stephen Skowronek explains in the "Foreword" of the book that accompanied the ten-part video series, "*The American President* invites readers to rethink presidential history and reconsider the men who have held America's top leadership positions" by offering "the most comprehensive visual accounting of the principal characters" combined with a "narrative supported by this artwork."[17] The Clinton episode, entitled "The Balance of Power," centered on the examination of "presidential leadership in an era of an increasingly divided government," and spotlighted, along with Clinton, Presidents Madison, Polk, and Taft. The Clinton installment in this episode was appropriately titled "Second Chances."[18]

These texts reflected larger cultural attempts to struggle with the postmodern angst inherent within late twentieth-century political culture and in current conceptions of presidentiality. Although both films offered differing interpretations through their narratives (visual and written), *BIOrhythm* and *The American President* ultimately articulated a redemptive, cathartic, and hopeful message that accentuated the stabilizing features of the presidency, transcending the foibles of the individual man. *BIOrhythm's* redemptive discourse, however, was at once private and cultural while *The American President's* discourse was much more institutional in its focus. Both videos also constructed an American public eager to reject "the politics of personal destruction" and thus determined to preserve the institutional and mythological status of the presidency. Oddly enough, Clinton's impeachment and the public's response actually proved how stabilizing and enduring the institution was; the majority of the American people maintained their allegiance to the office through their disapproval of the impeachment proceedings. The cultural response surrounding Clinton's impeachment, however, ultimately reaffirmed the public, futuristic, masculine, white, and war-like images of a more conservative presidentiality, resolving, at least in that moment, the cultural anxiety that enveloped the presidency from Kennedy through Clinton. For Clinton himself, his hyperreal image helped save him from impeachment; that same image, however, simultaneously worked to delimit his legacy because of the widespread unease about the "real" Bill Clinton. It seems, thus, that the level of uncertainty that surrounds the authenticity of image increases as the image becomes more hyperreal.

Impeachment and Bill Clinton's Redemption

For Bill Clinton, the impeachment crisis was an ironic though unsurprising moment for the first baby-boomer president. Culturally, it was a moment that functioned as a site of ideological contestation over conceptions of presidentiality. It was ironic that Clinton's private life became a subject he could no longer control fully given his past proclivity for using the private to define his public image in ways that few others had done before.[19] Yet, the scandal over a White House intern was hardly surprising given the turmoil that Bill Clinton's alleged sexual activities created during his 1992 presidential campaign.

In the midst and aftermath of the impeachment trial, many sought to understand this unprecedented presidential moment; the controversy thus generated a wealth of public debate and political commentary. The eventual verdict to the ideological paradox created by Bill Clinton's presidency was rendered, at least by some, in a discourse of redemption. Such a redemptive spirit was likewise evident in the U.S. public's response to the crisis of confidence that encircled President Bill Clinton and the presidency, illustrating the ways in which the American public helped preserve the institution. Bill Clinton's presidency, thus, functioned as the cultural apex over the confusion about the nature and role of presidentiality in the postmodern United States while also demonstrating the endurance of the public's voice and influence in a political environment dominated by hyperreal images.

Relying on redemptive themes during a time of national exigency is not unexpected. Kenneth Burke, for example, assumes the presence of a hierarchy that becomes disrupted during times of drama, ultimately inciting conflict. One primary way that order is restored, according to Burke, is through punishment and redemptive action, which allows for the sustenance of social order through the sacrificing of the scapegoat,[20] who "performs the role of vicarious atonement."[21]

Moreover, when redemption does occur, in Burke's scheme, there is always the presence of a redeemer, a force or agent that brings about the symbolic redemption of the guilty sinner.[22] As such, insofar as the impeachment of Bill Clinton involved his individual sins, the scapegoating of various parties and individuals, and ultimately the redemption of the sinner through the Senate's not-guilty verdict, the cultural markers of this redemption cycle are critical to understanding the symbolic meaning of this event in American political life. We examine two texts that offered different levels of symbolic redemption and that figure prominently in the post-impeachment imaging of Bill Clinton.

The Private and Cultural Redemption of Bill Clinton

Bill Clinton's common strategy of using the private as a salient feature of his public image resulted in a cultural battle during the impeachment debate over whether the Lewinsky matter constituted a public or private matter. *BIOrhythm* situated Clinton's private turmoil within the larger cultural (and thus public) turbulence of the 1960s and 1970s as a means by which to understand his successes and failures. In the end, the music video documentary implied that to convict Clinton would be to condemn an entire generation. In a macroscopic view, Clinton's successes loomed large in the face of great private and cultural adversity; the scapegoat was Clinton's aberrant childhood and the confused countercultural context in which he lived, both of which helped produce the president's demons.

From the outset, the fast-paced style of *BIOrhythm* was obvious, marking it as a different imaging text from the usual news-oriented documentaries. Images changed constantly to the accompaniment of congruent music, moving from a slower rate to a very rapid pace within a matter of seconds. This style of editing and filming reflected W. J. T. Mitchell's concept of a "'composite'" art, integrating "different codes, discursive conventions, channels, sensory and cognitive modes."[23] When juxtaposing the cultural turmoil of the 1960s with Clinton's graduation from Georgetown University, for example, some 65 visual images flashed across the screen in approximately 17 seconds. These images likewise exhibited a strobe effect as the colors blinked from blue to orange to red to black and white while the camera panned in and out with dizzying rapidity, reflecting postmodernity's disruption of textual unity. Such "speed and style" of contemporary video practices, Mitchell Stephens contends, reflects the "montage" motif that captures the "pace of modern and postmodern life and thought," producing "something much greater than the sum of their parts," including "new patterns and connections."[24]

Clinton's turbulent childhood was thus situated within the postmodern and chaotic editing presented by *BIOrhythm*. Most eerily, when the images turned to Clinton's disturbed family life, they slowed and blurred, and the music became morose, "involving both the spectator and the image in the discursive circuit which it directs."[25] As the episode addressed the alcoholism and domestic abuse of Clinton's stepfather (Roger Clinton, Sr.), we first saw the lips of an individual taking a drink in an extreme close-up shot filmed in bright white and orange hues. We then witnessed an image of a gun being fired that was superimposed over Virginia Clinton's face; we hear the sound of gun fire and read two captions: "Roger pulls out a gun . . . and fires a bullet over Virginia's head." In the next frame, an extreme close-up photo of an elementary school-aged Bill Clinton was featured with the captions: "The abuse continues for years . . . Billy keeps it a secret." To take us further into the psyche of Bill Clinton's childhood, the camera slowly moved us closer and closer to his face, freezing the image on Clinton's youthful eyes. *BIOrhythm*'s practice of morphing the young Bill Clinton into the adult Bill Clinton early on in the program cemented the conflation of the two images, suggesting visually that to understand the latter's behaviors we must understand the former's home environment. This psychological perspective reflects the lens assumed by certain presidential scholars; James David Barber alleges, for example, that an individual's childhood offers insight into a person's character, which is "the most important thing to know about a president or candidate."[26] *BIOrhythm*'s practice of referring to Bill Clinton as "Bill" throughout the film further exacerbated the morphing of the boy with the man/president, highlighting this psychological explication of his presidency.

Bill Clinton's image as an adolescent was likewise conflated, but this time it was fused with two of his idols, President John Kennedy and Elvis. In this montage of images, the song "Little Willie" was the sound track to visuals of a youthful Clinton dancing and playing the saxophone, with lyrics like, "little Willie wears the crown, he's the king around town" accompanying these mediated images. As Bill Clinton danced with a young girl, the image of him smiling at the camera was frozen as the caption read: "He's elected Junior Class President." This vision of Clinton then flowed into a moving video of a smiling John F.

Kennedy; as JFK interacted with a group of reporters, Clinton's image lingered on the screen before fading from view. The caption read: "He idolizes President Kennedy." Another Kennedy-like image trailed as we saw a teenaged Bill Clinton playing football with a group of friends. This image progressed to a photo of Elvis Presley with an accompanying caption: "He idolizes Elvis, too." Elvis's black and white photo then morphed into an image of a youthful yet older Bill Clinton, encouraging the fusion of these past and future celebrities. Like his two idols, Clinton was portrayed as being "very popular around town . . . especially with the ladies;" we then viewed a teenaged Bill Clinton surrounded by laughing girls. These production techniques echo the observations of Gunther Kress and Theo van Leeuwen: "For participants to be put together in a syntagm which establishes a classification means they were judged to be members of the same class and are to be read as such. As in language, naturalization is not natural. The picture itself constitutes the relation."[27]

This visual montage, in part, highlighted Clinton's heterosexist masculinity. *BIOrhythm* suggested that just like his idols and many adolescent boys, Clinton exhibited typical sexual interests. Such constructions reified Clinton's masculine image, normalizing it within the context of male celebrity and the sexual mores of the rock-and-roll generation. When women appeared in *BIOrhythm*, they were either objectified as sexual objects or were members of Clinton's family. In all cases, women were relegated to the private sphere (e.g., wife, mother, potential sexual conquest); men's actions transcended the private realm and became part of the public sphere of celebrity culture, naturalizing, in the process, the public/private split of men's/women's actions. Such visual representations are significant. John Hartley contends that "politics and truth become extricably bound up with notions of visualizations, representation, pictorial power" because the democratic process is "performed" via pictures.[28]

The scene, though, likewise accentuated Clinton's whiteness. In *The Man from Hope*, Clinton mentioned the significant impact that Martin Luther King, Jr.'s death had on him as a teen. *BIOrhythm* did not morph Clinton with King even though its producers relied heavily on Clinton's 1992 campaign video to frame its music documentary, featuring Clinton's first-person narratives and the campaign film's visuals in their own biography. Clinton's heroes, according to *BIOrhythm*, just happened to be two of America's past white idols, which weakened the magnitude of Clinton's future indiscretions even as it set up the comparison between Clinton's sexual propensities and his white idols' questionable practices.

The coupling of Clinton with JFK continued in *BIOrhythm* and centered on politics rather than sexual conduct. To the backdrop of very upbeat music, we saw photographs of Clinton preparing for his Boys' Nation trip, which *BIOrhythm* described as a "political training program for young men." Images of Bill Clinton were then superimposed over the Washington monument as he seemingly readied to meet his presidential hero. Once again, we heard Bill Clinton's voice from *The Man from Hope* narrating the story of that legendary moment. Multiple images appeared of the president shaking hands with participants at Boys' Nation. The camera, though, zoomed in on the handshake between the past and future presidents to the point that we only see a close-up of their interlocked hands; when the camera zoomed out, we saw the handshake that continues to permeate our collective memory of John F. Kennedy and Bill Clinton. Such an image accentuated the profound quality of that exchange, situating Clinton squarely within the mythos of JFK in a manner suggested by *The Man from Hope* and the 1996 campaign film. The Clinton campaign's co-optation of the JFK myth worked precisely because, as Michael Griffin maintains, the visual discourse "symbolize[d] socially shared concepts,"[29] grounded in assumptions of presidential destiny.

Clinton's "hope" theme, thus, represented the extension of JFK's promise as the president was assassinated only "four months" after the predestined exchange, *BIOrhythm* reported. The significance of the loss was not only personal; *BIOrhythm* transitioned from multiple images of Clinton and Kennedy's more private moments to the public memory of Walter Cronkite's disclosure of Kennedy's death. The import of these cultural moments of JFK's death are "replayed as markers of the nation's collective memory each time the story of Kennedy's death is recounted," Barbie Zelizer notes.[30]

JFK's assassination triggered *BIOrhythm*'s recounting of the cultural anxieties that plagued Clinton's generation, including the Vietnam War; Bill Clinton's college years were thus situated within the cultural conflict surrounding the war. To begin with, the ominous nature of the impending crisis was signified by a black and white image of a lightening bolt and accompanying thunder, which was placed between JFK's assassination images and Clinton's high school graduation photos. *BIOrhythm* then visually superimposed what appeared to be Clinton's senior photo with images of the war. We saw a black and white video of men with military helmets digging a hole in front of a helicopter flying low in the background. The caption read, "As American troops move into Vietnam . . . he moves to Washington, D.C." A close-up photograph of a smiling Bill Clinton was intertextualized over a video of soldiers being carried on stretchers. Clinton's coming of age period was thus defined by war; *BIOrhythm* captioned: "The Vietnam War will force Bill to choose between his political future . . . and his life." Clinton's ambivalence over war and peace was accentuated as *BIOrhythm* continued to juxtapose images of Clinton and the international conflict, noting how "torn" he was "between his duty to serve and his opposition to the war." Even though Clinton allegedly chose war by facing the draft lottery and rejecting service in the Army Reserve, *BIOrhythm* indicated the depth of his turmoil, claiming that in a letter he sent home from England, Clinton professed: "I feel like I'm losing my mind." Clinton's thoughts thus reflected the view of many young men at the time, who "experienced," Peter N. Carroll argues, "deep feelings of revulsion and disaffiliation from the policies of the national leadership."[31]

Unlike many of his peers, however, Clinton chose to enter politics in order to address such problems rather than reject the system that produced them; *BIOrhythm* thus moved beyond the conflation of Clinton and the countercultural generation of the 1960s to juxtapose Clinton with his peers. Clinton's experiences at Georgetown University, for example, were portrayed as a period where he "works 18 hours a day," combining school work with such leadership positions as class president and Capitol Hill clerk. His Yale Law School years were likewise detailed against images of naked people attending a concert and twenty-somethings strolling around a college campus. Clinton's visual images, conversely, were frenetic, exhibiting a dynamic, youthful, and energetic Bill Clinton repeatedly running for office, declaring, "there's so little time, there's so precious little time." Thus, despite the turmoil that surrounded Clinton, *BIOrhythm* accented Clinton's futurism, his unusual political mindset at a time when many of his generation shunned politics, and his ability to transcend the personal and cultural disruption, achieving remarkable feats at a very young age.

Despite the successes, *BIOrhythm* did not ignore the future problems that Clinton faced over his alleged sexual indiscretions. In the latter part of the film, *BIOrhythm* contextualized such scandals, not surprisingly, within his political ascendancy to the presidency. Yet, *BIOrhythm* continued to intersect these sexual issues with Clinton's youth, the cultural turmoil of the 1960s and 1970s, as well as with JFK. Just prior to captioning that "Bill's road to the White House is marred by scandal," *BIOrhythm* included images of a car rolling down a hillside, an image used earlier in the film to reference his biological father's death; this visual was followed by yet another viewing of the Clinton and Kennedy handshake. Also included within Clinton's 1992 scandal-in-review, *BIOrhythm* offered a montage of sexual images of Gennifer Flowers and a bare-backed Marilyn Monroe image shot in black and white footage (associating Clinton's Flowers with JFK's Monroe), which was interspersed with images from the Vietnam War and the protests against it. As Clinton accepted the Democratic nomination in 1992, *BIOrhythm* featured numerous images of his mother when Clinton attributed her with his "fighting spirit;" such comments were followed by childhood photos of the young Clinton and yet another vision of the Kennedy handshake. In the process of tracing Clinton's presidency, *BIOrhythm*'s producers accentuated Virginia Kelley's death, featuring photos of a mournful Clinton at a gravesite in 1994, with his voice superimposed over somber music, stating: "My mother taught me a lesson in courage . . . and always, always, she taught me to fight." Throughout the film, Clinton's fighting spirit was represented metaphorically by images of a boxing match, which offered a clear sense of *BIOrhythm*'s analogous "perspective."[32] This approach ordered the relationships present in the film by reference to their "similarity-in-difference."[33]

Clinton's fighting spirit, which is attributed to his mother's courage, functioned as the means by which *BIOrhythm* framed the Monica Lewinsky chapter of Clinton's presidency. Analogously, Kenneth Starr was repeatedly imaged with visions of a digging weasel superimposed over the smiling independent prosecutor as *BIOrhythm* reviewed the number of investigations into Clinton's past. The media's frenzy surrounding Monica Lewinsky was juxtaposed with graphic video footage of lions attacking and eating a zebra. The boxing match image appeared and reappeared as *BIOrhythm* reviewed Clinton's reactions to the scandal. *BIOrhythm* rendered a more psychological evaluation of the entire scandal by captioning: "Starr discovers that the only person who can defeat Bill Clinton . . . is Bill Clinton." *BIOrhythm* ended its 30-

minute music documentary with a montage of close-up photographs of Bill Clinton. The final caption reads: "Bill Clinton's most important battle . . . remains," as Bill Clinton, Hillary Rodham Clinton, and Chelsea Clinton were shown in a black and white photo walking away from the camera.

For *BIOrhythm*, the impeachment spectacle was clearly depicted as a private family matter. This interpretation was reinforced by repeated references to the lack of public interest in the scandal. In one caption, *BIOrhythm* stressed that "the public shows little interest in Starr's investigation." In another caption, *BIOrhythm*'s producers again emphasized that "the Paula Jones sex scandal garners little public interest." Clinton's redemption was likewise evidenced in the aside that *BIOrhythm* offered in response to Clinton's impeachment in the House of Representatives: "Bill's approval rating rises despite the scandal." For *BIOrhythm*, at least, the American public shunned the unending inquiries into the president's personal life and ultimately championed the "boxer" president over the "weasel" independent prosecutor and the "lions" of the news media.

In the process of redeeming Clinton, *BIOrhythm* scapegoated many but kept the president relatively blameless. In addition to Kenneth Starr and the news media, the personal and cultural contexts that produced Bill Clinton functioned as the primary culprits. Bill Clinton's crisis-centered childhood coupled with the turbulence of the 1960s and 1970s and produced a man tormented by the demons of his generation. To reject Clinton would be to reject an entire generation of his peers, the film suggested. *BIOrhythm* replayed a clip from Clinton's 1993 "Inaugural Address," where the baby-boomer president declared: "We will rise and fall together." As constructed by Clinton and rearticulated by *BIOrhythm*, Clinton was us and we were Clinton, and the documentary cast Clinton as the heroic victim rather than the scapegoat. P. David Marshall explains this phenomenon as a process of constructing "solidarity" between a politician and the voting public, culminating in the ability "to win the affection of a crowd or an audience." Yet, the political celebrity must simultaneously "construct an aura and a distance to sustain legitimacy."[34] The hyperreal conflation of Clinton with JFK (and Elvis) helped the president transcend the common man image and enter the domain of mythic celebrity—roles that many presidential heroes of the past performed.

The Institutional Redemption of Bill Clinton

The writers of *The American President* likewise used the exigency of the impeachment scandal as an opportunity to assess Bill Clinton's presidency. Rather than accentuate Clinton's childhood, *The American President*'s "Second Chances" segment was situated instead within the matrix of U.S. history, particularly the history of the institution and all of the men who served in the "most exclusive of clubs." The larger mission of *The American President* was to issue "a presidential portrait gallery" that showcased the "original words of presidents."[35] It is not surprising therefore that Bill Clinton's redemption was institutionally focused. Like *BIOrhythm*, however, *The American President* constructed the American people as the redeemer in its redemption drama about this president; the ultimate scapegoat was the partisanship that defined U.S. politics during the last decade of the century.

"Second Chances" began (and ended) with a discussion of the men who preceded Clinton in office, noting the changes in presidential power over the course of the twentieth century:

> After Taft, the balance of power shifted again under the force of Franklin Roosevelt, leading to an era when the executive branch dominated like it never had before. It wasn't until after Watergate that Congress seized back its powers and restored an earlier sense of balance.

In addition to its historical rendering, Bill Clinton's presidency was further contextualized within what *The American President* cast as an "intense new level of partisanship" and "political divisiveness" that affected Bill Clinton more than any other president in modern times. The significance of the balance of power crisis was evidenced by historian Richard E. Neustadt, who contended, "only once have our national parties fractured. When they did, we had a civil war; we're not at such a point but we have dangerous potentials in the country." The institutional ambiance of the film was furthered by the combined presentation of soothing, nostalgic music with a visual memorial to sites of American nationalism and mythology.[36] *The American President*, thus, took us inside the Oval Office, to a picturesque vision of the Capitol Building, and on to an outside view of the White House brilliantly lit in the dark of night.

Bill Clinton, who is interviewed by Hugh Sidey in the White House for *The American President*, enhanced the institutional *mythos* surrounding the office. Clinton's sentiments about the presidency at once reflected its perceived power as well as the postmodern critique of that power: "the presidency can still be a place of great influence and power—it's still the central office in the country, particularly in times of adversity or crisis—but . . . there's not an automatic deference to the presidency." Clinton likewise showed humility toward the office, which enhanced its institutional aura: "I was also humbled by it . . . any person who's not a little humbled by being given this responsibility doesn't understand what he or she's got a hold of." Clinton concluded his rendering of the presidency with an even greater subservience to the institution: "You feel always never quite adequate to do the work; no one is smart enough, or wise enough, or strong enough."

The camera positioning as well as the images that accompanied Clinton's testimony intensified this sentiment of respect and honor for the office. Joshua Meyrowitz suggests that audiences "react to the picture in terms of [mediated] distance, not size," indicating the "nature of a character's physical and psychological orientation to the scene."[37] The camera distance during the interview portions of the segment evidenced deference toward the president unlike many news cameras (or *BIOrhythm*'s shots),[38] which often visually invade a politician's privacy. *The American President* distanced the camera from Clinton such that we could see his hand gestures as well as his shoulders and head. Such visual privacy enhanced the level of respect offered the president that, when combined with the mythic pictures of the White House, accentuated Clinton's presidential aura. When Clinton, for example, discussed his humility relating to his position, *The American President* moved to black and white still photographs of the Oval Office under construction, and this context for the president's comments added historicity to the images.[39]

Grounding Clinton further within the sweep of presidential history, *The American President* defined the 42nd president as a "democratic reformer." *The American President* traced his reform interests to his childhood, featuring Clinton's testimony that he was "always, always interested in civil rights," calling it "the defining political issue of [his] childhood." Clinton's reform-mindedness was evidenced by his appointment of "minorities to his administration" where he "initiated a national dialogue on race." *The American President* thus defined

Clinton's key issue as one involving civil rights, situating his legacy with others who came before him (e.g., Lincoln, FDR, Johnson).

Bill Clinton's life and presidency, thus, were clearly contextualized within this institutional reverence that assumed a level of presidential destiny as the producers dealt with Clinton's childhood. To begin with, *The American President* relied on a destiny monomyth to frame Clinton's early years. Unlike *BIOrhythm*, which centered its narrative on the problems of Clinton's youth, *The American President* instead, focused on the characteristics that made him presidential, characteristics that were visible even in his earliest days.[40] Sidey noted, for example, that even in grade school, Clinton "was so outgoing, he was already recognized as a young man with a future in politics;" Neustadt went so far as to call Clinton a "natural politician." Throughout the narrative, Sidey and Neustadt referenced Clinton's qualities that implicitly made him presidential, including his "self-confidence," his "intelligence," his "sharp instinct," his "ideas," and his "energy," which combined with high levels of ambition and "popular[ity]" to explain his political success. Like *BIOrhythm*, *The American President* also highlighted the importance of the Clinton-Kennedy handshake. Of that momentous occasion when Clinton met his "political hero," Sidey asserted: "The encounter changed Bill Clinton's life forever." The way in which *The American President* accentuated what were Clinton's earliest inklings of presidential qualities reflects Barber's theory that the presidency is an institution impacted by the psychology of the individual and is shaped largely by childhood influences.[41] Stephen Hess likewise explicates, "some people are more fit psychologically to be president than others."[42]

The American President, at least in part, allowed for a psychological assessment of Clinton's preparedness for the presidency. As in *BIOrhythm*, Clinton's mother also functioned in *The American President* as "his greatest influence." Clinton reinforced this sentiment, asserting that "she taught me, never give up, never forget where you came from, and never lose your compassion for people who are less fortunate than you are." Delving further into his psychological make-up, Sidey asked Clinton to reflect on one of his own statements: "When you ran in 1992, you said, 'you may only be fit to be President when you are not obsessed with it.'" As Clinton responded, *The American President* panned over a still, color photo of Clinton's eyes; the close-up was so extreme, Clinton's forehead and nose are not even fully visible. The more respectful distance that epitomized the earlier interview portions of Clinton's sentiments disappeared in that moment as we were allowed to gaze into Clinton's eyes for evidence of his obsession with the position. *The American President* thus let the audience make up its own mind on this psychological quest. And, the president was given the last word on the question: "I was able to run with great passion but with less obsession than would have been the case, for example, if I had been a candidate in 1988."

The American President moved next to questions over Clinton's "infidelity in his personal life." Throughout the discussion over Clinton's sexual indiscretions, *The American President* repeatedly articulated implications of his private behavior that were virtually dismissed in the context of his victory. Its producers promulgated Clinton's own construction of his alleged infidelities during the 1992 campaign:

> Bill Clinton became the first presidential candidate ever to publicly admit to marital problems. "But it was behind them now," he said. "And entirely a private matter." The candidate insisted that he be judged not on his private life, but by his performance and his political record.

Noting that "his words made sense to a public that seemed to be growing more tolerant," *The American President* portrayed an energetic Clinton with enthusiastic crowds against a sound track of upbeat music. Sidey thus quickly moved beyond such character concerns, concluding: "And from a position low in the polls, Bill Clinton soared to second place in the New Hampshire primary, earning the nickname, 'The Comeback Kid.'" Furthering the Kennedy-Clinton parallel, Sidey concluded the section on the 1992 presidential campaign, calling Clinton "a young man of a new generation" who won a "resounding victory . . . in November." As Sidey detailed this new generation of Clinton enthusiasts, we viewed images of cheering young, white males gazing up at the young, white, southern president—images similar to the new generation of supporters for another white male president in 1961.

From the outset of Clinton's first term, partisanship defined the state of politics in Washington, D.C. and the political scandals that plagued the Clinton presidency, according to *The American President*. Partisanship explained the failure of the Clinton health care reforms, the Contract With America, and the GOP takeover of Congress in 1994.

Grounded in the 1995 governmental shutdowns, Sidey noted that "partisanship in the government reached epidemic proportions by the end of Bill Clinton's first term. . . . The spirit of compromise, key to the workings of the Madisonian system of government, was degenerating into a system of mutual antagonism." The music in this section was grim. The images showed Clinton sandwiched between Congressman Newt Gingrich (R-GA) and Senator Trent Lott (R-MS); he was also the recipient of Senator Alphonse D'Amato's ire. Sidey likewise identified the Supreme Court ruling that "a sitting President could be sued over actions taken prior to his term" in the Paula Jones sexual harassment lawsuit as a further challenge to the Madisonian system of government. *The American President* situated the actions of Kenneth Starr and the subsequent impeachment scandal squarely within what Sidey called a "politically charged atmosphere" such that the independent counsel, "with virtually unlimited investigative powers, intensified his scrutiny." Demonstrating the severity of the threat while utilizing a language of war, Sidey concluded: "the presidency was now under siege on all fronts."

Once *The American President* again ventured into allegations surrounding Clinton's sexual conduct, public/private distinctions reappeared and the partisanship of the debacle remained paramount. Sidey expressed the private and political motives of the independent counsel, noting that after "Failing to uncover incriminating evidence in what became known as Whitewater . . . Kenneth Starr shifted his focus from Clinton's business dealings to his personal life." Of the final impeachment vote and its partisan roots, Sidey deciphered: "The official charges were perjury and obstruction of justice, but throughout the trial, the underlying dynamic was political." *The American President* then detailed the constitutional debate over what constituted a "high crimes and misdemeanor." Sidey expressed the sentiment of some: "that if an elected President could be removed, scholars warned, on the basis of his personal relationships and an effort to cover them up, the Madisonian system itself could be in danger of collapse." Neustadt furthered the bifurcation of the public/private split in presidential behavior, claiming that Clinton "had the good fortune to have a personality which encourages discrimination between himself as President and himself as a private individual, and his personality has conquered all kinds of doubts about him." In the end, Sidey returned to the institutional legacy of Clinton, offering an upbeat assessment of his service: "Over time,

Bill Clinton reoriented the Democratic Party toward mainstream issues, including balancing the budget and reforming welfare. And, he presided over one of the strongest economies in the twentieth century."

The visual images that predominated throughout this section furthered the institutional rendering of *The American President*'s overall assessment of the Clinton presidency. The photos of Clinton assumed an *archetype of presidential form*, which encapsulated a history of presidential photography in its contemporary rendition of presidentiality.[43] Part of the U.S. collective memory of presidentiality is the black and white images of presidents often pictured alone in the White House who bear the burden of the country's hardships. These archetypal images often feature quite pensive if not pained expressions and capture the president in allegedly private moments of quiet reflection, facing the camera or turning away as if to heighten their solitude and privacy. Certainly, Clinton's "hero," John F. Kennedy, popularized such images,[44] and both Kennedy and Clinton were strategic about the ways in which their images were photographed and promulgated.[45]

In *The American President*, Clinton like Kennedy was shown in black and white, close-up images with the facial expression reflective of "the thinker" during the film's discussion of the impeachment process. Clinton's distress was vivid as the camera often centered on his eyes, which allowed for a scopophiliac moment on the part of the viewer. Such images accentuated a sense of realism devoid of image-making artificiality because of the assumed backstage behavior where the camera was perceived to be unobtrusive.[46] The black and white nature of the photographs, however, likewise "provoke" what Roger Rosenblatt contends, is a sense of "mystery" and "ambiguity," and is attention-getting for audiences as they attempt to glean insight from such apparently "private" moments of access. Their use furthered the hyperreality of this example of presidential image-making.[47] Presidential mediated forms are thus reliant on genre memory,[48] which shapes cultural interpretations of textual genres while simultaneously relying on a strong sense of nostalgia for times past. In discussing the relationship between photography and nostalgia, Nancy Martha West imbues photography with a function of "retrieval, as a means of reclaiming the past and even of shaping the future," offering feelings of "necessity, resistance, and even *hope*."[49] The familiarity of this presidential mediated form in the collective memory of audiences allows for a cathartic redemption of Bill Clinton as the soothing form of the photographs promoted a sense of assurance and hope that the institution of the presidency would survive. Such familiar and cathartic images, thus, overpowered the spectacle of the private scandal in *The American President*.

The scandal was so privatized in *The American President* that images of the women who brought forth the allegations were rendered invisible in the film as the producers of the series opted not to include visuals of Gennifer Flowers, Paula Jones, or Monica Lewinsky. Such invisibility communicated that presidential sexual conduct belongs to the private sphere and is reminiscent of the media coverage of JFK where the women were not given public exposure. These rhetorical choices by *The American President*'s producers emphasized the implicit narrative judgment that what matters in the assessment of a president is his public behaviors. Images, thus, of the white, masculine, president, who belonged within the historical lineage of the archetypal presidential form, represented the centerpiece of the program, which ideologically reified the power of the presidency and all of its ideological and institutional trappings. As Stephens notes, moving images like those devoted to President Clinton formulate "impressions and moods."[50]

In the end, the final verdict for *The American President* was communicated by its producers' construction of a forgiving and wise American public. Sidey reported on the role of the public, concluding, "Despite impassioned calls for his resignation throughout the trial, Clinton's approval ratings remained very high." *The American President*, however, went beyond *BIOrhythm* in its depiction of the audience's role in the impeachment process. In summarizing the Senate trial, Sidey stated that "In the end, the Senate listened to the people. As a body, it could not muster the required two-thirds vote or even a simple majority to convict Bill Clinton of any charges." Sidey then asked Bill Clinton to reflect upon the public's role throughout the impeachment process:

> Sidey: "The American people spoke out loud and clear throughout 1998, you know that better than anybody. . . . Well, what did you learn about the power of the people and the role the public plays in exercising political power?"
>
> Clinton: "The American people almost always get it right. They gave me a second chance and I think if we think about life as getting second chances, as

> long as you learn from your mistakes, I think it's a helpful way to look at life, and so I do believe in a God of second chances."

As the film neared its conclusion regarding the presidency of Bill Clinton, Sidey's empowerment of the people's role in the impeachment process was further enhanced. He projected:

> The only Democrat to be re-elected President since FDR, Bill Clinton both reflected and benefited from an increasingly tolerant America, and while most Americans deplored his personal acts in the Lewinsky case, they refused to judge his public role by his private behavior.

Neustadt returned the program's focus back to the politics of personal destruction, which functioned as the scapegoat for the Clinton impeachment and threatened the institution as a whole. Neustadt's final words were spoken as images of Clinton walking to his presidential helicopter that took off to the backdrop of the Washington Monument (images not unlike Nixon's departure from the White House in 1974) appeared on the screen:

> From Nixon's time on . . . it is now plain that every President immediately upon election attracts the serious intent of political opponents and the professional interests of the media in tearing him down and pushing him toward resignation. It used to be that one of the most fundamental powers underlying a President's position was a fixed term. We now see that the Nixon presidency has unfixed that term and has created both for media and for politicians, incentives to try to shorten the term. Well I find that sad in a way that goes far beyond Bill Clinton; it affects all successive Presidents as far as we can see.

With such closing words, *The American President* clearly contextualized the Clinton impeachment within a post-Watergate era of destructive partisanship. And even though *The American President* accentuated the threats to the presidency in the final words of Clinton's segment, its producers returned to the institutional vivacity of the office by accenting the historical legacy of the institution that is simultaneously dependent upon, yet transcends, the individual officeholders.[51] Immediately following Clinton's segment, Sidey ended the ten-part video series with the following words as we witnessed a slow moving montage of black and white historical presidential inaugurals, representing the past, dissolve into a colorized, vivacious, and aesthetically exquisite photograph of the White House surrounded by springtime foliage, representing the vibrant future:

> From humble beginnings, an almost baffling complexity has arisen, and yet through it all there remains a single person at the center who must shoulder the office. However, he, someday she, has arrived at the White House . . . each inherits and builds upon the work of his predecessors, bringing to bear talents and also human flaws and sometimes a rare capacity to rise to greatness. These individuals together embody the American President.

The Post-Impeachment Image of Bill Clinton

BIOrhythm offered a more future-oriented message—a message centered on coming to terms with not only Clinton's private behavior, but more importantly, with the anxieties of the unfulfilled possibilities and the lost hope of the past that weighed heavily on U.S. cultural identity and memory. Bill Clinton had to continue to address his own private affairs; the country, however, needed to move on to the business of public affairs and accept Clinton's private foibles just as it had to accept the disappointments of a generation. Bill Clinton thus shouldered this cultural burden, complete with its heartaches and its hopes. To convict Bill Clinton would be to condemn our past, our present, and our future, the documentary suggested.

The American President centered its attention not on the cultural context but on the institutional setting of the presidency. For the most part, the private actions of the president were rendered off-limits, even in a segment that was forced to address the private machinations of a controversial president. To the extent that Clinton's childhood prophesied his presidential behaviors, his private life did enter into *The American President*'s assessment. Noticeably absent, though, were the details of his dysfunctional childhood so clearly emphasized in *BIOrhythm*. They were replaced by the positive relationship with his mother and his ambitious childhood dreams. Otherwise, Clinton's private "issues" represented the political maneuverings of an over-zealous and hyper-political independent prosecutor bent on destroying this popular Democratic reformer.

Interestingly, both films accepted and promulgated Clinton's own hyperreal image. *BIOrhythm*'s repeated rendering of the Kennedy-Clinton handshake evidenced just how effective Clinton's attempt to "exploit the image of John F. Kennedy" in 1992 and beyond really was.⁵² *The American President* likewise imbued that fateful moment with considerable prominence, revealing the nostalgia surrounding the resurrection of the Kennedy mystique. Both texts also apparently accepted Clinton's response to the Lewinsky scandal; they both relegated marital improprieties to the private sphere, furthering a public/private dichotomy for presidential behavior. As Clinton expressed in *The American President*, "I made a personal mistake that became a matter of public debate. I tried to acknowledge my wrongdoing and say that I was sorry about it. But I also tried to demonstrate presidential character by standing up for the interests of the country and doing what I told the American people I would do when I ran for office."

In both texts, then, Clinton received redemption and evaded the scapegoat. For *BIOrhythm*, the scapegoat represented the private and public/cultural environment that produced the future president. For *The American President*, the institutional practices of partisanship received the ire of the filmmakers. While the scapegoat was less apparent in public opinion polling during the time of the impeachment process, *BIOrhythm*'s and *The American President*'s assessment of the public's views appeared congruent with the poll data and the interpretations of others. In short, the public was Bill Clinton's redeemer. And in the public opinion polls from 1998 through 1999, some 60 percent of the public reported that the president should not be impeached while approximately 40 percent supported the House impeachment decision. Similar results were recorded in response to whether or not the Senate should convict the president in light of the impeachment verdict.⁵³ Susan Schmidt and Michael Weisskopf's interpretation of the public's response to the impeachment reinforced the poll's results. According to the two journalists, "People had no trouble believing Clinton had an affair. But they saw it as a private matter not fit for criminal investigation. . . . The results rolled in: Americans don't prosecute people for having an affair; if Clinton interfered with the legal system, he did so to protect his privacy."⁵⁴

Despite such renderings, ambivalence existed in the larger culture over the constructed and implied scapegoats within these two cultural texts. Burke argues that the "scapegoat is dialectically appealing, since it combines in one figure contrary principles of identification and alienation."⁵⁵ The cultural tensions of the 1960s is at once revered and scapegoated in our public memory with Bill Clinton acting as a metonymy for the cultural angst of his generation.[56] The private lives of politicians at once incite scopophiliac excitement as they simultaneously evoke strong feelings of guilt and disgust. Thus, even as *BIOrhythm* and *The American President* rendered a popular verdict on the Clinton impeachment, such conclusions continue to evoke cultural ambivalence over the contemporary state of presidentiality in the United States

BIOrhythm and *The American President* reified a more traditional vision of presidentiality at the turn of the twentieth century. Such presidentiality was still highly dependent upon masculinity that was similarly imbued with a naturalized whiteness. Clinton often articulated messages of peace while a simultaneous mentality of war, especially as expressed through the political language surrounding this President, expressed a larger cultural commitment to militarism. And although Clinton and the larger culture is at once reliant on the private constructions of political candidates, the ultimate verdict suggested the valorization of a public presidentiality, one that often banished women to the private sphere. Presidentiality as constructed by Clinton and rearticulated by *BIOrhythm* and *The American President*, while demonstrating nostalgia for a traditional past, encouraged a futuristic gaze that promised to bring such traditional values of public masculinity, whiteness, and militarism into the twenty-first century. These continuing ideological conflicts would not surprise Mitchell, who suggests that "the notion of ideology is rooted in the concept of imagery, and reenacts the ancient struggles of iconoclasm, idolatry, and fetishism."[57]

Notes

1. Bill Clinton, "Statement By the President," http://www.pub.whitehouse.gov/ uri-res/I2R?urn:pdi://oma.eop.gov.us/1998/8/18/1.text.1. For an analysis of this statement, see Herbert W. Simons, "A Dilemma-Centered Analysis of Clinton's August 17th Apologia: Implications for Rhetorical Theory and Method," *Quarterly Journal of Speech* 86 (2000): 438-53.

2. Bill Clinton, "Remarks of the President in Commemoration of the 35th Anniversary of the March on Washington," August 28, 1998, http://www.pub.whitehouse.gov/uri-res/I2R?urn:pdi://oma.eop.gov.us/1998/8/31/3.text.1. See also Shawn J. Parry-Giles and Trevor Parry-Giles, "Collective Memory, Political Nostalgia, and the Rhetorical Presidency: Bill Clinton's Commemoration of the March on Washington, August 28, 1998," *Quarterly Journal of Speech* 86 (2000): 417–37.

3. As John Fiske contends, the postmodernist "refutes any hierarchialization of the different truths produced by the different modes of representation." As a result, concentrations of power are critiqued, distinctions between truth and falsehood are problematized, politicized, and associated with "specific historical time and geographical region." See John Fiske, *Media Matters: Race and Gender in U.S. Politics* (Minneapolis: University of Minnesota Press, 1996), 62. See also Linda J. Nicholson, ed., "Introduction," in *Feminism/Postmodernism* (New York: Routledge, 1990), 4.

4. Several commentators have commented on the disruption of the contemporary presidency. As Thomas Brown asserts, "The obsequies had grand, almost dynastic features that reinforced the sense that Kennedy's death was a national catastrophe." See Thomas Brown, *JFK: History of an Image* (Bloomington: Indiana University Press, 1988), 3. Stephen Paul Miller asserts, "After the rifts of the Vietnam War, the presidency began to lose much of its power as an ideological organizing mechanism." He further addresses the ineffectiveness of Nixon, Ford, Carter, and Bush in particular. See Stephen Paul Miller, *The Seventies Now: Culture as Surveillance* (Durham: Duke University Press, 1999), 362. Bruce J. Schulman suggests, "Nixon's ambitious and cunning agenda would poison American politics and fragment American society. His Presidency, often deliberately, sometimes unintentionally, drilled a deep well of cynicism about national politics . . . about the dignity and necessity of public service itself." See Bruce J. Schulman, *The Seventies: The Great Shift in American Culture, Society, and Politics* (New York: The Free Press, 2001), 24.

5. Mark J. White explains that the 1970s marked the period when a "radically different version of the private Kennedy [as well as FDR] emerged." In the aftermath of "Vietnam, Watergate, and the Edward Kennedy—Chappaquiddick

controversy . . . [t]he twin ideas that leaders were often corrupt and that their personal lives were worthy of scrutiny became accepted by the press." Hart argues that "Between 1958 and 1988 political cynicism grew prodigiously," often associated with such causes as Vietnam, Watergate, the economic conditions of the late 1970s and the 1980s, and for Hart, in particular, the "overexpos[ure]" of politics by the news media. Several scholars note the role of the news media in fostering a sense of cynicism, brought on by a journalistic commitment to adversarial journalism, which W. Lance Bennett calls "empty adversarialism" that actually produces more of a "posture of antagonism than . . . a no-holds-barred approach to the content of the news." See W. Lance Bennett, *News: The Politics of Illusion* (New York: Longman, 1988), 125; Roderick P. Hart, *Seducing America: How Television Charms the Modern Voter* (New York: Oxford University Press, 1994), 81–82; Mark J. White, "Behind Closed Doors: The Private Life of a Public Man," in *Kennedy: The New Frontier Revisited*, edited by Mark J. White (New York: New York University Press, 1998), 257, 260. See also Joseph N. Cappella and Kathleen Hall Jamieson, *Spiral of Cynicism: The Press and the Public Good* (New York: Oxford University Press, 1997); William Chaloupka, *Everybody Knows: Cynicism in America* (Minneapolis: University of Minnesota Press, 1999); and Thomas E. Patterson, *Out of Order* (New York: Alfred A. Knopf, 1993).

6. See Richard W. Waterman, Robert Wright, and Gilbert K. St. Clair, *The Image-Is-Everything Presidency: Dilemmas in American Leadership* (Boulder: Westview Press, 1999), 161.

7. Richard Bradley, *American Political Mythology from Kennedy to Nixon* (New York: Peter Lang, 2000), 170. Bob Woodward also talks about the impact of the Nixon scandal and resignation on his successors. See Bob Woodward, *Shadow: Five Presidents and the Legacy of Watergate* (New York: Simon & Schuster, 1999). Stephen Paul Miller also argues that during the Vietnam War era, "the American presidency also lost much of its backing and credibility." See Miller, *The Seventies Now*, 350.

8. Steven E. Schier, "A Unique Presidency," in *The Postmodern Presidency: Bill Clinton's Legacy in U.S. Politics*, edited by Steven E. Schier (Pittsburgh: University of Pittsburgh Press, 2000), 1, 3.

9. John Hellmann, *The Kennedy Obsession: The American Myth of JFK* (New York: Columbia University Press, 1997), 146.

10. Brown, *JFK*, 44.

11. See W. J. T. Mitchell's discussion of the images that function "like an actor on the historical stage, a presence or character endowed with legendary status, a history that parallels and participates in the stories we tell ourselves about our own evolution from creatures 'made in the image' of a creator, to creatures who make

themselves and their world in their own image." See W. J. T. Mitchell, *Iconology: Image, Text, Ideology* (Chicago: University of Chicago Press, 1986), 9.

12. Bradley, *American Political Mythology*, 43.

13. James MacGregor Burns and Georgia J. Sorenson, *Dead Center: Clinton-Gore Leadership and the Perils of Moderation* (New York: Scribner, 1999), 24.

14. Miller, *The Seventies Now*, 4.

15. See *BIOrhythm*, MTV, wysiwyg://bottomf/126/http://www.mtv.com/mtv/tubescan/biorhythms/; *BIOrhythm*: President Bill Clinton, MTV, http://www.mtv.com/mtv/tubescan/biorhythms/bill_clinton/producer.html; and *BIOrhythm: President Bill Clinton* (New York: MTV Productions). All future references to *BIOrhythm* will be to this particular source.

16. See Philip B. Kunhardt, Jr., Philip B. Kunhardt III, and Peter W. Kunhardt, *The American President* (New York: Riverhead Books, 1999); and Philip B. Kunhardt, Jr., Philip B. Kunhardt III, and Peter W. Kunhardt, *The American President* (New York: Kunhardt Productions, Inc., and Thirteen/WNET New York, 1999). Philip B. Kunhardt is the former managing editor of *Life* and has been producing documentaries with Peter W. Kunhardt for years. Philip B. Kunhardt has co-authored and produced such projects as *Lincoln: An Illustrated Biography*. Hugh Sidey covered the White House for forty years with *Time* magazine.

17. Stephen Skowronek, "Foreword," *The American President* (New York: Riverhead Books, 1999), xii–xiii.

18. *The American President*, "The Balance of Power," wysiwyg://epmain.149/http://www.pbs.org/wnet/amerpres/episode10.html. All future references to *The American President* will be to the this source (e.g., the video) unless otherwise noted.

19. Other scholars note that JFK's 1960 campaign as well as his presidency were shaped in large measure by a highly organized image-making campaign. See Hellmann, *The Kennedy Obsession*; and Bruce Miroff, *Icons of Democracy: American Leaders as Heroes, Aristocrats, Dissenters, and Democrats* (New York: Basic Books, 1993).

20. Burke equates the "scapegoat" as a "vessel of certain unwanted evils, the sacrificial animal upon whose back the burden of these evils is ritualistically loaded." See Burke, *The Philosophy of Literary Form: Studies in Symbolic Action* (Berkeley: University of California Press, 1973), 39–40. See also Joseph R. Gusfield, ed., *Kenneth Burke: On Symbols and Society* (Chicago: University of Chicago Press, 1989), 32–34.

21. Kenneth Burke, *A Grammar of Motives* (Berkeley: University of California Press, 1969), 406.

22. See Kenneth Burke, *The Rhetoric of Religion: Studies in Logology* (Berkeley and Los Angeles: University of California Press, 1970), 174–8.

23. W. J. T. Mitchell, *Picture Theory: Essays on Verbal and Visual Representation* (Chicago: University of Chicago Press, 1994), 95.

24. Mitchell Stephens, *the rise of the image the fall of the word* (New York: Oxford University Press, 1998), 103, 108–9, 125, 181, 187–8, 193–4. For more information on MTV's style of imaging, see Stephens, *the rise of the image*, 135.

25. Rick Altman, "Television/Sound." In *Studies in Entertainment: Critical Approaches to Mass Culture*, edited by Tania Modleski (Bloomington: Indiana University Press, 1986), 51.

26. James David Barber, *The Presidential Character: Predicting Performance in the White House*, 3rd ed. (Englewood Cliffs, NJ: Prentice-Hall, Inc., 1985), 4. See also Michael Nelson, "The Psychological Presidency," in *The Presidency and the Political System*, 5th ed., Michael Nelson (Washington, D.C.: CQ Press, 1998), 199–222; and Robert A. Wilson, ed., *Character Above All: Ten Presidents from FDR to George Bush* (New York: Simon & Schuster, 1995).

27. Gunther Kress and Theo van Leeuwen, *Reading Images: The Grammar of Visual Design* (London: Routledge, 2000), 81.

28. John Hartley, *The Politics of Pictures: The Creation of the Public in the Age of Popular Media* (London: Routledge, 1992), 3, 6.

29. Michael Griffin, "The Great War Photographs: Constructing Myths of History and Photojournalism," in *Picturing the Past: Media, History, and Photography*, edited by Bonnie Brennen and Hanno Hardt (Urbana: University of Illinois Press, 1999), 147.

30. Barbie Zelizer, *Covering the Body: The Kennedy Assassination, the Media, and the Shaping of Collective Memory* (Chicago: University of Chicago Press, 1992), 5.

31. Peter N. Carroll, *It Seemed Like Nothing Happened: America in the 1970s* (New Brunswick: Rutgers University Press, 2000), 21.

32. Burke details the relationship between metaphor and perspective. See Kenneth Burke, *Permanence and Change: An Anatomy of Purpose*, 3rd ed. (Berkeley: University of California Press, 1984), 89–96. See also, Burke, *A Grammar of Motives*, 503–5.

33. Barbara Maria Stafford, *Visual Analogy: Consciousness as the Art of Connecting* (Cambridge, MA: The MIT Press, 1999), 9. These explicit visual analogies substantiate Paul Messaris's theory that images "convey a message which would probably not go over at all well if it were made verbally." See Paul Messaris, "Visual 'Manipulation': Visual Means of Affecting Responses to Images," *Communication* 13 (1992): 191.

34. P. David Marshall, *Celebrity and Power: Fame in Contemporary Culture* (Minneapolis: University of Minnesota Press, 1997), 219, 225–26.

35. Kunhardt, Jr., Kunhardt III, and Kunhardt, "Preface," *The American President* (New York: Riverhead Books, 1999), vii–viii. At times, the visuals used in *The American President*'s video series replicated those used in *BIOrhythm*, especially relating to Clinton's childhood. The producers of both films undoubtedly relied on the same video bank.

36. John Ellis notes that "sound and image exist in relation to one another." See John Ellis, *Visible Fictions: Cinema, Television, Video* (London: Routledge, 1992), 129.

37. Joshua Meyrowitz, "Television and Interpersonal Behavior: Codes of Perception and Response," in *Inter/Media: Interpersonal Communication in a Media World*, edited by Gary Gumpert and Robert Cathcart (New York: Oxford University Press, 1982), 226, 230.

38. For a discussion of the use of close-up shots in the television news, see Shawn J. Parry-Giles, "Mediating Hillary Rodham Clinton: Television News Practices and Image-Making in the Postmodern Age," *Critical Studies in Media Communication* 17 (2000): 205–26.

39. Deborah Willis views photography as a connotation of "history and identity." See Deborah Willis, ed., "Preface," *Picturing Us: African American Identity in Photography* (New York: The New Press, 1994), xii. Roger Rosenblatt details the uniqueness of black and white photographs in his "Prologue" to P. F. Bentley's inside look at Bill Clinton's 1992 presidential campaign. See Roger Rosenblatt, "Prologue: In Black and White," in *Clinton: Portrait of Victory*, edited by P. F. Bentley (New York: Warner Books, 1993), 9–12.

40. Fred I. Greenstein perhaps jests (at least in part) that Bill Clinton's "political aspirations seem almost to have been incubated in the womb." See Fred I. Greenstein, *The Presidential Difference: Leadership Style from FDR to Clinton* (New York: Martin Kessler Books, 2000), 194.

41. Barber, *The Presidential Character*, 1–11.

42. Stephen Hess, *Presidents & the Presidency* (Washington, DC: The Brookings Institution, 1996), 138.

43. Such archetypal images serve as "proposition," Rudolf Arnheim, suggests, that make "a declaration about the nature of human existence," be it consciously or unconsciously. See Rudolf Arnheim, *Visual Thinking* (Berkeley: University of California Press, 1969), 296.

44. For examples of Kennedy's contributions to this archetype of presidential form, see "Kennedy and His Family in Pictures," *Look* (1963): n.p.; Evelyn Lincoln, "My Twelve Years with Kennedy," *The Saturday Evening Post* (1965, August 14): 23–27, 62–63; and Conover Hunt, *JFK: For a New Generation* (Dallas: The Sixth Floor Museum and Southern Methodist University Press, 1996).

45. Hellmann notes that "Kennedy carefully controlled the production of photographs to ensure that he was always presented as the character he had chosen to play." Bradley likewise argues that Clinton "consciously attempt[ed] to exploit the image of John F. Kennedy." Irving J. Rein contends that Clinton "was a star made for TV—prepared, polished, and potent." See Bradley, *American Political Mythology*, 170; Hellmann, *The Kennedy Obsession*, 132; and Irving J. Rein, "Imagining the Image," in *Bill Clinton on Stump, State, and Stage: The Rhetorical Road to the White House*, edited by Stephen A. Smith (Fayetteville: University of Arkansas Press, 1994): 192.

46. Joshua Meyrowitz, "New Sense of Politics: How Television Changes the Political Drama," *Research in Political Sociology* 7 (1995): 122.

47. Rosenblatt, "Prologue," 10.

48. See M. M. Bakhtin, *Speech Genres and Other Late Essays*, trans. (Austin: University of Texas Press, 1986), 60–102. See also Gary Saul Morson and Caryl Emerson, *Mikhail Bakhtin: Creation of a Prosaics* (Stanford, CA: Stanford University Press, 1990), 89, 295–97.

49. Nancy Martha West, *Kodak and the Lens of Nostalgia* (Charlottesville: University Press of Virginia, 2000), 10–11, emphasis added.

50. Stephens, *the rise of the image*, 181.

51. Other scholars like Philip Abbott contend in a manner similar to *The American President* that "later presidents draw strength and support from their predecessors"—a "major ritual of American political culture." See Philip Abbott, *Strong Presidents: A Theory of Leadership* (Knoxville: University of Tennessee Press, 1996), 1.

52. Bradley, *American Political Mythology*, 170.

53. The most widely circulated polls taken during the 1998 and 1999 impeachment process are available at *Hotline*, http://www.nationaljournal.com.

54. Susan Schmidt and Michael Weisskopf, *Truth at Any Cost: Ken Starr and the Unmaking of Bill Clinton* (New York: HarperCollins Publishers, 2000), 93.

55. Burke, *A Rhetoric of Motives*, 140.

56. See Miller's discussion of the ambivalence over the role that the 1960s plays within our popular memory. Miller, *The Seventies Now*, 1–6.

57. Mitchell, *Iconology*, 4.

Afterword

Postmodern Presidentiality and the Future of Image Politics

Bill Clinton was, if nothing else, a memorable and enduring president. Even after the inauguration of his predecessor, the media and the larger public continued to discuss Clinton at length, debating the merits of his presidential pardons, his role in the 2000 election campaign, the location of his post-presidential office, and the lucrative advance he received for his memoirs. The Bush administration routinely positions their actions and policies against Clinton's and blames many of the country's lingering problems on him and his administration. Even Al Gore wrestles with the Clinton legacy as he ponders his political options for 2004.

Why does this particular president linger on the U.S. political scene? What is it about Bill Clinton that continually motivates attention and invites such polarized reactions when other presidents fade quickly from view upon leaving office? Perhaps it is the enticing, often contradictory, but always intriguing, constructions of his personal and political image. Those images dominated U.S. political discourse for the better part of a decade, and Clinton brought political image construction to the foreground in ways that other presidents have not. Indeed, the images of Bill Clinton that commanded public attention during the 1990s and beyond were in many ways unprecedented in U.S. political history in both their range and their scope. Those powerful images are hard to forget and even harder to abandon.

Of course, political leaders have always been concerned with their projected images.[1] Andrew Jackson penned the first campaign biography in 1832, convincing voters that he was a Cincinnatus who would not seek but would reluctantly accept the presidency if pressed into service.[2] The U.S. political system has always packaged its presidents; William Henry Harrison was a war hero with "log-cabin" roots, Abraham Lincoln the backwoods rail-splitter, Theodore Roosevelt the Rough Riding war hero, and Jimmy Carter the simple southern peanut farmer. Constructed images of presidents, whatever their source, become critical in the demarcation and evolving articulation of a presidentiality that defines the presidency and the people who occupy the office. Such depictions also reveal how there really is no meaningful distinction between image and "reality" for the U.S. political culture, and how, at bottom, U.S. presidents are the personification of hyperreality.

Bill Clinton emerged out of this political history. His hyperreal presidency offers a compelling lens through which we can assess the nature of presidentiality in contemporary U.S. politics. In part, Clinton's presidency is meaningful and intriguing because it occurred at a pivotal moment in U.S. political life. The nation's economy was shifting and its place in the world was altered. In the post–Cold War era, enduring moral foundations were challenged and conceptions of personal identity and conduct were evolving in a myriad of directions. Old paradigms no longer dominated, and new technologies took hold of an increasingly fragmented U.S. public. Any president during such times of meaningful and profound change becomes significant to the understanding of that change and the nation it affects.

But Clinton's presidency was also critical for what it reveals about the evolution of presidentiality—the rhetorical means by which the culture enacts and performs its construction of the nation's chief executive. Attending to Clinton's images also offers lessons about the state of presidential politics in the postmodern United States. We use our reading of Clinton's constructed images and the presidentialities enacted by those images to suggest five basic axioms about the nature of postmodern presidential politics.

The Visuality of Postmodern Presidential Politics Exacerbates the Hyperreal

When Horatio Greenough sought to capture the character and persona of George Washington in stone, he chose to depict the first president as a Greek god sitting on an Olympian throne. Since those initial renditions of our first president, the U.S. political culture has continually fixated on the *visual* likenesses of its chief executives. Indeed, the presidentialities of postmodern life are reliant on visual rhetorics of image construction and manipulation. Cartoonists and caricaturists satirize presidents visually, exaggerating their flaws and highlighting their weaknesses. Presidents pose for countless portraits and statues and are photographed and filmed wherever they go, creating a powerful visual repository of collective memory that defines the presidency and the men who occupy the office. And our presidents seek more and more control over their visual depiction, recognizing, as they always have, the immense power of the visual in the construction and maintenance of political image.[3]

Postmodern presidential politics, though, emphasizes and exploits the visual focus of presidentiality and the power of presidential image-making. Visual images of presidents reflect the highly mediated constructions of presidentiality in the postmodern era. Sometimes those images are generated by campaigns and administrations to put forth a positive and electorally appealing image to garner votes and political support.[4] Often, political opponents or news media sources manufacture those images to reveal an unflattering dimension of a president's persona.

The proliferation of such visual images, more than anything else, manifests the inherent hyperreality of contemporary presidential politics. Voters cannot discern the difference between image and reality, because there is no difference between image and reality. Past presidential images were also hyperreal, but the technology of today's political imaging and the blurring of genre and form to achieve political and electoral success amplifies the hyperreality of postmodern presidential image-making with potentially serious consequences for the U.S. democratic system.

On one level, the hyperreality of visual imaging in contemporary political life invites voters to the mistaken conclusion that what they see and what is reported via the news media is truer because of its visual depiction.[5] The technologies of political communication practices in the postmodern age capitalize on the perception of visual truth; political communicators exploit that perception for political reasons. When voters see, for instance, the same image of Bill Clinton embracing Monica Lewinsky over and over again, that visual image reflects the "truth" of this relationship, metonymically symbolizing all that voters are told by the news media. Or when camera angles and close-ups beckon voters into the private and personal realms of a candidate's life, as they did in *The Man from Hope*, the discourse asks them to trust and believe the presented biographical information. The camera becomes, thus, the barometer of truth and character.

Ultimately, the decidedly visual nature of postmodern presidential politics may mask the constructed quality of constructed presidential personas. Nowhere was this more evident than in the Clinton campaign's skilled use of meta-imaging in *The War Room*. Through visual depiction, clever examples of image construction were presented in ways that suggested verisimilitude and invited judgments of believability from voters. The constructed quality of such texts are ignored and hidden from view as the discourse taps into and borrows from other genres that possess high levels of credibility. As political commercials mirror visually the form of newscasts, or campaign films resemble documentaries, voters are asked to trust the truth value of such highly crafted displays.

The increased visual sophistication of presidential imaging is likely to continue as candidates and presidents explore new technologies and seek new ways to appeal to broader groups of voters. No longer will constituencies only be unified by interest or geography or ethnicity. Instead, they will also achieve identity as citizens from the visual images offered for their consumption. And voters, being the scopophiliac persons that they are, respond to visual imaging with confidence and familiarity, trusting in the power of the gaze to provide knowledge, pleasure, and understanding. At the same time, these same voters grow increasingly suspicious of political imaging and the manipulation of emotion through visual pleasantries and constructions.

Because political candidates and presidents strive for control of the all-important visual images, the adversarial relationship between those who practice politics and those who write news is magnified. At the same time, political leaders depend on the news media for the presentation of their visual images to a larger public, enhancing their already symbiotic relationship. Journalists willingly allowed the Clinton campaign control over access to campaign operations and gladly used such access for commercial and reputational success, as in *The War Room*. Yet, these same journalists often condemned the Clintons for manufacturing images for public consumption. And the two Clinton campaigns and the president's White House press office were happy to use the media as image disseminators yet plead an invasion of privacy if the journalists came too close to the unsavory and unflattering.[6] Managing the complexities of the politics/journalism relationship, therefore, is increasingly difficult for both parties as media outlets proliferate and candidates/presidents become more sophisticated in their image-making strategies.[7] In the end, voters become suspicious of both politicians and journalists, wondering continually what to believe and who to trust.[8]

"Americans are no keener," Jean Baudrillard observed during the Reagan years, "than anyone else today to think about whether they believe in the merits of their leaders, *or even in the reality of power.*" Instead, these same Americans accept the view that "governing today means giving acceptable signs of credibility."[9] These "acceptable signs of credibility" are increasingly visual, and political leaders and presidents in the United States must adapt to the expanding sophistication of audiences who are schooled in consuming visual images discerningly. These voters are aware that such images can distort and manipulate. They are keenly conscious of the deployment of emotion through visual imagery and they are trapped in a political system where visual images are both trustworthy and suspicious. The result, for postmodern U.S. presidents, is an increasingly complex negotiation of symbolism, visual imagery, and institutional ethos. That negotiation process occurs at a time when powerful paradigms governing the communicative relationships among voters, presidents, and the news media are shifting. At bottom, both voters and presidents have come to know that seeing is no longer believing, that visual images are controlling political discourse, and that a successful postmodern presidentiality is as much about appealing to the eye as it is informing and enlightening the mind.

Postmodern Presidential Politics Redefines Traditional Image Expectations

Bill Clinton was the "first" on many measures—the first president from Arkansas, the first "baby-boomer" president, the first Democrat reelected to second term since FDR, and the first elected president tried for impeachment. Toni Morrison designated Clinton America's first "black" president, while Tyler Curtain hailed him as America's first "queer" president because of his sexual behaviors and fondness for Walt Whitman.[10] Each of these designations represents how Clinton complicated the prevailing images of the U.S. presidency. In this sense, he epitomized the tendency of postmodern presidential politics to reshape the traditional image expectations of the institution and to rewrite a new presidentiality for the U.S. community. This reshaping occurs on both a textual and an ideological level.

Textually, image discourses are more complicated and more visually intrusive in this postmodern age. Cameras and microphones transport contemporary viewers of such texts to new places. In the case of *The War Room*, *Primary Colors*, and *BIOrhythm*, at least, viewers are taken "behind-the-scenes" and into the backstage realm of politics with increasing frequency and intensity. Such texts invert traditional campaign images that largely viewed campaigns from the outside in. Now, images show us the inside out version of the campaign experience and, in the process, redefine both the ways that campaigns function and the histories that we tell about campaigning and politics.

As viewers are taken into the intimate, backstage regions of politics, they are further invited to believe that what they see is the reality of political experience. These viewers find themselves watching political actors in previously private sites—hotel rooms, debate spin rooms, campaign headquarters ("war rooms")—and they are asked to suppose that the discourse and events they witness are authentic. Lost in these texts, and masked by their presentational styles, is their strategic value for campaigns and candidates. As we have demonstrated, campaigns reap tactical benefits on political and ideological levels by engaging in meta-imaging, or by controlling the images of the images that define their campaign. Postmodern presidential politics, thus, is increasingly becoming a politics ordered by illusory intimacy and hyperreal knowledge of the private, hidden world of political life and behavior.

Within particular image texts, camera placement and perspective have tremendous impact on the presidentiality put forth for the citizen-voter. The talking head of yesterday's political interview has become the talking face of today's postmodern imaging, as producers of political image texts take us closer and closer to political leaders. In so doing, these texts beckon voters directly into the political text to interrogate the veracity of the political leader. The camera's extreme close-up speaks to the media's attempt to penetrate the private world of politics, much as *BIOrhythm* and *The American President* worked visually to take us as close to Bill Clinton as possible. Clinton embraced this video grammar, moreover, as he used intense close-ups as markers of his trustworthiness and character in *The Man from Hope* and the 1996 campaign film.

There are also ideological challenges to presidential imaging manifested in the construction of Bill Clinton. As evidenced in *The Man from Hope*, contemporary campaign imaging requires candidates who are more feminized and better able to project a sincere sense of self to a large television audience. Eroded are the interpersonal distances that are reflective of historical images of presidentiality in this new postmodern time, and candidates and presidents are forced to adjust. Unwilling to abandon the masculine totally, politicians, like Clinton, develop new skills and craft new images that appear feminized, or more intimate and personal. Those same images rely on masculine touchstones and ideologically limit the power of the image to create a meaningfully feminine/feminist political discourse. In this way, postmodern presidentialities are in a state of negotiation, managing the competing demands of a historical image of the presidency with the expectations of audiences attuned to television and its grammars of political discourse.

Postmodern presidents also face more layers of image construction than existed in less media-saturated times. Bill Clinton contended with his political images as constructed in fictional works, on a variety of television networks, and through numerous new media, from talk radio to tabloid television. Presidential images are found in stand-up comedy, literature, and film. Of course, as Murray Edelman remarks, "works of art may bring new ways of seeing and understanding."[11] The impact of an expansion of presidentialities provides new opportunities for construction and rhetorical definition of the institution and the people who occupy it. The sheer range and volume of image constructions of presidents, and Clinton in particular, point to the resulting interrogation of presidential image in this postmodern environment. Whether it is the demand for a more feminized persona, higher levels of personal intimacy and private revelation, or the exploitation of history and memory for political purposes, the presidential office and its image for U.S. democracy are undergoing profound changes.

Among Bill Clinton's many "firsts" was his status as the first president to engage citizens in an online discussion; the advent of new communication and computer technologies promises even further change in presidential imaging for the postmodern age. The exploitation of a new medium or technology becomes a marker of the time even though it may take years to realize the power of the medium on presidential leadership. While Warren Harding was the first president to speak over the radio, it was not until FDR that the power of that medium for presidential leadership purposes was realized. Harry Truman was the first president to speak on television, but it took JFK to demonstrate the extent of television's influence on presidential imaging. Similarly, though Clinton was the first chief executive to make use of the Internet and new media technologies, the impact of such technologies on the construction of presidential image may not be known for some time. Campaign organizations, political entities, and other public interest groups are only now discovering the power of the Internet to communicate and proliferate messages to wider, worldwide publics. Nonetheless, the interrogation of presidential image that is supremely evident in Bill Clinton's televisual constructions will only continue as new media and technological change alter and challenge defined understandings of the U.S. presidency.

Postmodern Presidential Politics Both Fragments and Unifies the U.S. Public

A prominent cliché of U.S. political life is that the public is fragmented and thus disconnected from civic life.[12] Citizens do not vote, they lack knowledge and understanding about political matters, are motivated by images and entertainment rather than serious policy discussions, and are ultimately self-absorbed, according to this view of U.S. political culture. These various behaviors and attitudes are evidence for scholars and political commentators of the decline of U.S. democratic life.[13]

There are several scapegoats for the fragmentation of U.S. political life. There are the citizens themselves, who, the critique suggests, are generally unable to see beyond their own selfish needs and desires. The news media are also complicit, this criticism maintains, because it panders to the public's cravings for entertainment in the search for ever-increasing ratings and advertising revenues. Political leaders fail to uphold their civic duty. These same leaders frequently employ political consultants who shame and defame the noble experiment of U.S. democracy through targeting, attacking, and polling. Each of these factors, say the harbingers of this decline in U.S. civic life, influences in some way the fragmentation of a society that deserves unity and active political participation.

This critique is a bit too easy in the complicated, image-saturated politics of postmodern U.S. culture. It ignores or simplifies the complexities of political life. And it reduces political behaviors and attitudes to the barest markers of political engagement. Bill Clinton's constructed images illuminate a more complicated vision of the fragmented U.S. political culture, particularly as that culture is oriented around specific rhetorics of presidentiality.

On one level, the constructed image of Bill Clinton manifested the fragmented nature of U.S. political life, and it speaks to the power of postmodern presidential politics to magnify and intensify such fragmentation. Certainly, Clinton elicited passionate reactions from both supporters and detractors. In their coverage of Clinton, the news media regularly segmented the public not according to their support for Clinton per se, but as demographic groups that favored or opposed Clinton as a result of identity. Women, thus, were largely pro-Clinton, the journalists said, because, as women, they agreed with his pro-choice positions and his general support of "family" issues. African Americans supported Clinton wholeheartedly while "whites" were mixed in their assessment, and so on.[14] Clinton became as a result not a cause of fragmentation, but a reification of fragmentations already present in U.S. society.

Given this predilection to order the public around favorability or opposition to Clinton, it is hardly surprising that his image was also defined by dualities or tensions at play in U.S. politics. Commentators and pundits routinely defined Clinton by reference to the "gender gap" or noted his unprecedented support among African Americans. These tendencies seeped into other image texts wherein Clinton is defined in important ways according to race and sex in sources like *Primary Colors*. Moreover, his self-constructed images played on these dualities, as in the references to Martin Luther King and the civil rights movement in *The Man from Hope*. The constructions of Bill Clinton's image, thus, addressed the fragmentations that characterize U.S. political life, speaking to the ways that presidentialities are implicated in the constitutive definition of political culture.

As such, the postmodern presidency may simply be a reflection of an inherent disconnectedness of U.S. culture. It intensifies a force and dimension of U.S. political life that has existed since the founding of the nation and that will not likely diminish, especially as the country becomes more diverse and polyvalent.

Moreover, this fragmentation may not signal an erosion of public life in the United States at all. In response to Putnam's thesis about the decline of social capital in contemporary America, Michael Schudson observes, "civic participation now takes place everywhere," existing in the "microprocesses of social life."[15] Put another way, it may be that civic life has not declined precipitously as feared, but rather has simply changed as a result of several factors—the mass media, higher levels of literacy, the erosion of political parties, sociological and economic realities, etc. Citizens engage in other forms and types of social interaction and civic involvement. They may no longer go to the YMCA, or to PTA meetings, and they may not find social interaction any longer in bowling leagues. Instead, they talk about politics at work, or in an Internet chat room and they interact with others at the fitness center, or via cell phone on a conference call. And the civic life of the nation is not in decline or on the verge of disappearance; it is simply transforming, as it has before, to another phase in its development. Often at the center of that evolution is the postmodern presidency that continues to put forth new and challenging presidentialities that are reflective of the time and meaningful as a constitutive force for the U.S. community.

Indeed, the case of Bill Clinton's constructed image speaks to the power of postmodern presidentialities to also unify a fragmented political culture. Few events in U.S. history were as polarizing and fragmenting as the impeachment of Bill Clinton. Yet the constructed images that defined those events frequently empowered the collective public and defined it as the redemptive agent in the 1998 drama unfolding in Washington. Both *BIOrhythm* and *The American President*, coming as they did from vastly different perspectives and sources, offered this interpretation of the impeachment trial. Above all of the bickering and partisanship that created the impeachment conflict, these texts suggested, was the transcendent American people, poised to rescue the sinner (Clinton) from the agents of his persecution (the Republicans; Kenneth Starr) and at the same time preserve the presidency as a critical institution of U.S. self-government.

Rather than simply assume that contemporary political culture and the larger public is fragmented and hopelessly disconnected from political life, we would do better to explore the means and texts that work to fragment and/or unite the public. In a postmodern time, when assumptions and presuppositions are questioned and challenged, the image texts of contemporary politics are critical in their ability to define and shape public culture. Indeed, in the wake of the terrorist attacks of September 11, 2001, the critical scrutiny of postmodern presidentialities as they create symbolic structures of nationalism and patriotism acquires even greater urgency and significance. Assumptions of fragmentation encourage scholars to miss the nuances and subtleties of political culture that in many ways resist fragmentation and provide citizens and voters with a powerful sense of unity and coherence.

Postmodern Presidential Politics Erodes the Connection Between Individual Presidents and the Institution of the Presidency

Though frequently underappreciated in narratives of presidential history, William McKinley ushered in a new presidentiality during his time in office at the dawn of the twentieth century. Put simply, it was McKinley who began the process of conjoining the presidency with the individual who occupied the office. The campaign of 1896 was unique, as McKinley's campaign made extensive, if unprecedented, use of campaign advertising and consultancy, with Mark Hanna directing the pilgrimages to Canton, Ohio, of voters and GOP dignitaries. McKinley's opponent, William Jennings Bryan, conversely also altered campaign practice by traveling around the country, giving speeches and asking for votes. McKinley later broke with nineteenth-century custom and defined his victory in 1896 as a popular mandate, or, as he said in his First Inaugural Address, as "the commanding verdict of the people."[16] McKinley began the process of increased presidential oratory and rhetoric as well, and he intensified presidential relations with the press.[17] Gunned down in 1901, McKinley was succeeded, of course, by Theodore Roosevelt, a president who viewed the presidency as his own "bully pulpit," and who furthered the fusion of president and the presidency that began with McKinley and that characterized much of the twentieth century.

Like William McKinley and Theodore Roosevelt, Bill Clinton was also an important and transitional figure in U.S. presidential history. Clinton's presidency may signal the eroding connection between individual presidents and the institution of the presidency. Indeed, a characteristic of postmodern presidential politics is the invitation to see presidents as individuals and as fleeting occupants of an office rather than as embodiments of the essence and legacy of the American government. There are several reasons for this development.

First, many twentieth century presidents were fused with the institution itself as a function of the challenges they faced and their powerful rhetorical constructions of the presidential role. Theodore Roosevelt created an imperial presidency with his trips abroad, his exertion of U.S. military might, and his robust personality. Woodrow Wilson represented the U.S. commitment to end the Great War; the greeting of his arrival in Europe to negotiate peace was unrivaled. He embodied the United States for the rest of the world in ways no other president had. Similarly, the consolidation of federal power with the executive branch during the Great Depression and World War II allowed for the fusion of the presidency as an institution with the persona of Franklin D. Roosevelt. It also helped that he served in the office longer than any other American. The Cold War and the accompanying fear of nuclear annihilation gave the president, whomever he was, the designation as "leader of the free world," and endowed him with a status and reach far beyond the parameters established in the Constitution and characteristic of U.S. government for most of its history.

But in the later decades of the twentieth century, presidential challenges changed and became more diffuse; public faith in an imperial presidency diminished. The need to embody the nation and the government in one individual declined.[18] In addition, other entities of government (Congress, the courts, local governments) began to perform more and critical governmental functions. The tripartite scheme of the Constitution was restored somewhat as Congress challenged presidential actions and investigated presidential behaviors constantly and the courts invalidated executive actions as unconstitutional. In part, this reassertion of congressional and legal authority occurred in response to presidential misbehaviors—LBJ's ill-begotten efforts in Vietnam and, most notably, Richard Nixon's abuse of executive power and privilege during Watergate. The imperious presidency of the Cold War was gone with the collapse of the Soviet Union and in the wake of presidential scandals. The subsequent reordering of U.S. political life and postmodern presidential politics disrupted the notion that presidents stood in for and embodied the nation.

A second reason for the decline of presidential embodiment is the disappearance of any public/private distinction in the mass media's coverage of the presidency. For much of the twentieth century, most Americans only saw their presidents as presidents, performing executive functions and acting presidential. There was a zone of privacy surrounding presidents and their families, adding to the aura of executive control and imperiousness. Certainly personal or private information would occasionally surface and may become fodder in campaign coverage. But the level of coverage devoted to "private" matters in the late twentieth century was largely unprecedented.

As more and more private and personal information about presidents becomes public, citizens are able to see these individuals as men with flaws and problems painfully similar to their own. In this way, such coverage fulfills what John B. Thompson identifies as the "subversion theory" of scandal, where the news coverage assaults the established norms of traditional journalism and exposes the underbelly of political life and power.[19] The result is the disruption of conventional presidentialities that fuse together the individual occupant of the office with the office itself. Rather, as we see the individual presidents with all of their flaws, they become individuals who are separate from the office they occupy temporarily.

All presidents, and Bill Clinton in particular, are swept up in the new cultural grammars of celebrity.[20] Those grammars necessitate both a public persona performing roles and expectations of a given position and a private persona revealed in the public dissemination of behaviors and conduct normally kept away from public scrutiny. Clinton tried to manage the private to suit his public, political purposes, with differing degrees of success. But Clinton was also the victim, of sorts, of a new presidentiality that makes the private dimensions of a president's behavior completely public. In this postmodern time, Lincoln's depressions, FDR's handicap, JFK's philandering, and LBJ's many idiosyncrasies would all be the stuff of talk and chatter on CNN and MSNBC, not hidden from view awaiting the diligent exposition of some future historian.

The increasing cultural preoccupation with previously private matters may explain, in part, how Bill Clinton was able to maintain high levels of support for his performance as president even as the most unsavory and scandalous dimensions of his personal life were widely reported. For much of the Clinton presidency, the personal and the private were grist for news, beginning with revelations about Gennifer Flowers and continuing to the end of his term. Our images of Bill Clinton were inseparable from the "behind-the-scenes" renditions of this president complete with glimpses of the "private" Bill Clinton.

Thanks to these new cultural grammars, we learned about Clinton's sexual life, personal habits, physicality, and personality. Clinton lost control of the discussion of the "private," leading to the decline in his personal popularity among many citizens who came to see him as immoral and personally corrupt. But Clinton also benefited from these new grammars. Americans judged him as an individual separate from his performance as a president, yielding a somewhat bipolar reaction to Clinton among polled Americans during the impeachment crisis of 1998. As our reading of *BIOrhythm* and *The American President* suggest, this separation of Clinton the man from Clinton the president created the conditions for Clinton's redemption and the not guilty verdict rendered by the Senate in his impeachment trial.

In addition, the impeachment trial of Bill Clinton and its accompanying images of this president proved, once again, the general fortitude of the presidency as an institution. Postmodern presidentialities reassure the political culture of its institutional stability in this way, such that by separating the individual from the office, the office survives the individual's frailties and faults. The symbolic constructions of the Vietnam War, Watergate, and the Clinton scandals allow for the maintenance of public faith in the institutional security of government.

These presidentialities tell us, complete with their powerful nostalgia for past presidents, that the presidency is the repository of public myth and expectations, not the flawed men who sit in the Oval Office.

Bill Clinton was our era's William McKinley and Theodore Roosevelt—a president who transitionally represented a new presidentiality, a new rhetoric for understanding how the presidency works and how the United States views and assesses its presidents. This new postmodern presidency will be more exposed and more consistent with the original constitutional framework of three, coequal, co-powerful branches of federal government. The postmodern spectacle of the presidency will be less grand, more human, and considerably more personal. And like McKinley and Roosevelt were to the imperial presidency of the twentieth century, so Bill Clinton will be to the postmodern presidency of the twenty-first century—the beginning of a new and radically different way of seeing and defining presidentiality.

Postmodern Presidential Politics Increases the Rhetorical and Image Demands Faced by Candidates and Presidents

As we have suggested, postmodern presidential politics is substantially different from presidential politics as practiced thus far in U.S. history. Such politics are hyperreal, more visual, more fragmenting of the U.S. public and more empowering of their voice, more likely to challenge existing conceptions of presidential leadership, and more likely to separate individual presidents from the institution itself. The spectacle of presidential leadership in this postmodern time thus significantly alters the political landscape in the United States and confronts existing realities in ways unusual for the U.S. polity. Bill Clinton was an early marker and a meaningful harbinger of these changes in the presidentialities that are so powerfully constitutive of U.S. political life.

Ultimately, what postmodern presidential politics means is that on several different levels, the rhetorical and image demands placed upon presidents will intensify. From the very outset of a presidential campaign to the final days in office, presidents will forever, in ways unheard of in U.S. history, be forced to attend to their rhetoric and their public image. Already, the sheer number of rhetorical occasions for presidents is on the rise. Harry Truman gave only 88 speeches and Ronald Reagan spoke only 320 times in a typical year. Bill Clinton spoke in public, on average, 550 times a year. Presidents are compelled by the increasing demands of their work, the ubiquity of news coverage, and the expectations of their office to speak publicly at increasing levels.[21] In addition, presidents are expected to speak well and with some measure of coherence. One of the early concerns about President George W. Bush, significantly, is his ability, or inability, at the art of public communication. In this time of a "highly personalized" presidency, Fred I. Greenstein concludes, presidents must be skilled at public communication as a critical marker of what he terms the "presidential difference."[22]

But these demands are so much deeper than simply higher expectations for the frequency and quality of presidential speechmaking. Postmodern presidential politics requires that contemporary presidents attend to their images constantly. They must manage the impressions of their past history and must project an image of future leadership more complicated than any of their predecessors. These images are the reality of U.S. political culture; everything in the postmodern political environment is fair game. Relationships from youth, indiscretions of all and any kind, and mistakes of even the smallest magnitude are legitimate topics of news and publicity in the postmodern political world. Some candidates and presidents may equivocate or minimize their past while others may tackle these issues directly, but they are nonetheless new demands on contemporary presidents. That which was private is no longer such, and the intensely new publicity of postmodern presidential politics makes managing images even more complicated.

On an even deeper level, existing paradigms of presidential leadership and expectations of presidential image are changing in this postmodern time, demanding of candidates and presidents higher levels of image flexibility and dexterity. Presidents must still project masculinity and conventional images of strength and power, but they must also appear feminine in their levels of self-disclosure and their capacity to identify with increasingly diverse audiences. Where once presidents could simply appeal to sectional groups or easily defined political aggregates, the postmodern president must grapple with an increasingly diverse and constantly morphing society where nothing is black or white anymore. On many competing dimensions, the imaging demands of postmodern presidential politics are multiplying and shifting in new and exciting ways.

If Bill Clinton's experience is any indication, and we believe that it is, then future presidential candidates and future presidents will face increasingly challenging and difficult image demands. But postmodern presidential politics has serious consequences for the voters who make up the audiences to whom such images are addressed. Fundamentally, the hyperreality that is so characteristic of all presidential image-making will only intensify and expand. As the images of presidents proliferate, the impossibility of discerning any sense of reality or truth behind such images will increase.

This may not be a bad thing. Intensified hyperreality may engender a healthy skepticism, further eroding presidential powers that, in the twentieth century, expanded far beyond their constitutional parameters. Contemporary voters do and will continue to see their leadership as a function of image construction, rather than as something else, something more noble and sacrosanct. Such increased skepticism may reflect a maturation of the U.S. political culture to challenge presidential images and motives. In so doing, the overextended idolatry commonly invested in the presidency and individual presidents may lessen, thus investing in the public a greater responsibility for the success of the U.S. democratic experiment.

So it was with Bill Clinton. The public constructed their own hyperreal Bill Clinton from all of the images they consumed of this political figure. He was not, for them, the savior of the Democratic Party who came back from so much hardship and trial to "feel the pain" of the suffering U.S. voter. He was not a reincarnation of Theodore Roosevelt, personifying the "bridge to the twenty-first century." He was not the evil interloper from the backwoods of Arkansas who brought corruption and slime with him to Washington, robbing the presidency of all its honor and dignity.

Instead, Bill Clinton was a man who was flawed, who was charismatic, who expressed empathy and pain, and who felt deeply. Bill Clinton was someone who was a generally successful president, undeserving of impeachment, but fully deserving of scorn and condemnation. He was, thus, an amalgam of images reflective of the many layers of contemporary political culture—a hyperreal creation molded from competing characters and biographies that represented a new, postmodern form of presidential politics.

Notes

1. A discussion of the imaging of political leaders beginning with medieval kings is offered by John B. Thompson, *Political Scandal: Power and Visibility in the Media Age* (London: Polity, 2000).

2. Joanne Morreale, *The Presidential Campaign Film: A Critical History* (Westport, CT: Praeger, 1993), 3, 10. Jackson's supporters also made use of "hickory sticks" that appeared nationwide to signal support for their candidate, and eight years later in the 1840 campaign organized construction of political image reached a new level in the construction of William Henry Harrison. For discussions of the 1840 campaign, see Robert Gray Gunderson, *The Log-Cabin Campaign* (Lexington: University Press of Kentucky, 1957); and Kathleen Hall Jamieson, *Packaging the Presidency: A History and Criticism of Presidential Campaign Advertising*, 3rd ed. (New York: Oxford University Press, 1996).

3. The classic case of controlling visual image, of course, is Franklin D. Roosevelt's prohibition of photographs displaying him in a wheelchair. See Richard W. Waterman, Robert Wright, and Gilbert St. Clair, *The Image-Is-Everything Presidency: Dilemmas in American Leadership* (Boulder, CO: Westview, 1999), 38–9. There is also evidence that Lyndon Johnson used images of himself as a propaganda weapon during the Vietnam conflict. See Fitzhugh Green, *American Propaganda Abroad* (New York: Hippocrene Books, 1988), 38.

4. Consider the two collections of Clinton photography. Upon his inauguration, a volume appeared featuring the black-and-white photography of *Time* photographer P. F. Bentley, and just before Clinton's departure from office, another volume was published with still more black-and-white photography of the Clinton years in the White House. It is almost as if along with an inaugural address at the beginning and a farewell address at the end, presidential terms are also defined by the photographic collections published about them. See P. F. Bentley, *Clinton: Portrait of Victory* (New York: Warner Books, 1993); and *The Clinton Years: The Photographs of Robert McNeely* (New York: Callaway, 2000). Of course, the fact that both volumes use black-and-white photography adds *gravitas* and mystery to the images and taps into powerful, Kennedyesque genre memories of presidential still photography. This is discussed more fully in Chapter 5.

5. The illusory capacity of televisual depictions of politics is the basis for Roderick P. Hart's call for a political New Puritanism. See Roderick P. Hart, *Seducing America: How Television Charms the Modern Voter* (New York: Oxford University Press, 1994).

6. Howard Kurtz simplifies the complex homeostatic relationship between journalists and the Clinton White House in his analysis of Clinton's "propaganda machine." From Kurtz's perspective, as a journalist, the news media was in no way complicit

in the creation and framing of news in the Clinton White House. Sadly, this "anti-politics" polemic achieved some level of credibility in defining how the Clinton White House managed communication with the public. See Howard Kurtz, *Spin Cycle: Inside the Clinton Propaganda Machine* (New York: Free Press, 1998). For a more balanced view from the "inside," see Michael Waldman, *POTUS Speaks: Finding the Words That Defined the Clinton Presidency* (New York: Simon & Schuster, 2000).

7. This tense relationship played out in the early days of the first Clinton term, when the president sought to circumvent official Washington by appealing directly to the public and by presenting them with highly visual images promoting the administration's policies. The strategy failed, of course, leading to, among other things, the doomed 1994 health care plan and Republican victories in the 1994 off-year elections. See Edwin Diamond and Robert A. Silverman, *White House to Your House: Media and Politics in Virtual America* (Cambridge, MA: MIT Press, 1997), 49–74.

8. There is also a technological dimension to the distortive capacities of image-based politics. Mitchell Stephens demonstrates how one of the aspects of increasingly technologized communication is the power to distort visual imagery. See Mitchell Stephens, *the rise of the image the fall of the word* (New York: Oxford University Press, 1998).

9. Jean Baudrillard, *America*, translated by Chris Turner (London: Verso, 1989), 108–9, emphasis added.

10. Dana D. Nelson and Tyler Curtain, "The Symbolics of Presidentialism: Sex and Democratic Identification," in *Our Monica, Ourselves: The Clinton Affair and the National Interest*, edited by Lauren Berlant and Lisa Duggan (New York: New York University Press, 2001), 41.

11. Murray Edelman, *From Art to Politics: How Artistic Creations Shape Political Conceptions* (Chicago: University of Chicago Press, 1995), 63.

12. Perhaps the most famous of the various scholars and commentators who advance this claim is Robert Putnam. His *Bowling Alone* project amasses a large array of data to demonstrate that, according to some measures of interconnectedness, Americans are less civic minded than in previous times. See Robert Putnam, *Bowling Alone: The Collapse and Revival of American Community* (New York: Simon & Schuster, 2000). Joseph Turow locates this fragmentation in the powerful discourses of advertising. See Joseph Turow, *Breaking Up America: Advertisers and the New Media World* (Chicago: University of Chicago Press, 1997).

13. An interesting analysis of this and other indictments of political communication and contemporary political culture is offered in Erik P. Bucy and Paul D'Angelo, "The

Crisis of Political Communication: Normative Critiques of News and Democratic Processes," *Communication Yearbook* 22 (1999): 301–39.

14. A compelling examination of African American support for Bill Clinton is found in Hanes Walton, Jr., *Reelection: William Jefferson Clinton as a Native-Son Presidential Candidate* (New York: Columbia University Press, 2000).

15. Michael Schudson, *The Good Citizen: A History of American Civic Life* (Cambridge, MA: Harvard University Press, 1999), 298.

16. Davis Newton Lott, ed., *The Presidents Speak: The Inaugural Addresses of the American Presidents, from Washington to Clinton* (New York: Henry Holt, 1994), 200.

17. For discussions of McKinley's transitional impact on the presidency, see Gerald Gamm and Renée M. Smith, "Presidents, Parties, and the Public: Evolving Patterns of Interaction, 1877–1929," in *Speaking to the People: The Rhetorical Presidency in Historical Perspective*, edited by Richard J. Ellis (Amherst: University of Massachusetts Press, 1998), 95–7; Samuel Kernell, *Going Public: New Strategies of Presidential Leadership*, 3rd ed. (Washington: CQ Press, 1997), 73–4; and Jeffrey K. Tulis, *The Rhetorical Presidency* (Princeton: Princeton University Press, 1987).

18. This may change, of course, in the future. As we write, the events of September 11, 2001, in New York City and at the Pentagon are still new, and the impact of these events on the presidency, as articulated by George W. Bush, is still uncertain. If, in fact, a "war" against terrorism erupts, the time-honored tendency to have the president embody the nation may resurface. Such a change, we would suggest, may only be temporary, as with George H. W. Bush's presidency where he was a successful war-time leader with a 91% approval rating who, only a few months later, was defeated for reelection, garnering only 38% of the popular vote.

19. Thompson, *Political Scandal*, 241–2.

20. An excellent discussion of this phenomenon is offered in Bruce E. Gronbeck, "Character, Celebrity, and Sexual Innuendo in the Mass-Mediated Presidency," in *Media Scandals: Morality and Desire in the Popular Culture Marketplace*, edited by James Lull and Stephen Hinerman (New York: Columbia University Press, 1997), 122–42.

21. See Waldman, *POTUS Speaks*, 16.

22. Fred I. Greenstein, *The Presidential Difference: Leadership Style from FDR to Clinton* (New York: Martin Kessler Books, 2000), 189.

Bibliography

Abbott, Philip. *Strong Presidents: A Theory of Leadership*. Knoxville: University of Tennessee Press, 1996.

Alter, Jonathan. "Documentary: The James and George Show." *Newsweek*, November 8, 1993.

Altman, Rick. "Television/Sound." In *Studies in Entertainment: Critical Approaches to Mass Culture*, edited by Tania Modleski. Bloomington: Indiana University Press, 1986.

Andrew, J. Dudley. *The Major Film Theories: An Introduction*. London: Oxford University Press, 1976.

Armstrong, Dan. "Wiseman and the Politics of Looking: *Manoeuvre* in the Documentary Project." *Quarterly Review of Film Studies* 11 (1990): 35–50.

Arnheim, Rudolf. *Visual Thinking*. Berkeley: University of California Press, 1969.

Aumont, Jacques, Alain Bergala, Michel Marie, and Marc Vernet. *Aesthetics of Film*, translated by Richard Neupert. Austin: University of Texas Press, 1992.

Bailey, Thomas A. *Presidential Greatness*. New York: Appleton-Century-Crofts, 1966.

Bakhtin, M. M. *Speech Genres and Other Late Essays*, translated by Vern W. McGee. Austin: University of Texas Press, 1986.

Barber, James David. *The Presidential Character: Predicting Performance in the White House*, 4th ed. Upper Saddle River, NJ: Prentice-Hall PTR, 1992.

Barilleaux, Ryan J. *The Post-Modern Presidency: The Office after Ronald Reagan*. New York: Praeger, 1988.

Barthes, Roland. *Mythologies*, translated by Annette Lavers. New York: Hill and Wang, 1972.

Barušs, Imantis. *Authentic Knowing: The Convergence of Science and Spiritual Aspiration*. West Lafayette, IN: Purdue University Press, 1996.

Bass, Jeff D. "Becoming the Past: The Rationale of Renewal and the Annulment of History." In *Argument in Transition: Proceedings of the Third Summer Conference on Argumentation*, edited by David Zarefsky, Malcolm O. Sillars, and Jack Rhodes. Annandale, VA: Speech Communication Association, 1983.

Baudrillard, Jean. *Simulations*, translated by Paul Foss, Paul Patton, and Philip Beitchman. New York: Semiotext(e), 1983.

———. *America*, translated by Chris Turner. London: Verso, 1989.

———. "Hyperreal America," translated by David Macey. *Economy and Society* 22 (1993): 243-52.

Bennett, W. Lance. "The Ritualistic and Pragmatic Bases of Political Campaign Discourse." *Quarterly Journal of Speech* 63 (1977): 219–38.

———. *News: The Politics of Illusion*, 2nd edition. New York: Longman, 1988.

———. *The Governing Crisis: Media, Money, and Marketing in American Elections*. New York: St. Martin's Press, 1992.

———. "The Cueless Public: Bill Clinton Meets the New American Voter in Campaign '92." In *The Clinton Presidency: Campaigning, Governing, and the Psychology of Leadership*, edited by Stanley A. Renshon. Boulder, CO: Westview Press, 1995.

Bennett, W. Lance, and Robert M. Entman. "Mediated Politics: An Introduction." In *Mediated Politics: Communication in the Future of Democracy*, edited by W. Lance Bennett and Robert M. Entman. Cambridge, UK: Cambridge University Press, 2001.

Benoit, William L. "Framing Through Temporal Metaphor: 'Bridges' of Bob Dole and Bill Clinton in Their 1996 Acceptance Addresses." *Communication Studies* 52 (2001): 70–84.

Benson, Thomas W., and Carolyn Anderson. *Reality Fictions: The Films of Frederick Wiseman*. Carbondale: Southern Illinois University Press, 1989.

Bentley, P. F. *Clinton: Portrait of Victory*. New York: Warner Books, 1993.

Benze, James G., and Eugene R. Declercq. "Content of Television Political Spot Ads for Female Candidates." *Journalism Quarterly* 62 (1985): 278–83, 288.

Berman, Marshall. *The Politics of Authenticity: Radical Individualism and the Emergence of Modern Society*. New York: Atheneum, 1970.

Bernstein, Amy. "The Hidden Life of the War Room." *U.S. News & World Report*, April 12, 1993.

Bertelsen, Dale A. "Media Form and Government: Democracy as an Archetypal Image in the Electronic Age." *Communication Quarterly* 40 (1992): 325–37.

Biesecker, Barbara A. "Rhetorical Studies and the 'New' Psychoanalysis: What's the Real Problem? or Framing the Problem of the Real" [review essay]. *Quarterly Journal of Speech* 84 (1998): 222–40.

Blair, Carole, Marsha S. Jeppeson, and Enrico Pucci, Jr. "Public Memorializing in Postmodernity: The Vietnam Veterans Memorial as Prototype." *Quarterly Journal of Speech* 77 (1991): 263–88.

Blankenship, Jane, and Deborah C. Robson. "A 'Feminine Style' in Women's Political Discourse: An Exploratory Essay." *Communication Quarterly* 43 (1995): 353–66.

Borch-Jacobsen, Michel. *The Emotional Tie: Psychoanalysis, Mimesis, and Affect*. Stanford, CA: Stanford University Press, 1992.

Bradley, Richard. *American Political Mythology from Kennedy to Nixon*. New York: Peter Lang, 2000.

Brown, Thomas. *JFK: History of an Image*. Bloomington: Indiana University Press, 1988.

Browne, Stephen H. "Reading Public Memory in Daniel Webster's Plymouth Rock Oration." *Western Journal of Communication* 57 (1993): 464–77.

Bryson, Lois. "Sport and the Maintenance of Masculine Hegemony." *Women's Studies International Forum* 10 (1987): 349–60.

Bucy, Erik P., and Paul D'Angelo. "The Crisis of Political Communication: Normative Critiques of News and Democratic Processes." *Communication Yearbook* 22 (1999): 301–39.

Burke, Kenneth. *Attitudes Toward History*. Berkeley and Los Angeles: University of California Press, 1984.

———. *Counter-statement*. Berkeley and Los Angeles: University of California Press, 1968.

———. *A Grammar of Motives*. Berkeley and Los Angeles: University of California Press, 1969.

———. *The Philosophy of Literary Form: Studies in Symbolic Action*, 3rd ed. Berkeley and Los Angeles: University of California Press, 1973.

———. *Permanence and Change: An Anatomy of Purpose*, 3rd ed. Berkeley and Los Angeles: University of California Press, 1984.

———. *The Rhetoric of Religion: Studies in Logology*. Berkeley and Los Angeles: University of California Press, 1970.

Burns, James MacGregor, and Gloria J. Sorenson. *Dead Center: Clinton-Gore Leadership and the Perils of Moderation*. New York: Scribner, 1999.

Butler, Judith. *Gender Trouble: Feminism and the Subversion of Identity*. New York: Routledge, 1990.

———. "Performative Acts and Gender Constitution: An Essay in Phenomenology and Feminist Theory." In *Performing Feminisms: Feminist Critical Theory and Theater*, edited by Sue-Ellen Case. Baltimore: Johns Hopkins University, 1990.

Campbell, James E. "Candidate Image Evaluations: Influence and Rationalization in Presidential Primaries." *American Politics Quarterly* 11 (1983): 293–313.

Campbell, Karlyn Kohrs. "Conventional Wisdom—Traditional Form: A Rejoinder." *Quarterly Journal of Speech* 58 (1972): 451–4.

———. *Man Cannot Speak for Her: A Critical Study of Early Feminist Rhetoric*, Volume I. New York: Praeger, 1989.

———. "The Sound of Women's Voices." *Quarterly Journal of Speech* 75 (1989): 212–20.

———. "The Discursive Performance of Femininity: Hating Hillary." *Rhetoric & Public Affairs* 1 (1998): 1–19.

Campbell, Karlyn Kohrs, and Kathleen Hall Jamieson. "Form and Genre in Rhetorical Criticism: An Introduction." In *Form and Genre: Shaping Rhetorical Action*, edited by Karlyn Kohrs Campbell and Kathleen Hall Jamieson. Falls Church, VA: Speech Communication Association, 1978.

Capella, Joseph N., and Kathleen Hall Jamieson. *Spiral of Cynicism: The Press and the Public Good*. New York: Oxford University Press, 1997.

Carmichael, Thomas. "Postmodernism, Symbolicity, and the Rhetoric of the Hyperreal: Kenneth Burke, Fredric Jameson, and Jean Baudrillard." *Text and Performance Quarterly* 11 (1991): 319–24.

Carrigan, Tim, Bob Connell, and John Lee. "Toward a New Sociology of Masculinity." *Theory and Society* 14 (1985): 551–604.

Carroll, Peter N. *It Seemed Like Nothing Happened: America in the 1970s.* New Brunswick, NJ: Rutgers University Press, 2000.

Ceaser, James W., and Andrew E. Busch. *Losing to Win: The 1996 Elections and American Politics.* Lanham, MD: Rowman & Littlefield, 1997.

Cha, Theresa H. K., ed. *Apparatus.* New York: Tanam Press, 1980.

Chaloupka, William. *Everybody Knows: Cynicism in America.* Minneapolis: University of Minnesota Press, 1999.

Charland, Maurice. "Constitutive Rhetoric: The Case of the *Peuple Québécois.*" *Quarterly Journal of Speech* 73 (1987): 133–50.

Chase, Malcolm, and Christopher Shaw. "The Dimensions of Nostalgia." In *The Imagined Past: History and Nostalgia,* edited by Christopher Shaw and Malcolm Chase. Manchester and New York: Manchester University Press, 1989.

Clinton, Bill. *Between Hope and History: Meeting America's Challenges for the 21st Century.* New York: Time Books, 1996.

The Clinton Years: The Photographs of Robert McNeely. New York: Callaway, 2000.

Cloud, Dana L. *Control and Consolation in American Culture and Politics: Rhetoric of Therapy.* Thousand Oaks, CA: Sage, 1998.

Combs, James. *The Reagan Range: The Nostalgic Myth in American Politics.* Bowling Green, OH: Bowling Green State University Press, 1993.

Conason, Joe, and Gene Lyons. *The Hunting of the President: The Ten-Year Campaign to Destroy Bill and Hillary Clinton.* New York: St. Martin's Press, 2000.

Condit, Celeste. "The Functions of Epideictic: The Boston Massacre Orations as Exemplar." *Communication Quarterly* 33 (1985): 284–98.

———. "The Rhetorical Limits of Polysemy." *Critical Studies in Mass Communication* 6 (1989): 103–22.

———. "Hegemony in a Mass-Mediated Society: Concordance About Reproductive Technologies." *Critical Studies in Mass Communication* 11 (1994): 205–30.

Connell, Robert W. *Gender and Power: Society, the Person, and Sexual Politics.* Stanford, CA: Stanford University Press, 1987.

———. "An Iron Man: The Body and Some Contradictions of Hegemonic Masculinity." In *Sport, Men, and the Gender Order: Critical Feminist Perspectives*, edited by Michael A. Messner and Dan F. Sabo. Champaign, IL: Human Kinetics Books, 1990.

Cox, J. Robert. "Memory, Critical Theory, and the Argument from History." *Argumentation & Advocacy* 27 (1990): 1–13.

Craib, Ian. *Psychoanalysis and Social Theory*. Amherst: University of Massachusetts Press, 1990.

Crouse, Timothy. *The Boys on the Bus*. New York: Random House, 1973.

Dames, Nicholas. *Amnesiac Selves: Nostalgia, Forgetting, and British Fiction, 1810–1870*. New York: Oxford University Press, 2001.

Daniels, Eugene B. "Nostalgia and Hidden Meaning." *American Imago* 42 (1985): 371–83.

Daughton, Suzanne M. "Women's Issues, Women's Place: Gender-Related Problems in Presidential Campaigns. *Communication Quarterly* 42 (1994): 106–19.

Davis, Fred. "Nostalgia, Identity, and the Current Nostalgia Wave." *Journal of Popular Culture* 11 (1977): 414–24.

———. *Yearning for Yesterday: A Sociology of Nostalgia*. New York: Free Press, 1979.

Davis, Richard, and Diana Owen. *New Media and American Politics*. New York: Oxford University Press, 1998.

Denton, Robert E., Jr. *The Symbolic Dimensions of the American Presidency: Description and Analysis*. Prospect Heights, IL: Waveland Press, 1982.

Denton, Robert E., Jr., and Rachel L. Holloway. "Clinton and Town Hall Meetings: Mediated Conversation and the Risk of Being 'In Touch.'" In *The Clinton Presidency: Images, Issues, and Communication Strategies*, edited by Robert E. Denton, Jr., and Rachel L. Holloway. Westport, CT: Praeger, 1996.

d'Entrèves, Maurizio Passerin, and Ursula Vogel, eds. *Public & Private: Legal, Political and Philosophical Perspectives*. London: Routledge, 2000.

Depoe, Stephen P. "Requiem for Liberalism: The Therapeutic and Deliberative Functions of Nostalgic Appeals in Edward Kennedy's Address to the 1980 Democratic National Convention." *Southern Communication Journal* 55 (1990): 175–92.

Devlin, L. Patrick. "Contrasts in Presidential Campaign Commercials of 1988." *American Behavioral Scientist* 32 (1989): 389–414.

Diamond, Edwin, and Robert A. Silverman. *White House to Your House: Media and Politics in Virtual America.* Cambridge, MA: MIT Press, 1995.

Dickinson, Greg. "Memories for Sale: Nostalgia and the Construction of Identity in Old Pasadena." *Quarterly Journal of Speech* 83 (1997): 1–27.

Dionne, E. J., Jr. *Why Americans Hate Politics.* New York: Simon & Schuster, 1991.

Doane, Janice, and Devon Hodges. *Nostalgia and Sexual Difference.* New York and London: Methuen, 1987.

Dow, Bonnie J., and Mari Boor Tonn. "'Feminine Style' and Political Judgment in the Rhetoric of Ann Richards." *Quarterly Journal of Speech* 79 (1993): 286–302.

Drew, Elizabeth. *Showdown: The Struggle Between the Gingrich Congress and the Clinton White House.* New York: Simon & Schuster, 1996.

Dunning, Eric. "Sport as a Male Preserve: Notes on the Social Sources of Masculine Identity and Its Transformation." *Theory, Culture & Society* 3 (1986): 79–90.

Eco, Umberto. *Travels in Hyperreality: Essays,* translated by William Weaver. San Diego, CA: Harcourt Brace Jovanovich, 1986.

Edelman, Murray. *Constructing the Political Spectacle.* Chicago: University of Chicago Press, 1988.

Edwards, George C., III. "Campaigning Is Not Governing: Bill Clinton's Rhetorical Presidency." In *The Clinton Legacy,* edited by Colin Campbell and Bert A. Rockman. New York: Chatham House, 2000.

Edwards, Gwenyth H. "The Structure and Content of the Male Gender Role Stereotype: An Exploration of Subtypes." *Sex Roles* 27 (1992): 533–51.

Ellis, John. *Visible Fictions.* London: Routledge & Kegan Paul, 1982.

Ellis, Richard J., ed. *Speaking to the People: The Rhetorical Presidency in Historical Perspective.* Amherst: University of Massachusetts Press, 1998.

Elshtain, Jean Bethke. "Feminist Political Rhetoric and Women's Studies." In *The Rhetoric of the Human Sciences: Language and Argument in Scholarship and Public Affairs,* edited by John S. Nelson, Allan Megill, and Donald N. McCloskey. Madison, WI: University of Wisconsin Press, 1987.

Erickson, Keith V. "Presidential Rhetoric's Visual Turn: Performance Fragments and the Politics of Illusionism." *Communication Monographs* 67 (2000): 138–57.

Farrell, Thomas B. "Rhetorical Resemblance: Paradoxes of a Practical Art." *Quarterly Journal of Speech* 72 (1986): 1–19.

Ferrara, Alessandro. *Reflective Authenticity: Rethinking the Project of Modernity.* London: Routledge, 1998.

———. *Modernity and Authenticity: A Study of the Social and Ethical Thought of Jean-Jacques Rousseau.* Albany: State University of New York Press, 1993.

Fields, Wayne. *Union of Words: A History of Presidential Eloquence.* New York: Free Press, 1996.

Fisher, Walter. "Rhetorical Fiction and the Presidency." *Quarterly Journal of Speech* 66 (1980): 119–26.

———. "Romantic Democracy, Ronald Reagan, and Presidential Heroes." *Western Journal of Speech Communication* 46 (1982): 299–310.

Fiske, John. *Television Culture.* London: Methuen, 1987.

———. *Media Matters: Everyday Culture and Political Change.* Minneapolis: University of Minnesota Press, 1996.

Flitterman, Sandy. "Woman, Desire and the Look: Feminism and the Enunciative Apparatus in Cinema." In *Theories of Authorship: A Reader*, edited by John Caughie. London: Routledge & Kegan Paul, 1981.

Flitterman-Lewis, Sandy. "Psychoanalysis, Film, and Television." In *Channels of Discourse: Television and Contemporary Criticism*, edited by Robert C. Allen. Chapel Hill: University of North Carolina Press, 1987.

Foss, Karen A., and Sonja K. Foss. *Women Speak: The Eloquence of Women's Lives.* Prospect Heights, IL: Waveland Press, 1991.

Foster, Donald. "Who Is Anonymous?" *New York*, February 26, 1996.

———. *Author Unknown: On the Trail of Anonymous.* New York: Henry Holt & Company, 2000.

Foster, Hal, ed. *Vision and Visuality.* New York: The New Press, 1988.

Frentz, Thomas S., and Janice Hocker Rushing. "Integrating Ideology and Archetype in Rhetorical Criticism, Part II: A Case Study of *Jaws*." *Quarterly Journal of Speech* 79 (1993): 61–81.

Freud, Sigmund. "Three Essays on the Theory of Sexuality." In *The Standard Edition of the Complete Psychological Works of Sigmund Freud*, volume 7, translated and edited by James Strachey. London: The Hogarth Press, 1957.

———. "Notes Upon a Case of Obsessional Neurosis." In *The Standard Edition of the Complete Psychological Works of Sigmund Freud*, volume 10, translated and edited by James Strachey. London: The Hogarth Press, 1955.

———. "Instincts and Their Vicissitudes." In *The Standard Edition of the Complete Psychological Works of Sigmund Freud*, volume 14, translated and edited by James Strachey. London: The Hogarth Press, 1957.

———. "Group Psychology and the Analysis of the Ego." In *The Standard Edition of the Complete Psychological Works of Sigmund Freud*, volume 18, translated and edited by J. Strachey. London: The Hogarth Press, 1955.

Furno-Lamude, Diane. "Baby Boomers Susceptibility to Nostalgia." *Communication Reports* 7 (1994): 130–5.

Gabler, Neal. *Life, the Movie*. New York: Vintage Books, 1998.

Gamm, Gerald, and Renée M. Smith. "Presidents, Parties, and the Public: Evolving Patterns of Interaction, 1877–1929." In *Speaking to the People: The Rhetorical Presidency in Historical Perspective*, edited by Richard J. Ellis. Amherst: University of Massachusetts Press, 1998.

Gane, Mike. *Baudrillard's Bestiary*. London: Routledge, 1991.

Gatens, Moira. *Imaginary Bodies: Ethics, Power and Corporeality*. London: Routledge, 1996.

Gelderman, Carol. *All the Presidents' Words: The Bully Pulpit and the Creation of the Virtual Presidency*. New York: Walker and Company, 1997.

Genovese, Michael A., and Seth Thompson. "Women as Chief Executives: Does Gender Matter?" In *Women as National Leaders*, edited by Michael A. Genovese. Newbury Park, CA: Sage, 1993.

Germond, Jack W., and Jules Witcover. *Mad as Hell: Revolt at the Ballot Box, 1992*. New York: Warner Books, 1993.

———. *Whose Broad Stripes and Bright Stars? The Trivial Pursuit of the Presidency 1988*. New York: Warner Books, 1989.

Giglio, Ernest. *Here's Looking at You: Hollywood, Film, and Politics*. New York: Peter Lang, 2000.

Goldman, Peter, Thomas M. DeFrank, Mark Miller, Andrew Murr, and Tom Mathews. *Quest for the Presidency, 1992*. College Station: Texas A&M University Press, 1994.

Goodman, Sharon, and Paul Manners. "Making It 'Real': Words and Pictures in Television News." *Language & Communication* 17 (1997): 53–66.

Goodnight, G. Thomas. "Reagan, Vietnam, and Central America: Public Memory and the Politics of Fragmentation." In *Beyond the Rhetorical Presidency*, edited by Martin J. Medhurst. College Station: Texas A&M University Press, 1996.

Gray, Herman. *Watching Race: Television and the Struggle for 'Blackness.'* Minneapolis: University of Minnesota Press, 1995.

Green, Fitzhugh. *American Propaganda Abroad*. New York: Hippocrene Books, 1988.

Greene, Gayle. "Feminist Fiction and the Uses of Memory." *Signs* 16 (1991): 290–321.

Greenstein, Fred I. "Popular Images of the President." *American Journal of Psychiatry* 122 (1965): 523–29.

———. *The Presidential Difference: Leadership Style from FDR to Clinton*. New York: Martin Kessler Books, 2000.

Griffin, Michael. "The Great War Photographs: Constructing Myths of History and Photojournalism. In *Picturing the Past: Media, History, and Photography*, edited by Bonnie Brennen and Hanno Hardt. Urbana: University of Illinois Press, 1999.

Gronbeck, Bruce E. "The Functions of Presidential Campaigning." *Communication Monographs* 45 (1978): 268–80.

———. "Celluloid Rhetoric: On Genres of Documentary." In *Form and Genre: Shaping Rhetorical Action*, edited by Karlyn Kohrs Campbell and Kathleen Hall Jamieson. Falls Church, VA: Speech Communication Association, 1990.

———. "Characterological Argument in Bush's and Clinton's Convention Films." In *Argument and the Postmodern Challenge: Proceedings of the Eighth SCA/AFA Conference on Argumentation*, edited by Raymie E. McKerrow. Annandale, VA: Speech Communication Association, 1993.

———. "Rhetoric, Ethics, and Telespectacles in the Post-everything Age." In *Postmodern Representations: Truth, Power, and Mimesis in the Human Sciences and Public Culture*, edited by Richard Harvey Brown. Chicago: University of Chicago Press, 1995.

———. "Character, Celebrity, and Sexual Innuendo in the Mass-Mediated Presidency." In *Media Scandals: Morality and Desire in the Popular Culture Marketplace*, edited by James Lull and Stephen Hinerman. New York: Columbia University Press, 1997.

Gunderson, Robert Gray. *The Log-Cabin Campaign*. Lexington: University Press of Kentucky, 1957.

Gurevitch, Michael, and Anandam P. Kavooris. "Television Spectacles as Politics." *Communication Monographs* 59 (1992): 415–20.

Habermas, Jürgen. *The Structural Transformation of the Public Sphere*, translated by Thomas Burger. Cambridge, MA: MIT Press, 1992.

Hacker, Kenneth L. "Virtual Democracy: A Critique of the Clinton Administration Citizen-White House Electronic Mail System." In *The Clinton Presidency: Images, Issues, and Communication Strategies*, edited by Robert E. Denton, Jr., and Rachel L. Holloway. Westport, CT: Praeger, 1996.

Hagstrom, Jerry. "War Room Secrets." *National Journal*, March 20, 1993.

Hahn, Dan F. "The Media and the Presidency: Ten Propositions." *Communication Quarterly* 35 (1987): 254–66.

Hahn, Dan F., and Ruth M. Gonchar. "Political Myth: The Image and the Issue." *Today's Speech* 20 (1972): 57–65.

Halbwachs, Maurice. *The Collective Memory*. New York: Harper Colophon Books, 1980.

Hanke, Robert. "Hegemonic Masculinity in *thirtysomething*." *Critical Studies in Mass Communication* 7 (1990): 231–48.

Hankins, Sarah Russell. "Archetypal Alloy: Reagan's Rhetorical Image." *Central States Speech Journal* 34 (1983): 33–43.

Hardt, Hanno. "Authenticity, Communication, and Critical Theory." *Critical Studies in Mass Communication*. 10 (1993): 49–69.

Hart, Roderick P. *Seducing America: How Television Charms the Modern Voter*. New York: Oxford University Press, 1994.

———. "The End of the American Presidency." Lecture presented as the Josephine Jones Lecture, University of Colorado, Boulder, CO, March 8, 1999.

Hartley, John. *The Politics of Pictures: The Creation of the Public in the Age of Popular Media*. London: Routledge, 1992.

Hearn, Jeff, and David H. J. Morgan. "Men, Masculinities and Social Theory." In *Men, Masculinities, and Social Theory*, edited by Jeff Hearn and David H. J. Morgan. London: Unwin Hyman, 1990.

Hedlund, R. D., P. K. Freeman, K. E. Hamm, and R. M. Stein. "The Electability of Women Candidates: The Effects of Sex Role Stereotypes." *Journal of Politics* 41 (1979): 513–24.

Hellmann, John. *The Kennedy Obsession: The American Myth of JFK*. New York: Columbia University Press, 1997.

Hellweg, Susan. "An Examination of Voter Conceptualizations of the Ideal Political Candidate." *Southern Speech Communication Journal* 44 (1979): 373–85.

Hellweg, Susan A., George N. Dionisopoulos, and Drew B. Kugler. "Political Candidate Image: A State-of-the-Art Review." In *Progress in Communication Sciences*, volume IX, edited by Brenda Dervin and M. J. Voigt. Norwood, NJ: Ablex, 1989.

Hess, Stephen. *Presidents & the Presidency*. Washington, D.C.: The Brookings Institution, 1996.

Hinckley, Barbara. *The Symbolic Presidency: How Presidents Portray Themselves*. New York: Routledge, 1990.

Hirschmann, Nancy J. "Freedom, Recognition, and Obligation: A Feminist Approach to Political Theory." *American Political Science Review* 83 (1989): 1227–44.

Hodgkinson, Georgine, and Chris M. Leland. "Metaphors in the 1996 Presidential Debates: An Analysis of Themes." In *The Electronic Election: Perspectives on the 1996 Campaign Communication*, edited by Lynda Lee Kaid and Dianne G. Bystrom. Mahwah, NJ: Lawrence Erlbaum, 1999.

Hoffman, Joyce. *Theodore H. White and Journalism as Illusion*. Columbia: University of Missouri Press, 1995.

Hogan, J. Michael. "Media Nihilism and the Presidential Debates." *Argumentation & Advocacy* 25 (1989): 220–5.

Holloway, Rachel L. "The Clintons and the Health Care Crisis: Opportunity Lost, Promise Unfulfilled." In *The Clinton Presidency: Images, Issues, and*

Communication Strategies, edited by Robert E. Denton, Jr., and Rachel L. Holloway. Westport, CT: Praeger, 1996.

———. "Taking the Middle Ground: Clinton's Rhetoric of Conjoined Values." In *The 1996 Presidential Campaign: A Communication Perspective*, edited by Robert E. Denton, Jr. New York: Praeger, 1998.

Hornig, Susanna. "Television's *NOVA* and the Construction of Scientific Truth." *Critical Studies in Mass Communication* 7 (1990): 11–23.

Hunt, Conover. *JFK: For a New Generation*. Dallas: The Sixth Floor Museum and Southern Methodist University Press, 1996.

Hunter, Jefferson. *Image and Word: The Interaction of Twentieth-Century Photographs and Texts*. Cambridge, MA: Harvard University Press, 1987.

Hyde, Michael J. "Jacques Lacan's Psychoanalytic Theory of Speech and Language." *Quarterly Journal of Speech* 66 (1980): 96–118.

Ignatieff, Michael. *Blood and Belonging: Journeys into the New Nationalism*. New York: Noonday Press, 1993.

"Inside the Campaign." *Time Extra: The Election of 1996*, Fall, 1996.

Isikoff, Michael. *Uncovering Clinton: A Reporter's Story*. New York: Crown, 1999.

Ivie, Robert L. "Literalizing the Metaphor of Soviet Savagery: President Truman's Plain Style." *Southern Speech Communication Journal* 51 (1986): 91–105.

———. "The Ideology of Freedom's 'Fragility' in American Foreign Policy Argument." *Journal of the American Forensic Association* 24 (1987): 27–36.

———. "Cold War Motives and the Rhetorical Metaphor: A Framework of Criticism." In *Cold War Rhetoric: Strategy, Metaphor, and Ideology*, edited by Martin J. Medhurst, Robert L. Ivie, Phillip Wander, and Robert L. Scott. New York: Greenwood Press, 1990.

———. "Scrutinizing Performances of Rhetorical Criticism." *Quarterly Journal of Speech* 80 (1994): n.p.

———. "Productive Criticism." *Quarterly Journal of Speech* 81 (1995): n.p.

———. "Tragic Fear and the Rhetorical Presidency: Combating Evil in the Persian Gulf." In *Beyond the Rhetorical Presidency*, edited by Martin J. Medhurst. College Station: Texas A & M University Press, 1996.

Jacoby, Mario. *The Longing for Paradise: Psychological Perspectives on an Archetype*, translated by Myron B. Gubitz. Boston: Sigo Press, 1985.

Jamieson, Kathleen Hall. *Eloquence in an Electronic Age: The Transformation of Political Speechmaking*. New York: Oxford University Press, 1988.

———. *Dirty Politics: Deception, Distraction, and Democracy*. New York: Oxford University Press, 1992.

———. *Beyond the Double Bind: Women and Leadership*. New York: Oxford University Press, 1995.

———. *Packaging the Presidency: A History and Criticism of Presidential Campaign Advertising*, 3rd edition. New York: Oxford University Press, 1996.

Janeway, Michael. *Republic of Denial: Press, Politics and Public Life*. New Haven, CT: Yale University Press, 1999.

Jasinski, James. "(Re)constituting Community Through Narrative Argument: *Eros* and *Philia* in *The Big Chill*. *Quarterly Journal of Speech* 79 (1993): 467–86.

Jay, Martin. *Downcast Eyes: The Denigration of Vision in Twentieth-Century French Thought*. Berkeley: University of California Press, 1993.

Johnson, Haynes. *Sleepwalking Through History: America in the Reagan Years*. New York: W. W. Norton, 1991.

Johnson, Mark. *Moral Imagination: Implications of Cognitive Science for Ethics*. Chicago: University of Chicago Press, 1993.

Johnson, Richard, Gregor McLennan, Bill Schwartz, and David Sutton. *Making Histories: Studies in History-Writing and Politics*. Minneapolis: University of Minnesota Press, 1982.

Jones, Steven. "A Sense of Space: Virtual Reality, Authenticity, and the Aural." *Critical Studies in Mass Communication* 10 (1993): 238–52.

Jorgensen-Earp, Cheryl R., and Lori A. Lanzilotti. "Public Memory and Private Grief: The Construction of Shrines at the Sites of Public Tragedy." *Quarterly Journal of Speech* 84 (1998): 150–70.

Katriel, Tamar. "Sites of Memory: Discourses of the Past in Israeli Pioneering Settlement Museums." *Quarterly Journal of Speech* 80 (1994): 1–20.

Keating, John P., and Bibb Latane. "Politicians on TV: The Image Is the Message." *Journal of Social Issues* 32 (1976): 116–32.

Kellner, Douglas. *Jean Baudrillard: From Marxism to Postmodernism and Beyond*. Stanford, CA: Stanford University Press, 1989.

———. *Television and the Crisis of Democracy*. Boulder, CO: Westview Press, 1990.

Kernell, Samuel. *Going Public: New Strategies of Presidential Leadership*, 3rd edition Washington: CQ Press, 1997.

[Klein, Joe]. *Primary Colors: A Novel of Politics*. New York: Random House, 1996.

———. *The Running Mate*. New York: The Dial Press, 2000.

Knapp, Steven. "Collective Memory and the Actual Past." *Representations* 26 (1989): 123–49.

Kress, Gunther. "Language in the Media: The Construction of the Domains of Public and Private." *Media, Culture, and Society* 8 (1986): 395–419.

Kress, Gunther, and Theo van Leeuwen. *Reading Images: The Grammar of Visual Design*. London: Routledge, 2000.

Kuhn, Annette. *Women's Pictures: Feminism and Cinema*. London: Routledge & Kegan Paul, 1982.

Kurtz, Howard. *Spin Cycle: Inside the Clinton Propaganda Machine*. New York: Free Press, 1998.

Lakoff, George, and Mark Johnson. *Metaphors We Live By*. Chicago: University of Chicago Press, 1980.

Levin, David Michael, ed. *Modernity and the Hegemony of Vision*. Berkeley: University of California Press, 1993.

Lewis, William F. "Telling America's Story: Narrative Form and the Reagan Presidency." *Quarterly Journal of Speech* 73 (1987): 267–79.

Loevy, Robert D. *The Manipulated Path to the White House, 1996*. Lanham, MD: University Press of America, 1998.

Lorber, Judith. *Paradoxes of Gender*. New Haven, CT: Yale University Press, 1994.

Lott, Davis Newton, ed. *The Presidents Speak: The Inaugural Addresses of the American Presidents, from Washington to Clinton*. New York: Henry Holt, 1994.

Louden, Allen. "Voter Rationality and Media Excess: Image in the 1992 Presidential Campaign." In *The 1992 Presidential Campaign: A Communication Perspective*, edited by Robert E. Denton, Jr. Westport, CT: Praeger, 1994.

Lowenthal, David. *The Past Is a Foreign Country*. Cambridge: Cambridge University Press, 1985.

———. "Nostalgia Tells It Like It Wasn't." In *The Imagined Past: History and Nostalgia*, edited by Christopher Shaw and Malcolm Chase. Manchester and New York: Manchester University Press, 1989.

Luke, Timothy. "Televisual Democracy and the Politics of Charisma." *Telos* 70 (1986–1987): 59–80.

———. "Power and Politics in Hyperreality: The Critical Project of Jean Baudrillard." *Social Science Journal* 28 (1991): 347–67.

Lyons, Gene. *Fools for Scandal: How the Media Invented Whitewater*. New York: Harper's Magazine Foundation, 1996.

MacCannell, Dean, and Juliet Flower MacCannell. "Social Class in Postmodernity: Simulacrum or Return of the Real?" In *Forget Baudrillard?*, edited by Chris Rojek and B. S. Turner. London: Routledge, 1993.

Mackey-Kallis, Susan. "Spectator Desire and Narrative Closure: The Reagan 18-Minute Political Film." *Southern Speech Communication Journal* 56 (1991): 308–14.

Makay, John J. "Psychotherapy as a Rhetoric for Secular Grace." *Central States Speech Journal* 31 (1980): 184–96.

The Man from Hope. Produced by Harry Thomason and Linda Bloodworth-Thomason. Democratic National Committee, 1992. Videocassette.

Maraniss, David. *The Clinton Enigma: A Four-and-a-Half Minute Speech Reveals This President's Entire Life*. New York: Simon & Schuster, 1998.

Maranhão, Tullio. *Therapeutic Discourse and Socratic Dialogue*. Madison: University of Wisconsin Press, 1986.

Maraniss, David, and Michael Weisskopf. *"Tell Newt to Shut Up!"* New York: Touchstone Books, 1996.

Marshall, P. David. *Celebrity and Power: Fame in Contemporary Culture*. Minneapolis: University of Minnesota Press, 1997.

Maslin, Janet. "Another Making of a President, Starring the New Spin Doctors." *The New York Times*, October 13, 1993, p. C15.

Mattina, Anne F. "'Rights as Well as Duties': The Rhetoric of Leonora O'Reilly." *Communication Quarterly* 42 (1994): 196–205.

McDaniel, James P. "Fantasm: The Triumph of Form (An Essay on the Democratic Sublime)." *Quarterly Journal of Speech* 86 (2000): 48–66.

McGee, Michael C. "'Not Men, but Measures': The Origins and Import of an Ideological Principle." *Quarterly Journal of Speech* 64 (1978): 141–54.

———. "The 'Ideograph': A Link Between Rhetoric and Ideology." *Quarterly Journal of Speech* 66 (1980): 1–16.

McGinniss, Joe. *The Selling of the President 1968*. New York: Pocket Books, 1969.

McKerrow, Raymie E. "Critical Rhetoric: Theory and Practice." *Communication Monographs* 56 (1989): 91–111.

Mechling, Elizabeth W., and Jay Mechling. "The Jung and the Restless: The Mythopoetic Men's Movement." *Southern Communication Journal* 59 (1994): 97–111.

Medhurst, Martin J., ed. *Beyond the Rhetorical Presidency*. College Station: Texas A&M University Press, 1996.

Medhurst, Martin J., and Thomas W. Benson. "*The City*: The Rhetoric of Rhythm." *Communication Monographs* 48 (1981): 54–72.

Messaris, Paul. "'Visual 'Manipulation': Visual Means of Affecting Responses to Images." *Communication* 13 (1992): 181–95.

———. *Visual Literacy: Image, Mind, & Reality*. Boulder, CO: Westview Press, 1994.

———. *Visual Persuasion: The Role of Images in Advertising*. Thousand Oaks, CA: Sage, 1997.

Metz, Christian. *The Imaginary Signifier: Psychoanalysis and the Cinema*, translated by Celia Britton et al. Bloomington: Indiana University Press, 1982.

Meyrowitz, Joshua. "Television and Interpersonal Behavior: Codes of Perception and Response." In *Inter/Media: Interpersonal Communication in a Media World*, edited by Gary Gumpert and Robert Cathcart. New York: Oxford University Press, 1982.

———. *No Sense of Place: The Impact of Electronic Media on Social Behavior.* New York: Oxford University Press, 1985.

———. "New Sense of Politics: How Television Changes the Political Drama." *Research in Political Sociology* 7 (1995): 117–38.

Miller, Arthur H., Martin P. Wattenberg, and Oksana Malanchuk. "Schematic Assessments of Presidential Candidates." *American Political Science Review* 80 (1980): 521–40.

Miller, Mark Crispin. *The Bush Dyslexicon: Observations on a National Disorder.* New York: W. W. Norton, 2001.

Miller, Stephen Paul. *The Seventies Now: Culture as Surveillance.* Durham: Duke University Press, 1999.

Miroff, Bruce. *Icons of Democracy: American Leaders as Heroes, Aristocrats, Dissenters, and Democrats.* New York: Basic Books, 1993.

———. "From 'Midcentury' to *Fin-de-Siècle*: The Exhaustion of the Presidential Image." *Rhetoric & Public Affairs* 1 (1998): 185–200.

———. "Courting the Public: Bill Clinton's Postmodern Education." In *The Postmodern Presidency: Bill Clinton's Legacy in U.S. Politics*, edited by Steven E. Schier. Pittsburgh, PA: University of Pittsburgh Press, 2000.

Mitchell, W. J. T. *Iconology: Image, Text, Ideology.* Chicago: University of Chicago Press, 1986.

———. *Picture Theory: Essays on Verbal and Visual Representation.* Chicago: University of Chicago Press, 1994.

Morreale, Joanne. *A New Beginning: A Textual Frame Analysis of the Political Campaign Film.* Albany: State University Press of New York, 1991.

———. "The Political Campaign Film: Epideictic Rhetoric in a Documentary Frame." In *Television and Political Advertising, Volume 2, Signs, Codes, and Images*, edited by Frank Biocca. Hillsdale, NJ: Erlbaum, 1991.

———. *The Presidential Campaign Film: A Critical History.* New York: Praeger, 1993.

———. "American Self Images and the Presidential Campaign Film, 1964–1992." In *Presidential Campaigns and American Self Images*, edited by Arthur H. Miller and Bruce E. Gronbeck. Boulder, CO: Westview Press, 1994.

Morris, Dick. *Behind the Oval Office: Getting Reelected Against All Odds.* Los Angeles: Renaissance Books, 1999.

Morson, Gary Saul, and Caryl Emerson. *Mikhail Bakhtin: Creation of a Prosaics.* Stanford, CA: Stanford University Press, 1990.

Mulvey, Laura. "Visual Pleasure and the Narrative Cinema." *Screen*, 16:3 (1975): 6–18.

Mumby, Dennis K., and Carole Spitzack. "Ideology and Television News: A Metaphoric Analysis of Political Stories." *Central States Speech Journal* 34 (1983): 162–71.

Murphy, John M. "Inventing Authority: Bill Clinton, Martin Luther King, Jr., and the Orchestration of Rhetorical Traditions." *Quarterly Journal of Speech* 83 (1997): 71–89.

———. "Knowing the President: The Dialogic Evolution of the Campaign History." *Quarterly Journal of Speech* 84 (1998): 23–40.

———. "The Heroic Tradition in Presidential Rhetoric." *Rhetoric & Public Affairs* 3 (2000): 466–70.

Nehamas, Alexander. *Virtues of Authenticity.* Princeton, NJ: Princeton University Press, 1996.

Nelson, Dana D., and Tyler Curtain. "The Symbolics of Presidentialism: Sex and Democratic Identification." In *Our Monica, Ourselves: The Clinton Affair and the National Interest*, edited by Lauren Berlant and Lisa Duggan. New York: New York University Press, 2001.

Nelson, Michael. "The Psychological Presidency." In *The Presidency & the Political System*, edited by Michael Nelson. Washington, D.C.: CQ Press, 1998.

Nichols, Bill. *Ideology and the Image: Social Representation in the Cinema and Other Media.* Bloomington: Indiana University Press, 1981.

———. *Representing Reality: Issues and Concepts in Documentary.* Bloomington: Indiana University Press, 1991.

Nicholson, Linda J. "Introduction." In *Feminism/Postfeminism*, edited by Linda J. Nicholson. New York: Routledge, 1990.

Nimmo, Dan. *The Political Persuaders: The Techniques of Modern Election Campaigns.* Englewood Cliffs, NJ: Prentice-Hall, 1970.

Nimmo, Dan, and Robert L. Savage. "Political Images and Political Perceptions." *Experimental Study of Politics* 1 (1971): 1–36.

Nora, Pierre. "Between Memory and History: *Les Lieux de Mémoire*." *Representations* 26 (1989): 7–25.

Novak, Janet. "Hope Springs Eternal: The Reinvention of America in Bill Clinton's 1996 Campaign Biography Video." *American Behavioral Scientist* 40 (1997): 1048–57.

O'Keefe, M. Timothy, and Kenneth G. Sheinkopf. "The Voter Decides: Candidate Image or Campaign Issue?" *Journal of Broadcasting* 18 (1974): 403–12.

O'Kelly, Charlotte G. *Women and Men in Society*. New York: D. Van Nostrand Co., 1980.

O'Leary, Stephen D., and Mark H. Wright. "Psychoanalysis and Burkeian Rhetorical Criticism." *Southern Communication Journal* 61 (1995): 104–21.

Orvell, Miles. *The Real Thing: Imitation and Authenticity in American Culture, 1880-1940*. Chapel Hill: University of North Carolina Press, 1989.

———. "Documentary Film and the Power of Interrogation: *American Dream* and *Roger and Me*." *Film Quarterly* 48 (1994–95): 10–9.

Owens, Craig. "The Discourse of Others: Feminists and Postmodernism." In *The Anti-Aesthetic: Essays on Postmodern Culture*, edited by Hal Foster. New York: The New Press, 1983.

Papa, Michael J., Arvind Singhal, Sweety Law, Saumya Pant, Suruchi Sood, Everett M. Rogers, and Corinne L. Shefner-Rogers. "Entertainment-Education and Social Change: An Analysis of Parasocial Interaction, Social Learning, Collective Efficacy, and Paradoxical Communication." *Journal of Communication* 50 (2000): 31–56.

Parenti, Michael. *Inventing the Politics of News Media Reality*, 2nd edition. New York: St. Martin's Press, 1993.

Parry-Giles, Shawn J. "The Rhetorical Tension Between 'Propaganda' and 'Democracy': Blending Competing Conceptions of Ideology and Theory." *Communication Studies* 44 (1993): 117–31.

———. "Mediating Hillary Rodham Clinton: Television News Practices and Image-Making in the Postmodern Age." *Critical Studies in Media Communication* 17 (2000): 205–26.

———. "Political Authenticity, Television News, and Hillary Rodham Clinton." In *Politics, Discourse and American Society: New Agendas*, edited by Roderick P. Hart and Bartholomew Sparrow. Lanham, MD: Rowman & Littlefield, 2001.

Parry-Giles, Shawn J., and Trevor Parry-Giles. "Gendered Politics and Presidential Image Construction: A Reassessment of the 'Feminine Style.'" *Communication Monographs* 63 (1996): 337–53.

———. "Collective Memory, Political Nostalgia, and the Rhetorical Presidency: Bill Clinton's Commemoration of the March on Washington, August 28, 1998." *Quarterly Journal of Speech* 86 (2000): 417–37.

Parry-Giles, Trevor. "Ideological Anxiety and the Censored Text: *Real Lives—At the Edge of the Union.*" *Critical Studies in Mass Communication* 11 (1994): 54–72.

Parry-Giles, Trevor, and Shawn J. Parry-Giles, "Political Scopophilia, Presidential Campaigning, and the Intimacy of American Politics." *Communication Studies* 47 (1996): 191–205.

———. "Reassessing the State of Political Communication in the United States" [forum essay]. *Argumentation & Advocacy* 37 (2001): 158–70.

Patterson, Thomas E. *Out of Order.* New York: Alfred A. Knopf, 1993.

Payne, David. *Coping with Failure: The Therapeutic Uses of Rhetoric.* Columbia: University of South Carolina Press, 1989.

———. "*The Wizard of Oz*: Therapeutic Rhetoric in a Contemporary Media Ritual." *Quarterly Journal of Speech* 75 (1989): 25–39.

Peck, Janice. "TV Talk Shows as Therapeutic Discourse: The Ideological Labor of the Televised Talking Cure." *Communication Theory* 5 (1995): 58–81.

Pettigrew, Lloyd. "Psychoanalytic Theory: A Neglected Rhetorical Dimension." *Philosophy & Rhetoric* 13 (1977): 46–59.

Pizzello, Stephen. "Waging a Film in *The War Room.*" *American Cinematographer* 75 (1994, January): 58–64.

Pomper, Gerald M., Walter Dean Burnham, Anthony Corrado, Marjorie Randon Hershey, Marion R. Just, Scott Keeter, Wilson Carey McWilliams, and William F. Mayer. *The Election of 1996: Reports and Interpretations.* Chatham, NJ: Chatham House, 1997.

Popkin, Samuel L. *The Reasoning Voter: Communication and Persuasion in Presidential Campaigns.* Chicago: University of Chicago Press, 1991.

Popular Memory Group. "Popular Memory: Theory, Politics, Method." In *Making Histories: Studies in History-Writing and Politics*, edited by Richard Johnson,

Gregor McLennan, Bill Schwartz, and David Sutton. Minneapolis: University of Minnesota Press, 1982.

Posner, Richard A. *An Affair of State: The Investigation, Impeachment, and Trial of President Clinton*. Cambridge, MA: Harvard University Press, 1999.

Pribram, E. Deidre. "Seduction, Control, and the Search for Authenticity." In *The Madonna Connection: Representational Politics, Subcultural Identities, and Cultural Theory*, edited by Cathy Schwichtenberg. Boulder, CO: Westview Press, 1993.

Putnam, Robert. *Bowling Alone: The Collapse and Revival of American Community*. New York: Simon & Schuster, 2000.

Rabinowitz, Paula. "Voyeurism and Class Consciousness: James Agee and Walter Evans, Let Us Now Praise Famous Men." *Cultural Critique* 21 (1992): 143–70.

———. *They Must Be Represented: The Politics of Documentary*. London: Verso, 1994.

Rafferty, Terence. "The Battle of Little Rock." *The New Yorker*, November 8, 1993.

Rawlins, William K. "Theorizing Public and Private Domains and Practices of Communication: Introductory Concerns." *Communication Theory* 8 (1998): 369–80.

Reese, Stephen D. "The News Paradigm and the Ideology of Objectivity: A Socialist at *The Wall Street Journal*." *Critical Studies in Mass Communication* 7 (1990): 390–409.

Rein, Irving J. "Imagining the Image." In *Bill Clinton on Stump, State, and Stage: The Rhetorical Road to the White House*, edited by Stephen A. Smith. Fayetteville: University of Arkansas Press, 1994.

Retter, James D. *Anatomy of a Scandal: An Investigation into the Campaign to Undermine the Clinton Presidency*. Santa Monica, CA: General Publishing, 1998.

Rogin, Michael P. *Ronald Reagan, the Movie: And Other Episodes in Political Demonology*. Berkeley and Los Angeles: University of California Press, 1987.

Rosaldo, Renato. "Imperialist Nostalgia." *Representations* 26 (1989): 107–22.

Rosenblatt, Roger. "Prologue: In Black and White." In *Clinton: Portrait of Victory*, edited by P. F. Bentley. New York: Warner Books, 1993.

Rossinow, Doug. *The Politics of Authenticity: Liberalism, Christianity, and the New Left in America*. New York: Columbia University Press, 1998.

Rosteck, Thomas. *See It Now Confronts McCarthyism: Television Documentary and the Politics of Representation*. Tuscaloosa: University of Alabama Press, 1994.

———. "The Intertextuality of 'The Man from Hope': Bill Clinton as Person, as Persona, as Star? In *Bill Clinton on Stump, State, Stage, and Stage: The Rhetorical Road to the White House*, edited by Stephen A. Smith. Fayetteville: University of Arkansas Press, 1994.

Rubin, Alan M., and Elizabeth M. Perse. "Audience Activity and Soap Opera Involvement: A Uses and Effects Investigation." *Human Communication Research* 14 (1987): 246–68.

Rubin, Alan M., Elizabeth M. Perse, and Robert A. Powell. "Loneliness, Parasocial Interaction, and Local Television News Viewing." *Human Communication Research* 12 (1985): 155–81.

Rudd, Robert. "Issues as Image in Political Campaign Commercials." *Western Journal of Speech Communication* 50 (1986): 102–18.

Rushing, Janice Hocker, and Thomas S. Frentz. "Integrating Ideology and Archetype in Rhetorical Criticism." *Quarterly Journal of Speech* 77 (1991): 385–406.

Ryan, Mary P. "Gender and Public Access: Women's Politics in Nineteenth-Century America." In *Habermas and the Public Sphere*, edited by Craig Calhoun. Cambridge: MIT Press, 1992.

Sabato, Larry J. *The Rise of Political Consultants: New Ways of Winning Elections*. New York: Basic Books, 1981.

Sabato, Larry J., Mark Stencel, and S. Robert Lichter. *Peepshow: Media and Politics in an Age of Scandal*. Lanham, MD: Rowman & Littlefield, 2000.

Sapiro, Virginia. *The Political Integration of Women: Roles, Socialization, and Politics*. Urbana, IL: University of Illinois Press, 1983.

———. "The Political Uses of Symbolic Women: An Essay in Honor of Murray Edelman." *Political Communication* 10 (1993): 141–54.

Sapiro, Virginia, and David T. Canon. "Race, Gender, and the Clinton Presidency." In *The Clinton Legacy*, edited by Colin Campbell and Bert A. Rockman. New York: Chatham House, 2000.

Schier, Steven E. "American Politics After Clinton." In *The Postmodern Presidency: Bill Clinton's Legacy in U.S. Politics*, edited by Steven E. Schier. Pittsburgh, PA: University of Pittsburgh Press, 2000.

Schlesinger, Philip. *Putting 'Reality' Together: BBC News.* London: Constable, 1978.

Schmidt. Susan, and Michael Weisskopf. *Truth at Any Cost: Ken Starr and the Unmaking of Bill Clinton.* New York: HarperCollins, 2000.

Schmuhl, Robert. *Statecraft and Stagecraft: American Political Life in the Age of Personality.* Notre Dame, IN: University of Notre Dame Press, 1992.

Schram, Sanford F. "The Post-Modern Presidency and the Grammar of Electronic Electioneering." *Critical Studies in Mass Communication* 8 (1991): 210–16.

Schudson, Michael. *The Good Citizen: A History of American Civic Life.* New York: Martin Kessler Books, 1998.

[Scott, Craig R.]. "To Reveal or Not to Reveal: A Theoretical Model of Anonymous Communication." *Communication Theory* 8 (1998): 381–407.

Shanley, Mary Lyndon, and Carole Pateman, eds. *Feminist Interpretations and Political Theory.* University Park: The Pennsylvania State University Press, 1991.

Shogan, Robert. *The Double-Edged Sword: How Character Makes and Ruins Presidents, from Washington to Clinton.* Boulder, CO: Westview, 1999.

Shyles, Leonard. "Defining 'Images' of Presidential Candidates from Televised Political Spot Advertisements." *Political Behavior* 6 (1984): 171–81.

Sigelman, Lee. "Taking Popular Fiction Seriously." In *Reading Political Stories: Representations of Politics in Novels and Pictures*, edited by Maureen Whitebrook. Lanham, MD: Rowman & Littlefield, 1992.

———. "There You Go Again: The Media and the Debasement of American Politics." *Communication Monographs* 59 (1992): 407–10.

Sigelman, Lee, and David Bullock. "Candidates, Issues, Horse Races, and Hoopla." *American Politics Quarterly* 19 (1991): 5–32.

Silverstone, Roger. "The Right to Speak: On a Poetic for Television Documentary." *Media, Culture and Society* 5 (1983): 145–52.

Simon, Roger. *Show Time: The American Political Circus and the Race for the White House.* New York: Times Books, 1998.

Simons, Herbert W. "Going Meta: Definition and Political Applications." *Quarterly Journal of Speech* 80 (1994): 468–81.

———. "A Dilemma-Centered Analysis of Clinton's August 17th Apologia: Implications for Rhetorical Theory and Method," *Quarterly Journal of Speech* 86 (2000): 438–53.

Simons, Herbert W., and Don J. Stewart. "Network Coverage of Video Politics: 'A New Beginning' in the Limits of Criticism." In *Television and Political Advertising, Volume 2, Signs, Codes, and Images*, edited by Frank Biocca. Hillsdale, NJ: Erlbaum, 1991.

Skowronek, Stephen. *The Politics Presidents Make: Leadership from John Adams to Bill Clinton*. Cambridge, MA: Belknap Press, 1997.

Smith, Kimberly K. "Mere Nostalgia: Notes on a Progressive Paratheory." *Rhetoric & Public Affairs* 3 (2000): 505–27.

Snyder, Joel. "Picturing Vision." In *The Language of Images*, edited by W. J. T. Mitchell. Chicago: University of Chicago Press, 1980.

Spence, Donald P. *The Rhetorical Voice of Psychoanalysis*. Cambridge, MA: Harvard University Press, 1994.

Spitzack, Carole, and Kathryn Carter. "Women in Communication Studies: A Typology for Revision." *Quarterly Journal of Speech* 73 (1987): 401–23.

Stafford, Barbara Maria. *Visual Analogy: Consciousness as the Art of Connecting*. Cambridge, MA: The MIT Press, 1999.

Stephanopoulos, George. *All Too Human: A Political Education*. Boston: Little, Brown, 1999.

Stephens, Mitchell. *the rise of the image the fall of the word*. New York: Oxford University Press, 1998.

Sullivan, Patricia A. "Women's Discourse and Political Communication: A Case Study of Congressperson Patricia Schroeder." *Western Journal of Communication* 57 (1993): 530–45.

Swanson, David. "The Political-Media Complex." *Communication Monographs* 59 (1992): 397–400.

Tannock, Stuart. "Nostalgia Critique." *Cultural Studies* 9 (1995): 453–64.

Taylor, Charles. *The Ethics of Authenticity*. Cambridge, MA: Harvard University Press, 1992.

Terrill, Robert E. "Put on a Happy Face: *Batman* as Schizophrenic Savior." *Quarterly Journal of Speech* 79 (1993): 319–35.

———. "Spectacular Repression: Sanitizing the Batman." *Critical Studies in Media Communication* 17 (2000): 493–509.

Thomas, Evan, Karen Breslau, Debra Rosenberg, Leslie Kaufman, and Andrew Murr. *Back from the Dead: How Clinton Survived the Republican Revolution*. New York: The Atlantic Monthly Press, 1997.

Thompson, John B. *Studies in the Theory of Ideology*. Berkeley: University of California Press, 1984.

———. *Ideology and Modern Culture*. Stanford, CA: Stanford University Press, 1990.

———. *Political Scandal: Power and Visibility in the Media Age*. Cambridge, UK: Polity Press, 2000.

Timmerman, David M. "1992 Presidential Candidate Films: The Contrasting Narratives of George Bush and Bill Clinton." *Presidential Studies Quarterly* 26 (1996): 364–73.

Tonn, Mari Boor, Valerie A. Endress, and John N. Diamond, "Hunting and Heritage on Trial: A Dramatistic Debate Over Tragedy, Tradition, and Territory," *Quarterly Journal of Speech* 79 (1993): 165–81.

Trilling, Lionel. *Sincerity and Authenticity*. Cambridge, MA: Harvard University Press, 1972.

Troy, Gil. *Mr. & Mrs. President: From the Trumans to the Clintons*. Lawrence: University Press of Kansas, 2000.

Trujillo, Nick. "Hegemonic Masculinity on the Mound: Media Representations of Nolan Ryan and American Sports Culture." *Critical Studies in Mass Communication* 8 (1991): 290–308.

Tuchman, Gaye. "Realism and Romance: The Study of Media Effects." *Journal of Communication* 43 (1993): 36–41.

Tulis, Jeffrey. *The Rhetorical Presidency*. Princeton, NJ: Princeton University Press, 1987.

Turow, Joseph. *Breaking Up America: Advertisers and the New Media World*. Chicago: University of Chicago Press, 1997.

"Victory March." *Newsweek*, November 18, 1996.

Wadsworth, Ann Johnston, Philip Patterson, Lynda Lee Kaid, Ginger Cullers, Drew Malcomb, and Linda Lamirand. "'Masculine' vs. 'Feminine' Strategies in Political Ads: Implications for Female Candidates." *Journal of Applied Communication Research* 15 (1987): 77–94.

Waldman, Michael. *POTUS Speaks: Finding the Words That Defined the Clinton Presidency.* New York: Simon & Schuster, 2000.

Walsh, Kenneth T. *Feeding the Beast: The White House Versus the Press.* New York: Random House, 1996.

Walton, Hanes, Jr. *Reelection: William Jefferson Clinton as a Native-Son Presidential Candidate.* New York: Columbia University Press, 2000.

Wander, Phillip. "The Ideological Turn in Modern Criticism." *Central States Speech Journal* 34 (1983): 1–18.

———. "The Rhetoric of American Foreign Policy." *Quarterly Journal of Speech* 70 (1984): 339–61.

The War Room. Produced and directed by Chris Hegedus and Da Pennebaker. MCA Home Video, 1994. Videocassette.

Waterman, Richard W., Robert Wright, and Gilbert K. St. Clair. *The Image-Is-Everything Presidency: Dilemmas in American Leadership.* Boulder, CO: Westview Press, 1999.

Weintraub, Jeff, and Krishan Kumar, eds. *Public and Private in Thought and Practice: Perspectives on a Grand Dichotomy.* Chicago: University of Chicago Press, 1997.

Weisberg, Jacob. "Southern Exposure." *The New Republic*, November 2, 1992.

———. "Revenge Fantasy," *New York*, February 26, 1996.

Wenner, Lawrence A. "Media, Sports, and Society: The Research Agenda." In *Media, Sports, & Society*, edited by Lawrence A. Wenner. Newbury Park, CA: Sage, 1989.

Werman, David S. "Normal and Pathological Nostalgia." *Journal of the American Psychoanalytic Association* 25 (1977): 387–98.

West, Nancy Martha. *Kodak and the Lens of Nostalgia.* Charlottesville: University Press of Virginia, 2000.

Wheeler, Wendy. "Nostalgia Isn't Nasty: The Postmodernising of Parliamentary Democracy." In *Altered States: Postmodernism, Politics, Culture*, edited by Mark Perryman. London: Lawrence & Wishart, 1994.

White, James Boyd. *When Words Lose Their Meaning: Constitutions and Reconstitutions of Language, Character, and Community.* Chicago: University of Chicago Press, 1984.

White, Mark J. "Behind Closed Doors: The Private Life of a Public Man." In *Kennedy: The New Frontier Revisited,* edited by Mark J. White. New York: New York University Press, 1998.

White, Theodore H. *America in Search of Itself: The Making of the President.* New York: Warner Books, 1982.

———. *The Making of the President 1960.* New York: Atheneum, 1961.

———. *The Making of the President 1964.* New York: Atheneum, 1965.

———. *The Making of the President 1968.* New York: Atheneum, 1969.

———. *The Making of the President 1972.* New York: Atheneum, 1973.

Whitson, David. "Sport in the Social Construction of Masculinity." In *Sport, Man, and the Gender Order: Critical Feminist Perspectives,* edited by Michael A. Messner and Don F. Sabo. Champaign, IL: Human Kinetics Books, 1990.

Whitson, Steven, and John Poulakos. "Nietzsche and the Aesthetics of Rhetoric." *Quarterly Journal of Speech* 79 (1993): 131–45.

Willis, Deborah. "Preface." In *Picturing Us: African American Identity in Photography,* edited by Deborah Willis. New York: The New Press, 1994.

Wills, Garry. *Reagan's America.* New York: Doubleday, 1987.

Wilson, Robert A. *Character Above All: Ten Presidents from FDR to George Bush.* New York: Simon & Schuster, 1995.

Windt, Theodore O., Jr. "Presidential Rhetoric: Definition of a Field of Study." *Central States Speech Journal* 35 (1984): 24–34.

Woodward, Bob. *The Choice.* New York: Simon & Schuster, 1996.

———. *Shadow: Five Presidents in the Legacy of Watergate.* New York: Simon & Schuster, 1999.

Wright, Sharon D. "Clinton and Racial Politics." In *The Postmodern Presidency: Bill Clinton's Legacy in U.S. Politics,* edited by Steven E. Schier. Pittsburgh, PA: University of Pittsburgh Press, 2000.

Wyckoff, Gene. *The Image Candidates: American Politics in the Age of Television*. New York: Macmillan, 1968.

Zarefsky, David. "Spectator Politics and the Revival of Public Argument." *Communication Monographs* 59 (1992): 411–14.

Zelizer, Barbie. *Covering the Body: The Kennedy Assassination, the Media, and the Shaping of Collective Memory*. Chicago: University of Chicago Press, 1992.

———. "Reading the Past Against the Grain: The Shape of Memory Studies." *Critical Studies in Mass Communication* 12 (1995): 213–39.

Index

21st Century Express, 83–84
60 Minutes, 33, 53, 138
1992 New Hampshire primary, 55, 69, 138, 144, 172
1992 New York primary, 24
1992 presidential campaign, 6, 8, 10–11, 24, 31, 52–54, 157, 159; and collective memory, 86, 88; and "hope" theme, 89; and whiteness, 71; defined metaphorically, 67; defined as war, 68; in *Primary Colors*, 139
1996 Clinton convention film, 6, 12, 85, 97–105, 116n.63, 143, 165, 192; and use of visual imagery, 100–1; displaying the 1992 inauguration, 98–99; feminizing Clinton, 99; photo montage at end of, 105–6
1996 presidential campaign, 53, 84, 157
Abbott, Philip, 185n.51
Adversarial journalism, 158
Affirmative Action, 9, 21n.29, 91
Ailes, Roger, 69
Altman, Roger, 129
The American President (PBS), 13–14, 160, 169–79, 196, 199; and camera positioning, 170; and construction of the public, 175, 178; and institutional ambiance, 169, 176–77; music in, 172
Anderson, Carolyn, 77n.10
Annulment of history, 98
Anonymous, 118–119
Anti-politics, 124
Archetype of presidential form, 174–75, 185n.44
Arnheim, Rudolf, 185n.43
Arsenio Hall Show, 126

Authenticity, 15, 39, 50n.50; and baby-boomer generation, 131–32, 146; and culture of imitation, 122–23 and hyperreality, 119, 122, 141, 146–47, 161; and identity politics, 131–32; and masculine sexuality, 136–39; and moral relevance, 122; and personal fulfillment, 123; and political culture, 129–30, 139, 147; and privacy, 192; and written discourse, 140; and visual technique, 55, 101–2; as philosophical question, 123; etymology of, 149n.9; history of, 78n.26; political, 120–21, 123–24; war room as site of, 63
Baker, James, 61
Bakhtin, Mikhail, 76n.5
Barber, James David, 163, 171
Barthes, Roland, 153n.44
Baruš, Imants, 78n.26
Bass, Jeff D., 98
Bates, Kathy, 141
Baudrillard, Jean, 190
Begala, Paul, 58–59, 128–29, 155n.66
Bennett, W. Lance, 31, 181n.5
Benson, Thomas W., 77n.10
Bentley, P.F., 203n.4
Berman, Marshall, 123
Between Hope and History, 6, 12, 85, 89–97, 104
Bill of Rights, 94
BIOrhythm (MTV), 13–14, 159–69, 191, 196, 199
Black/white, 6, 131
Bloodworth–Thomason, Linda, 31, 97, 116n.65
Blumenthal, Sidney, 128
Booknotes (C–Span), 113n.32

Boys' Nation, 37, 107, 165
Bradley, Richard, 158
Bridge metaphor, 6, 20n.20, 84–85, 109n.4
Broadcast News, 61
Brown, Ron, 99
Brown, Thomas, 180n.4
Browne, Stephen, 86–87
Bryan, William Jennings, 197
Bully pulpit, 197
Burgoyne, Robert, 67
Burke, Kenneth, 127–28; and scapegoating, 161–62, 182n.20; on metaphor, 183n.32
Burns, James MacGregor, 154n.54, 159
Burton, Henry, 127, 132, 135–36, 138–39, 142, 144–46
Bush, George H. W., 59–62, 68, 71, 81n.54, 120, 180n.4, 205n.18; and 1992 convention film, 116n.63, 148n.6
Bush, George W., 7, 21n.27, 120, 148n.6, 187, 201, 205n.18
Bush, Neil, 148n.6
CBS, 61
Camelot, 37, 103, 108
Campaign Manager, 78n.15
Campbell, Karlyn Kohrs, 111n.18
Carrigan, Tim, 30
Carter, Jimmy, 124, 180n.4, 187; and "crisis of confidence" speech, 150n.20
Carter–Clark, Daria, 137–38
Cartesian dualism, 122
Carville, James, 11, 55, 57–63, 65, 68–70, 73, 81n.54
Celebrity, 4; and cultural grammars, 198; Clinton fused with, 168; leaders as, 119–120, 164
Channock, Foster, 17n.6
Character, 3–4, 18n.9
Chechnya, 118
Cheney, Richard, 7, 21n.27
Chernomyrdin, Viktor, 118
Cincinnatus, 187
Cinéma vérité, 11, 55, 143

Civic Virtue, 36, 41
Civil rights, 8–9, 37, 131–33, 136, 170–71, 195
Civil War, 96
Clinton, Chelsea, 33–34, 40–41, 97, 99, 103, 168
Clinton, Hillary, 97; and *The Man from Hope*, 31, 33–34, 36, 40–41; and public/private distinction, 120; as a nostalgia character, 99; as portrayed in *Primary Colors*, 142; in 1996 convention film, 98–104; in *BIOrhythm*, 168
Clinton, Jr., Roger, 36, 39
Clinton, Sr., Roger, 32, 38, 163
Clinton, Tyler, 103
Clinton, William Jefferson, 2; adolescence of, 163–64; and the 1950s, 90–91; and African embassy bombings, 157; and alcoholism, 32, 163; and American Dream, 13, 35, 100; and authenticity of character, 126, 145; and balanced budget, 174; and character issues, 41, 98; and health care reforms, 172, 204n.7; and hope theme, 165; and impeachment, 13, 15–16, 126, 159–60, 168–69, 173, 175–76, 178, 196, 199, 202; and Jefferson's "yeoman farmer," 95; and marijuana, 126; and personal nostalgia, 99; and presidential character, 178; and presidentiality, 188; and public/private distinction, 120; and race, 114n.43, 134–36, 154n.54, 170, 205n.14; and themes of opportunity, responsibility, and community, 89, 94–95; and Watergate, 127; and whiteness, 157, 164; and women's issues, 157; approval ratings, 15; as agent of collective memory, 91, 107; as amalgam of images, 202; as baby-boomer, 8, 127, 158, 161, 168, 178–79, 191; as "The Comeback Kid," 172; as commander in chief, 7–8; as draft evader, 32, 55, 127, 166; as

INDEX • 239

epitome of inauthentic politics, 124; as first "black" president, 9, 191; as first "queer" president, 191; as first virtual president, 126; as governor of Arkansas, 37, 125; as New Democrat, 71; as preemptive president, 14; as site of ideological contestation, 161; as "womanizer," 36, 55, 103, 137, 166–67, 172; at Yale Law School, 166; authentication of in *Primary Colors*, 131–40; cathartic redemption of, 175; childhood of, 163, 170–71, 177, 184n.35; Clinton image, 2, 5, 7–9, 13–14, 16; commitments to nonviolence, 8; dualities of, 6–10, 131; First Inaugural Address, 168; graduation from Georgetown University, 162, 166; in 1992 presidential debate, 151n.28; institutional redemption of, 169; legacy of, 15–16, 159–61; "Mend it, don't end it," 9, 91; militarism, 8; move to Washington, DC, 166; photographs of, 203n.4; post-impeachment imaging, 162; psychological evaluation of, 167, 171–72; public oratory, 200; redemption of, 160–61, 178, 199; Second Inaugural Address, 8; struggles with legacy, 96; use of political nostalgia, 96, 105; use of presidential mythology, 93; views of opponents, 125; views of supporters, 125
Clinton–Kennedy handshake, 34, 37, 107–8, 158–59, 167, 171, 177
Close–ups, 31–33
CNN, 199
Cold War, 67, 96, 197–98
Collective memory, 6, 12, 85, 96, 174; and visuality, 189, 193; as partial and usable, 87; as political tool, 88; defined, 86; in epideictic oratory, 87; in public argument, 110n.12; of Bill Clinton, 103, 165; of John F. Kennedy, 165
Columbia, 36
Common sense, 30
Condit, Celeste Michelle, 39, 42
Congress, 169, 198
Connell, Robert W., 29, 37
Constitutive rhetoric, 17n.7
Contract with America, 172
Cronkite, Walter, 165
Crouse, Timothy, 53
Cuomo, Mario, 144
Currie, Betty, 71
Curtain, Tyler, 191
Cynicism, 15, 151n.24; in journalism, 124
D'Amato, Alphonse, 173
Dames, Nicholas, 104
Daniels, Eugene, 92
Davis, Fred, 88
Declaration of Independence, 92, 94
Deep Throat, 128, 152n.34
Democratic National Convention (1992), 11, 52, 55, 63, 81n.54
Democratic National Convention (1996), 12, 83–85
Depoe, Stephen, 95, 111n.18
Destiny monomyth, 171
Diamond, Edwin, 66
Direct address, 31–32
Documentary, 53–54, 66; as subject for rhetorical analysis, 77n.10
Dole, Elizabeth, 109n.1
Dole, Robert, 53, 84, 109n.1
Donahue, 24
Donaldson, Sam, 128
Dow, Bonnie, 29
Eco, Umberto, 1
Edelman, Murray, 41, 68, 193
Edmonds, J. Terry, 22n.31
Edwards, George, 14
Electoral College, 74
Epideictic oratory, 86–87, 110n.14, 111n.16, 111n.18
Epistemophilia, 28, 35, 42
Erickson, Keith V., 62

Evans, Harold, 129
Exnomination, 153n.44
Face watching, 31
Fatalism, 15
Feminine style, 6–7, 11, 20n.22, 25–26; and presidential image construction, 28–30; and feminized politics, 29, 192–93; and marginalization of women, 48n.30; as result of socialization, 48n.29; defined, 50n.48; in *The Man from Hope*, 36–43
Fiske, John, 1, 81n.57, 180n.3
Fleetwood Mac, 6
Fleischer, Ari, 148n.6
Flowers, Gennifer, 32–33, 51n.59, 59–60, 69, 104, 126, 137–38, 167, 175, 199
Ford, Gerald, 17n.6, 180n.4
Foster, Donald, 129, 131
Foster, Vince, 99, 125
Founders, 13, 92–95
Fragmentation, 194–96
Frentz, Thomas, 27
Freud, Sigmund, 25, 27–28, 45n.14; and group psychology, 47n.21
Gatens, Moira, 70
Genre memory, 53, 174, 203n.4
George, 155n.66, 155n.70
GI Bill, 90
Gingrich, Newt, 8, 173
Goddess of Liberty, 36
Golden rule, 40
Goldwater, Barry, 78n.15
Goodnight, G. Thomas, 111n.18
Gore, Al, 100, 105, 187
Government shutdown (1995), 173
Gray, Herman, 71
Great Depression, 84, 96, 106, 197
Greenough, Horatio, 188
Greenstein, Fred I., 184n.40, 201
Grenier, John, 78n.15
Griffin, Michael, 165
Gronbeck, Bruce E., 5, 55
Grunwald, Mandy, 58, 70, 129
Guinier, Lani, 9, 135

Hagstrom, Jerry, 57
Hahn, Dan, 87
Halbwachs, Maurice, 85
Halperin, Mark, 128
Hanna, Mark, 197
Harding, Warren G., 193
Hardt, Hanno, 123
Harlem, 132, 136–37
Harrison, William Henry, 187, 203n.2
Hart, Gary, 158
Hart, Roderick P., 24, 31, 181n.5; and New Puritanism, 203n.5
Hartley, John, 164
Heaney, Seamus, 89
Hegedus, Chris, 55, 57
Hegemonic masculinity, 7, 20n.23, 25, 29–30, 179; and familial patriarchy, 38–39; and occupational achievement, 37; and the military, 37; as result of socialization, 47n.29; in *The Man from Hope*, 36–43
Hegemony, 39, 42
Heimweh (homesickness), 88
Hellman, John, 158, 185n.45
Heroism, 24
Hess, Stephen, 18n.8, 171
Hodgkinson, Georgine, 109n.3
Hoffman, Joyce, 18n.8
Hogan, J. Michael, 150n.22
Holden, Libby, 138
Holloway, Rachel, 114n.34
Homophobia, 106
Hope, Arkansas, 33–35, 90–91
Hot Springs, Arkansas, 90–91
Hubris, 67
Hyperreal history, 12–13, 104–8
Hyperreal intimacy, 41–42
Hyperreal politics, 28
Hyperreality, 1, 5–6, 9–13, 20n.17, 24–25, 43, 54; and authenticity, 120–21, 146–47; and Clinton marriage, 100; and public confusion, 147; and image-making, 119–20, 142–43, 146, 159; and journalism, 72; and meta–imaging, 73; and mimesis, 141, 146; and militarism, 75; and

political nostalgia, 85, 89, 97; and political spectacle, 83; and polysemy, 67; benefits of, 202 in *Primary Colors*, 142–43; presidents as personification of, 188
Ideology, 66, 72, 87
Image–makers, 60, 68–72
Imperial presidency, 197–98, 200
Individual memory, 85–86
Industrial age, 96, 122–23
Information age, 4, 96
Insider access, 53; and authenticity, 72, 119, 129; and "backstage" politics, 56, 63, 65, 174, 191–92, 199; and *Primary Colors*, 121, 139, 144; and visuality, 56, 59, 61–64; as political genre, 76n.5
Internet and new media, 193, 195
Intimacy, 10, 24–26, 28, 192; and celebrity, 51n.59; and visual images, 101; in 1996 convention film, 101; in *The Man from Hope*, 31–35, 41, 51n.59; politics of, 148n.4
Inverted gaze, 53, 61
Iran–Contra, 61, 124, 158
Ivie, Robert L., 67
Jackson, Andrew, 187, 203n.2
Jackson, Jesse, 9, 22n.35, 134–35
Jamieson, Kathleen Hall, 25, 29, 111n.18
Japanese internment, 106
Jasinski, James, 148n.4
Jefferson, Thomas, 95
Johnson, Lyndon, 90, 124, 158, 171, 198–99, 203n.3
Johnson, Mark, 67
Jones, Paula Corbin, 125, 137, 168, 173, 175
Jones, Steven, 123
Kakutani, Michiko, 130
Kelley, Virginia, 32, 38–41, 99, 103, 163, 167, 171, 177
Kemp, Jack, 53
Kennedy, Edward M., 158, 180n.5
Kennedy, John F., 18n.8, 35, 37, 78n.15, 89, 103, 108, 160, 163–68, 193; and photographic images of, 174; assassination of, 124, 158–59; nostalgia for, 178; privacy of, 175, 199
Kennedy, Robert F., 37, 106, 133–34, 158
Kerrey, Bob, 129
King, Jr., Martin Luther, 37–38, 106, 133–34, 157, 164, 195
Klein, Joe, 129, 131, 137, 140, 144–47, 152n.38
Koppel, Ted, 83, 109n.1
Kosovo, 15, 21n.26
Kress, Gunther, 164
Krispy Kreme, 144
Ku Klux Klan, 106
Kunhardt, Peter W., 160, 182n.16
Kunhardt, Philip B, Jr., 160, 182n.16
Kunhardt, Philip B., III, 160, 182n.16
Kurtz, Howard, 153n.38, 203n.6
Lamb, Brian, 113n.32
Larry King Live, 126, 128
Late–night comedy, 100
Latino farm workers, 106
Leland, Chris M., 109n.3
Lester, Adrian, 141
Lewinsky, Monica, 105, 157, 167, 175, 189
Lewinsky scandal, 13, 20n.21, 22n.35, 126, 141, 162, 178
Lewis, John, 157
Lincoln, Abraham, 171, 187, 199
Little Rock, Arkansas, 99
Little, Rich, 144
Little Willie, 163
Lott, Trent, 173
Lyons, Gene, 130
Machiavelli, Niccolo, 147
Madison, James, 160
Madisonian system, 173
The Man from Hope, 6–7, 9, 11, 14, 21n.25, 24–51, 52, 83, 98, 100–101, 107, 116n.63, 120, 143, 164–65, 189, 192, 195
Mandela, Nelson, 157
Maraniss, David, 9

March on Washington, 20n.21, 157
Marshall, P. David, 70, 168
Masculine/feminine, 6, 11, 29, 42, 131, 201
Matalin, Mary, 60, 70
May, Elaine, 141
McCarthyism, 77n.10
McGee, Michael Calvin, 18n.9
McKinley, William, 196–97, 200, 205n.17
McLeod, Cashmere, 138
McMurran, Kristin, 130
McNeely, Robert, 117n.68
Media images, 3
Media nihilism, 150n.22
Memoria, 111n.18
Messaris, Paul, 32, 35, 106, 184n.33
Meta–imaging, 11, 52–82; and hyperreality, 65; as polysemic, 74; as trapped by hyperreality, 75; defined, 52; ignoring republican government, 74
Metaphor, 67, 73
Meyers, Dee Dee, 59, 128
Meyrowitz, Joshua, 56, 63, 170
Middle East, 7
Middle region behavior, 65–66
Military metaphors, 8; and governance, 74; and nationalism, 74; as normative, masculine, and white, 54; force in American culture, 67–68; in *The American President*, 173, 179; in *The War Room*, 66–75
Miller, Mark, 129
Miller, Stephen Paul, 180n.4, 181n.7
Miroff, Bruce, 4, 14
Mitchell, Andrea, 65
Mitchell, W.J.T., 62, 162, 179, 181n.11
Monroe, Marilyn, 167
Montage, 162, 164
Morreale, Joanne, 26
Morrison, Toni, 9, 191
Mosbacher, Georgette, 69
MSNBC, 199
MTV, 126–27, 183n.24
Mumby, Dennis, 66

Murphy, John M., 9
Myths, 54, 66
Narratives, 54, 66, 73
Nationalism, 196
Native America displacement, 106
Neustadt, Richard E., 169, 171, 173, 176
A New Beginning, 26, 98, 116n.63
New Left, 124, 136
New video, 150n.17
New World Order, 67
New York, 131
New York Times, 126, 130
The Newshour with Jim Lehrer, 129
Newsweek, 52–53
Nichols, Mike, 140, 146
Nightline, 83
Nixon, Richard, 158, 180n.4, 198; resignation of, 159, 176, 181n.7
Nora, Pierre, 111n.21
Northern Ireland, 7
Nostalgia, 88, 200; and feminism, 112n.28; and identification, 88; and psychoanalytic qualities, 112n.25; and temporal dislocation, 104; as progressive ideology, 112n.24; as Western concept, 112n.25
Nothdurft, William E., 113n.32
Novak, Janet, 116n.65
Office of Civil Rights, Justice Department, 135
Orvell, Miles, 122–23
Oval Office, 103, 169, 200
Ozio, Orlando, 144
Parasocial interaction, 44n.5
Partisanship, 169, 172–73, 176–78, 196
Past/future, 6, 84–85, 89, 91–92, 96, 104, 108
Patterson, Thomas, 124
Patriarchy, 7, 38–39, 42, 106
Patriotism, 196
Pennebaker, Da, 55, 57–58, 78n.15
People Magazine, 129–30
Perot, H. Ross, 60
Persian Gulf War, 67
Personalized presidency, 201

Photography, 33; and authenticity, 123; and nostalgia, 174–75; black-and-white, 33–34; in 1996 convention film, 102, 117n.68; in *The American President*, 171–77; in *BIOrhythm*, 165–67
Plato's cave parable, 121–22
Political advertising, 197
Political authenticity, defined, 125
Political culture, 2, 5, 10, 15–16, 26; and Clinton marriage, 100; and collective memory, 87; and meta-imaging, 72–75; and political nostalgia, 107; and *Primary Colors*, 118; and uncertainty, 104; and *The War Room*, 53–54; as reflected in *The Man from Hope*, 42–43
Political images, 4, 6, 16, 24–27, 87, 204n.8
Political nostalgia, 6, 12, 20n.21, 86; affective power of, 12; and characterology, 90; and Clinton marriage, 102–3; and Ike's America, 91–92; and *mythos*, 107; and political image-making, 97–98; and Theodore Roosevelt, 93; and visual images, 103; as distortive, 91–92; defined, 88; in *Between Hope and History*, 89–97; trains as tool of, 84
Political scandal, 119, 139, 168, 172, 175, 198–99
Political spectacle, 5, 14, 42, 47n.23, 68, 83, 148n.5, 200
"Politics of personal destruction," 10, 157, 160, 176
Polk, James K., 160
Polysemy, 67
Postmodern politics, 26, 55, 73, 86–87, 191
Postmodern presidency, 14, 195, 200
Postmodernity, 5, 11, 16, 20n.17, 180n.3; and hyperreality, 124; and modernity, 120; disruption of texual unity, 162; turn to, 124–25
Premiere, 142

Presidential image construction, 5, 10, 35, 43, 174, 202; and authenticity, 121; and ideological challenges, 192; and meta-imaging, 57, 67; and military metaphors, 73; and political nostalgia, 104–5; and postmodern presidentiality, 191–94; as hyperreal, 174; Clinton's legacy on, 187; shifting image demands, 200–2
Presidentiality, 3–4, 17n.6, 26, 158; and gender, 30, 36–37; and hyperreal history, 104; and new media, 193–94; and photography, 174; and political authenticity, 120; and scopophilia, 30; as postmodern, 28, 158, 161, 170, 187–202; in 1996 convention film, 97; in *BIOrhythm* and *The American President*, 160, 179; in *The Man from Hope*, 43; in *The War Room*, 72–75
Presley, Elvis, 163–64, 168
Pribram, E. Deidre, 150n.16
Primetime Live, 128
Primary, 78n.15
Primary Colors, 10, 12, 118–56, 191, 195; and personal/private, 139; and U.S. political culture, 145–47; and product placement, 144; anonymity of author, 128–30, 145; as authenticating text, 121; as commentary on political culture, 128; as feature film, 142–45; as hyperreal, 140; as satire, 127–28
Private sphere, 7, 36, 164, 178–79, 192
Progressivism, 13, 85, 92–93, 95–96, 124; characteristics of, 92
Psychoanalytic theory and rhetoric, 45n.14
Public memory, 110n.12, 178
Public/private, 6, 9–12, 85, 89, 97, 104, 119–120, 130, 153n.45, 154n.46, 157, 161–62, 164, 168, 173, 176, 178, 198–99
Putnam, Robert, 95, 195, 204n.12
Putting People First, 89
Race Initiative, 8, 21n.29

Random House, 128–29, 137
Reagan, Ronald, 26, 98, 111n.18, 124, 190, 200; and epideictic oratory, 110n.14; and nostalgia, 113n.31; and whiteness, 71
Reaganism, 71
Rein, Irving J., 185n.45
Republican National Convention (1992), 61
Republican National Convention (1996), 83–84
Republican Party, 62, 68–69, 196
Rhetorical presidency, 14, 110n.13
Richards, Ann, 35, 41
Rodham, Dorothy, 40–41, 101–3, 105
Rodham, Hugh, 99
Roosevelt, Franklin, 1, 169, 171, 176, 191, 193, 197, 199
Roosevelt, Theodore, 85, 92–93, 187, 196–97, 200, 202
Rosaldo, Renato, 112n.25
Rosenblatt, Roger, 174
Rosteck, Thomas, 77n.10
Rossinow, Doug, 78n.26, 124, 131–32, 136
Rousseau, Jean–Jacques, 122
The Running Mate, 129
Rushing, Janice, 27
Ryan, Mary, 36
Sabato, Larry, 119
San Juan Hill, 93
Sapiro, Virginia, 39
Saturday Night Live, 144
Schier, Steven, 14, 158
Schmidt, Susan, 178
Schram, Sanford, 119
Schudson, Michael, 148n.5, 195
Schulman, Bruce J., 180n.4
Scopophilia, 11, 15, 25–26, 179; as political phenomenon, 27–30, 190; as opposed to voyeurism, 27; in *The American President*, 174; in *The Man from Hope*, 31, 35, 42
Segregation, 90–91, 106, 124, 134
See It Now, 77n.10
September 11, 2001, 196, 205n.18

Serbia, 15, 21n.26
Shogan, Robert, 18n.8
Showbiz Today, 128
Sidey, Hugh, 170–73, 182n.16
Silverman, Robert A., 66
Simons, Herbert W., 57
Sirhan, Sirhan, 133
Skowronek, Stephen, 14
Sorenson, Georgia, 154n.54, 159
Souljah, Sister, 9, 134
Soviet Union, 198
Spectator positioning, 31–32
Specularity theory, 27
Speechwriters, 8
Spitzack, Carole, 66
Stanton, Jack, 12, 127; as baby-boomer, 131, 146; as "real" Bill Clinton, 131–40, 147
The Star, 126, 138
Starr, Kenneth, 8, 15, 167, 173, 177, 196
Stephanopoulos, George, 11, 55, 57–60, 64, 68–71, 73, 128, 142, 152n.38, 154n.54
Stephens, Mitchell, 150n.17, 162, 204n.8
Supreme Court, 173
Synchronous sound, 64–65
Tabloid journalism, 120, 126
Taft, William Howard, 160, 169
Talk radio, 100, 126
Talking head style, 31
Tannock, Stuart, 95
Taylor, Charles, 122
Television, 4, 28
That's My Bush (Comedy Central), 144
Thomason, Harry, 31, 83, 97, 116n.65
Thompson, Emma, 141–42
Thompson, John B., 67, 198
Thornton, Billy Bob, 141
Time, 53, 126; and Primary Colors cover, 141–42, 146
Tocqueville, Alexis de, 95, 107
Tonn, Mari Boor, 29
Travolta, John, 140–46, 155n.70
Triangulation, 89, 95, 113n.34

Trilling, Lionel, 149n.9
Truman, Harry S., 193, 200
Turow, Joseph, 115n.52
Unity, 194–96
Universal Pictures, 141, 155n.68
Urban Cowboy, 142
U.S. Capitol, 169
U.S. Constitution, 2, 92, 94, 197–98
U.S. Senate, 175
V–chip, 115n.47
van Leeuwen, Theo, 164
Vasser College, 129, 131
"Vast right–wing conspiracy," 8
Vietnam War, 37, 123–24, 131, 158, 165–67, 180n.4, 180n.5, 198–99
Virtual inclusivity, 64
Visual grammars, 30, 35
Visuality, 5, 20n.17; and epistemology, 28, 47n.19; and filming/production techniques, 31, 35, 62; and FDR, 203n.3; and postmodern presidentiality, 188–91; in *BIOrhythm*, 162–68
Voyeurism, 27
Waldman, Michael, 22n.31, 84
War/peace, 6, 12
War rooms, 21n.28, 43; and diversity, 71, 157; and militaristic symbolism, 68; Little Rock campaign headquarters, 55, 57, 59–60, 63, 70; New Hampshire primary headquarters, 63, 71, 81n.54
The War Room, 8, 10–11, 52–82, 130, 143, 189–91; Academy Award nomination, 76n.8; and campaign speechwriting, 58; and cinema verite technique, 55, 64; and hyperreality, 62; as adventure story, 55; as documentary, 55, 62, 66
Washington, George, 188
The Washington Post, 129
Watergate, 13, 123–24, 131, 158, 169, 180n.5, 198–99
Waterman, Richard W., 158
Weisberg, Jacob, 131
Weisskopf, Michael, 178

Welfare reform, 174
West, Nancy Martha, 174
White House, 169–70, 177
White House Map Room, 157
White House Situation Room, 68
White, James Boyd, 17n.7
White, Mark J., 180n.5
White, Theodore, 18n.8, 53, 76n.6
Whiteness, 70, 179; and militarism in *The War Room*, 71; defined, 81n.57; in *The American President*, 172; in *Primary Colors*, 134
Whitewater, 32, 125, 173
Wilson, Robert A., 3
Wilson, Woodrow, 92–93, 197
Wiseman, Frederick, 77n.10
Women's movement, 136
Woodward, Bob, 181n.7
World War I, 197
World War II, 84–85, 106, 124, 197
Wright, Betsey, 138
Yeltsin, Boris, 118
Young, Josh, 155n.70
Zelizer, Barbie, 85, 87, 165

General Editors
Lynda Lee Kaid and Bruce Gronbeck

At the heart of how citizens, governments, and the media interact is the communication process, a process that is undergoing tremendous changes as we embrace a new millennium. Never has there been a time when confronting the complexity of these evolving relationships been so important to the maintenance of civil society. This series seeks books that advance the understanding of this process from multiple perspectives and as it occurs in both institutionalized and non-institutionalized political settings. While works that provide new perspectives on traditional political communication questions are welcome, the series also encourages the submission of manuscripts that take an innovative approach to political communication, which seek to broaden the frontiers of study to incorporate critical and cultural dimensions of study as well as scientific and theoretical frontiers.

For more information or to submit material for consideration, contact:

BRUCE E. GRONBECK
Obermann Center for Advanced Studies
N134 OH
The University of Iowa
Iowa City, IA 52242-5000

LYNDA LEE KAID
Political Communication Center
Department of Communication
University of Oklahoma
Norman, OK 73109

To order other books in this series, please contact our Customer Service Department:
   (800) 770-LANG (within the U.S.)
   (212) 647-7706 (outside the U.S.)
   (212) 647-7707 **FAX**

Or browse online by series:
   www.peterlangusa.com